We are now ready to start on our way down the Great Unknown. Our boats tied to a common stake, are chafing each other, as they are tossed by the fretful river. . . . We are three quarters of a mile in the depths of the earth, and the great river skrinks into insignificance, as it dashes its angry waves against the walls and cliffs, that rise to the world above, they are but ripples and we but pigmies. . . . We have an unknown distance yet to run; what rocks beset the channel, we know not; what walls rise over the river, we know not. The men talk as cheerfully as ever; jests are bandied about freely this morning; but to me the cheer is somber and the jests are ghastly. . . .

JOHN WESLEY POWELL,
13 August 1869

The Great Unknown

The Journals of the Historic First Expedition Down the Colorado River

BY JOHN COOLEY, 1937–

Northland Publishing

Frontispiece : *Gunnison's Butte at the foot of Gray Canyon.*

Map on page 18 courtesy the *Utah Historical Quarterly*.
Maps on pages 66, 94, 154 reprinted with permission from *Beyond the Hundredth Meridian: John Wesley Powell and the Second Opening of the West,* by Wallace Stegner.

Library of Congress Cataloging-in-Publication Data
The great unknown.
   Bibliography: p. 203
   Includes index.
   1. Colorado River (Colo.-Mexico)—Description
and travel. 2. United States—Exploring
expeditions. 3. Powell, John Wesley, 1834-
1902—Journeys—Colorado River (Colo.-Mexico)
I. Cooley, John, 1937-
F788.G774   1988   917.91'3044   88-22420
ISBN 0-87358-475-9

917. 91
C

C . 1

Dedication

Readers familiar with the Green and Colorado River system know that it is impossible today to follow the route of the Powell party by boat down these rivers. Because of impoundments like the Glen Canyon Dam, which forms Lake Powell, America's greatest wild river system has become a patchwork of dams so extensive it no longer meets the Gulf of California. Even in the Grand Canyon itself, water levels rise and fall in response to electrical power needs in southern California, rather than spring thaw and summer aridity. Although John Wesley Powell became a strong proponent for the orderly development of the arid West and of the wise use of its scarce water resources, it is hard to believe that he and his fellow explorers would not be shocked at the disappearance of America's wild waterways. According to American Rivers, Inc., 600,000 miles of once free-flowing rivers are now buried behind dams. Even in our protected national parks and wildlife refuges, our wild waterways are constricted by 280 dams. Against America's insatable need for power and water, we must set the equally great need to preserve the most important remaining stretches of our wild and scenic rivers. By keeping these rivers free-flowing we also help preserve wildlife habitat, plant diversity, and wilderness integrity. As much as this edition is a testament of the strength of character and endurance of the first explorers of the Green and Colorado rivers, it is a testament to the beauty, wildness, and grandeur of our national heritage, the wild rivers of America. Unlike journals of exploration, which are preserved in archives and editions such as this one, our natural heritage can be kept intact only through citizen effort and protective legislation.

This book, then, is dedicated to the preservation of America's remaining Wild and Scenic Rivers.

Light-House Rock in the Canyon of Desolation.

Contents

Swallow Cave.

A Note about the Illustrations

The illustrations chosen for this book are based chiefly on photographs taken on the second Powell expedition of 1871-72. Powell, having seen the canyons of the Green and Colorado and secured sufficient financial support, was determined to bring back a photographic record that would capture the moods of the river and the incomparable canyon scenery. He engaged photographer E. O. Beaman of New York for the task, and one of the three boats of the second expedition was devoted to the transport of the bulky photographic supplies and equipment—they weighed about 1 ton! Beaman left the Powell party during its winter encampment at Kanab, Utah. With some training, boatman John K. Hillers, then mastered the difficult art of wet-plate photography and was responsible for the plates taken during the Grand Canyon portion of the trip.

Most of the photographs taken were stereoscopic pairs. Powell used the photographs, in the form of lantern slides, to give illustrated lectures; he was often accompanied by Hillers who served as projectionist. The plates also were copied as stereographic prints and sold for use in hand-held stereoptican viewers that were popular in the late nineteenth century.

Powell intended the photographs to provide illustrations for his printed reports. As the technique of halftone printing had not yet come into use, he employed a number of artists, including Thomas Moran, H. H. Nicols, and E. S. King, to prepare engravings that could be readily reproduced by the printer. An advantage of this process was that blemishes in the original photograph could be eliminated and the scene enhanced by imaginary clouds or the veiled moon. The artists also took the liberty of enlivening some of the scenes with figures working about the campfire or boats running a rapid. As fast-moving water was blurred in the long exposures of the fine-grained wet plates, the artists depended to a considerable extent on their imaginations to provide details of the rapids. Generally, the rendition of the background scene and much of the foreground detail is sufficiently accurate that the site of the photograph can be easily determined from the printed engraving. Some scenes, however, were invented from whole cloth. Very likely, Powell himself collaborated in these contrivances.

The illustrations were published in a series of articles by Powell in Scribners Monthly (November 1874–April 1875) and in his famous Smithsonian Institution report, *Exploration of the Colorado River of the West*. Among those who had a major hand in bringing these images to the public, Hillers went on to enjoy a distinguished career as chief photographer of the U.S. Geological Survey, and Moran, already famous for his paintings of Yellowstone, became well known for his paintings of the Grand Canyon.

EUGENE M. SHOEMAKER
June 28, 1988
Flagstaff, Arizona

Acknowledgments

I wish to express great appreciation to Lloyd Schmaltz, professor of geology at Western Michigan University, for inviting me to join his field trip on the Colorado River and for providing a good introduction to the geography and geology of the Grand Canyon. My indebtedness also extends to another colleague, Professor Larry Syndergaard, for reading the manuscript and making many wise suggestions, and to R. V. Rusho, Bureau of Land Management, who served as historical consultant. I am also mindful of good efforts by my student research assistant Randolph Smith, and by Sandy S. Lemley in preparing the manuscript. As projects of this sort require time and financial support, I am indebted to Research and Sponsored Programs at Western Michigan for a Faculty Research Grant, and to the Western Michigan Department of English for assigned time to complete the project.

Among those scholars who have paved the way for this book, I wish especially to acknowledge Wallace Stegner for his classic biography of Powell and the story of the opening of the West, *Beyond the Hundredth Meridian,* for permission to reprint three maps from that volume, and for some helpful suggestions by correspondence. William Culp Darrah is another to be acknowledged for his valuable biography of Powell and for editorial contributions, along with O. Dock Marston, to the special volumes of the *Utah Historical Quarterly* in which most of these journals first appeared.

I would like to thank the editors of the *Utah Historical Quarterly* for permission to reprint materials that first appeared in that publication. All other materials appearing in this volume have come from Powell's 1875 and 1895 publications, from the Library of Congress photo archives, and from the archives of the Smithsonian Institution.

The Grand Canyon.

Introduction

On 10 May 1869, rail crews from the Central Pacific and Union Pacific railroads met at Promontory, Utah. A diverse crowd of frontiersmen, celebrities, and laborers watched as the last rails were set in place between the cowcatchers of the two facing locomotives, and the world's first transcontinental railroad became a reality. Two weeks later and a few hundred miles east of Promontory, at Green River, Wyoming, a small band of townsfolk watched as Major John Wesley Powell and his crew of nine set out on their harrowing, but history-making expedition of the Green and Colorado rivers. Although this event received little of the attention paid to the ceremony at Promontory, it marked the beginning of one of the last and most significant and dramatic, explorations through unknown, uncharted country in American history.

In 1869, almost nothing was known about the Green, Grand, and Colorado River system, for a thousand-mile stretch of its circuitous, canyon-girded course. The government maps of the period registered a great uncharted, untraveled void in the region that is today known as the Colorado Plateau. Powell and his men set out to travel the major artery of this vast unknown, observing, recording, and charting both the river and many of its side canyons as they worked their way downriver. Three months and a thousand miles downstream, six of the ten adventurers emerged from their greatest challenge, the Grand Canyon, and beached their boats in placid waters at the mouth of the Rio Virgin.

It is a wonder that Powell's expedition ever survived. The explorers were expecting great rapids, of course, but neither of the size nor frequency they encountered, sometimes by the dozen in a single day. Nor were their problems confined to the river and its rapids. As Powell's crew floated into the depths of the Colorado canyon system and watched the walls rise and tower a thousand, three thousand, finally six thousand feet above them they realized they were prisoners of the very river they were exploring.

The river and its canyon walls were not the only sources of trial for the voyagers; time and food supplies also worked against them. When they finally encountered the great rapids of the Grand Canyon's inner gorge, they were living on nothing more than flour biscuits and coffee! With each bend of the river, the crew witnessed what no white man had seen before*—the glory and wonder of the Grand Canyon. Yet so preoccupied were they with survival that none except Major Powell was able to marvel in their discovery.

The ordeals of the river, the growing fear of this great unknown, and their own gradual starvation, preyed continually on the physical strength and mental outlook of the crew. In his excitement, Major Powell was seemingly oblivious to his crew's deteriorating morale, as they reveal in their journal entries. Major Powell had a serious tangle of personal conflicts on his hands, and was perhaps himself the cause of much of the animosity and discontent. The awesome Separation Rapids, at the lower end of the Grand Canyon, unraveled the last threads of loyalty and leadership that held Powell's party together. On 28 August 1869, three members left the expedition, not out of cowardice, it can fairly be said, but because they could no longer tolerate the river ordeal, the slow starvation, the endless rapids, and growing personal conflicts. Refusing to go another foot by water, the three climbed up a break in the canyon wall, taking food, guns, and some of the journals with them. To this day Separation Rapids is a reminder of their fateful decision. Their choice also highlights one of the river's many harsh ironies. Although no one knew it at the time, Separation was the last of the river's great rapids.

Not only did the majority of Powell's men survive their river ordeal to give report of this vast unknown, they emerged with written records of their day-to-day adventures. In 1875, Major Powell published his report, *Exploration*

---

*James White claimed to have rafted the Colorado in 1867 from the junction of the Grand and Green to Callville, Nevada, a Morman settlement well below the canyons. White and George Strole had apparently stolen horses from Indians and fled to the river, where they built a cottonwood log raft and set out on their journey. Although Strole drowned in one of the rapids, White survived to tell of his fourteen-day ordeal on the river. One of the great controversies of the Colorado is over the distance White traveled. Although the newspapers of the day, and White himself, claimed he started at the junction of the Grand and Green, Stanton, Dellenbaugh, and Powell believed the more realistic point of entry to be somewhere near Grand Wash.

of the Colorado River, which is based on his hastily written and often water-soaked river journals of this expedition and the one that followed it in 1871. Although this account of the voyage does not capture the immediacy of the raw journal entries, it is finely crafted writing and expresses his deep interest in the Colorado Plateau country. The novelist and western historian Wallace Stegner has called Powell's report of the exploration "probably the finest narrative of exploration in all of American literature."

Major Powell's account of the 1869 expedition need not stand alone, however, for members of his crew also kept journals; some of them wrote letters that were eventually published in newspapers, and two wrote their recollections of the expedition quite a few years later. These journals and letters written during the trip, and the accounts written afterward, have never before been assembled in one volume. Arranged as a continuous narrative from 24 May to 1 September 1869, they present a richly textured and more colorful story of this amazing adventure into the unknown than could any single account.

The journal entries for each given day appear first, their raw, hastily written comments reflecting the most immediate concerns of the men for safety and survival, food and shelter, and their relative position on the river. The accounts that follow them were written between five and thirty-five years later, and their distance from the voyage is reflected in their occasional discrepancies and exaggerations. Generally, the accounts agree with each other and with the events recorded in the journals. What the accounts provide, which the journals by their nature and necessity do not, are the impressions and feelings of some of the crew members as the journey became more severe. Whether or not the accounts written by Billy Hawkins and Jack Sumner are exaggerated, it is impossible to know, although it does seem likely. In any event, they agree with each other in recalling increasing hostility and conflict among the crew during that harrowing summer of 1869.

Large portions of the narrative are missing, most notably the journals kept by William Dunn, Oramel and Seneca Howland, and the first two months of the Powell and Sumner journals. These journals were lost when the Howland brothers and William Dunn left the expedition at Separation Rapids. Lost with them are the stories these three could have told and the light they might have shed on the gloomy outlook and strained unity that plagued the party as it labored through the inner gorge of the Grand Canyon.

Running a rapid.

The Adventurous Ten

What sort of men were these who followed Powell across Colorado and were willing to risk their lives on so perilous a voyage with no sure sign of financial gain? John Wesley Powell, a Civil War veteran, was born in Mount Morris, New York, in March 1834. His father, Joseph Powell, was an exhorter in the Methodist Episcopal Church and had emigrated from England in 1830 along with his wife and two young daughters. In 1838, the Powells moved to Jackson, Ohio. Young John was tutored by a neighbor and self-taught naturalist, George Cookham. Cookham and his fellow naturalist George Mather took Powell with them on nature study trips, during which they collected and identified specimens of plants, birds, animals, and minerals. Mather and Cookham had previously worked on the first geological survey of Ohio and were thus excellent tutors in mapping and surveying as well as in nature study.

The Powell family moved to Wisconsin in 1846 and purchased a farm, the management of which, in large part, fell to John Wesley. He left the family farm four years later, however, to continue his education. By 1852, he was teaching in a one-room district school in Illinois. His life during the next seven years alternated between teaching school, attending classes at several colleges, and exploring the Midwest. His intermittent college education included sojourns at Illinois College, Illinois Institute (later Wheaton College), and Oberlin College. His practical education centered on that great midwestern university of the nineteenth century, the Mississippi River system. Outdoing even Samuel Clemens, he rafted down the full length of the Mississippi itself, as well as the Ohio, Illinois, Des Moines, and lesser rivers of the system. During these solo expeditions he was already gaining valuable experience against the challenges that awaited him both as a natural scientist and an explorer.

Powell's teaching career and river adventures were brought to a halt by the advent of the Civil War. Powell responded quickly by enlisting as a private in the Twentieth Illinois Infantry on 8 May 1861. At the time of induction, he was described in his personnel records as "age 27, height 5'6½" tall, light complected, gray eyes, auburn hair. . . ." He rose through the ranks rapidly, soon being elected the sergeant major of his regiment; not long afterward he was commissioned a second lieutenant. His regiment bivouaced in the St. Louis area, and Powell was assigned to work on the fortifications for the town and the camp.

In November 1861, he was promoted to captain and given leave for a hasty trip to Detroit to marry his cousin, Emma Dean. A rushed honeymoon it was, too, as the courageous Emma Dean Powell accompanied her new husband back to St. Louis.

Captain Powell's artillery battery was soon moved to Pittsburg Landing on the Tennessee River. On 6 April 1862, during the Battle of Shiloh, Powell was badly wounded. Raising his right arm to give his battery the signal to fire, he was struck by a minieball, which plowed up his arm almost to the elbow. So severe was the damage, his arm was amputated just below the elbow two days later.

This did not end Powell's military career, however; the courageous Major returned to active duty several months later, along with his wife. She was given permission by General Grant to accompany Powell and remained with her husband from then on. During the next several years, the Powells took part in the siege of Vicksburg and the Battle of Nashville. Powell did not altogether abandon his former interest in nature study, however. During his inspections of earthworks and fortifications, he picked up many samples of rocks and fossils. Some of these samples were later deposited in the Illinois State Museum.

Soon after the war, Powell became a geology professor at Illinois Wesleyan College; two years later he accepted a similar appointment at Illinois State Normal University. In 1867, Professor Powell led a party of students to western Colorado to collect specimens for the Illinois State Natural History Museum, of which he had also been appointed curator. Although Powell contributed much of his own money to finance the trip that year, he did receive contributions totaling five hundred dollars from Illinois Industrial University and the Chicago Academy of Sciences. The Smithsonian Institution loaned

Powell scientific instruments, and in return, he agreed to give the Smithsonian copies of the measurements and maps he made during the trip.

Although Powell collected samples, explored, and kept records much as he had learned to do from Cookham and Mather, and as he had done on his own during those many river trips throughout the Midwest, this was all new country, with markedly different flora and fauna. Little could he have known that this trip into the Colorado Rockies marked the beginning of a new career for Powell. As Professor Powell and his students made their way past Denver into the Rampart Range and then on to the South Park area, they discovered just how wild and how little traveled the Rockies were at the end of the Civil War. But the trip was made with perfect timing, for national attention was just turning to this vast, open, but forbidding land, filled with both opportunity and danger.

In September, most of the little group returned to Illinois, but Powell, his wife, and a few others remained to explore Middle Park and the headwaters of the Grand River (later renamed the upper Colorado).

The proprietor of the trading post at Hot Springs in Middle Park was a man named Jack Sumner. He was an all-purpose mountaineer but with an amateur's interest in the natural sciences. Sumner was attracted to Powell and took an interest in showing him the Middle Park area and its fur-bearing mammals. He helped Powell collect specimens to take back home and told many a good tale about life in this untamed mountain country.

John Colton Sumner was also a Civil War veteran. Born in Newton, Indiana, 16 May 1840, he spent most of his boyhood on farms in Indiana and Iowa. Sumner became an excellent marksman early in life by shooting at prairie chickens, ducks, passenger pigeons, and almost anything else that moved. He had also become a proficient boatsman before he enlisted in the Iowa Volunteer Infantry in 1862. His company muster roll records that Jack Sumner was five feet five, light complected, and had auburn hair. His regiment saw extensive action in Arkansas and Louisiana. Toward the end of the war he was promoted to corporal, and then mustered out on 24 August 1865.

Sumner traveled west to visit his sister in Denver, but found city life too confining. He moved into the Rockies, setting up his trading and outfitting post in Middle Park in 1866. Jack Sumner's business apparently prospered from the influx of new settlers as well as from the patronage of mountaineers and Indians. But Sumner was obviously ready for new adventure and took readily to Powell's suggestion that he join the field trip the following summer and help them explore farther west. In fact, Sumner asserts in his account that the idea of exploring the Colorado by boat was originally his, not Powell's. Although there is no sure way to authenticate or deny his claim, it seems more likely that Powell, with his extensive background in river explorations, would have seized on the idea early in his encounters with this region. The Colorado was the challenge Powell was waiting and preparing for without knowing it—the last unnavigated, unmapped river system in the nation and its territories.

Not only did Sumner close down his trading post to join Powell, he also enlisted the services of the men who made up half of Powell's river expedition: Seneca Howland, Oramel G. Howland, Bill Dunn, and Billy Hawkins. Although something of a braggart and complainer in his journal accounts, Sumner proved to be a strong and fearless boatsman. He navigated Powell's lead boat and on at least one occasion saved the Major from drowning.

As Sumner records in his account, Powell and his wife returned in June of the following year with twenty-five students for more exploring and collecting. For this second field trip, Powell received authority from Congress to draw supplies for his party from any western army post. As the summer progressed, Powell turned his attention to a study of the nearby Ute Indians, the first of years of ethnological studies that he would make. After accomplishing the summit of 14,000-foot Long's Peak and exploring the central Colorado Rockies, Powell was ready to move on.

The Powell party gained an important addition during the summer, when Sumner introduced Powell to Billy Hawkins. As Powell soon discovered, Billy Hawkins was a rough-cut and somewhat mysterious fellow who traveled with several aliases: he was variously known as "Missouri" and Billy Rhodes. Hawkins did have at least one known run-in with the military law, having been reported absent without leave from his cavalry unit in the Missouri militia. He was mustered out of the Union Army in May 1865 and made his way west. Whether or not Billy "Missouri" Rhodes-Hawkins was a fugitive from justice, he proved himself a valuable member of the preliminary expedition and the river voyage.

Major Powell's younger brother, Walter Powell, came along on the 1868 trip and accompanied his brother on the river voyage as well. Walter Henry Powell was born in Jackson, Ohio, in 1842. He was educated at Illinois Institute (Wheaton College) and, like his brother, taught in a district school until the coming of the war. Initially he enlisted in the home guards and then joined his brother's artillery unit in 1862. He saw active duty combat during a number of battles and campaigns, including the battles of Shiloh and Atlanta. In the latter, he was captured and sent to a Confederate prison at Camp Sorghum, where he suffered severely from fever and near starvation. Placed in the prison hospital, Captain Powell escaped, but was recaptured several days later. Although he was returned to the North in a prisoner exchange in 1865, he had suffered mentally from the experience and never fully recovered. The war rendered him an excessively moody and temperamental man, sudden and intense in his anger, undependable, and unfit for most occupations, especially teaching. Although some of the journal entries refer to Walter Powell's moods and hot temper, he seems to have held his own in the work of the expeditions. He had a good bass voice and was dubbed "Old Shady" by the crew, a reference to a popular ballad of the time, which he frequently sang at their campfires.

By the end of August 1868, Powell was becoming restless to move on and he was not thinking of Illinois. He had in mind even wilder and more remote country, the valley of the White River. He knew that E. L. Berthoud and his guide, Jim Bridger, had blazed a trail to the White River in 1861 and was intent on following this rather uncertain track through high mountain country. Since most of his college students had returned to Illinois by now, he needed a few more hands to round out a workable crew. These were provided for him by the ever resourceful Jack Sumner; soon two brothers, O. G. and Oramel Howland, and their friend Bill Dunn had thrown in with Powell. The Howlands were raised on a farm in Pomfret, Vermont. In additon to farming, Oramel had been trained as a printer. In 1860, he made his way west and found employment with William Byers, editor of the *Rocky Mountain News*. Howland became vice-president of the Denver printers' union and a member of the board of trustees of a mining company. In addition to his diverse business interests, however, Oramel was an outdoorsman.

Oramel's younger brother, Seneca, served as a private in the Vermont Military Infantry. He was wounded, although not seriously, in the Battle of Gettysburg, and was mustered out of the army in 1863. Seneca came west on the urging of his older brother, and soon after his arrival, the two joined Powell's expedition. Nothing is known about William Dunn, except that he, too, was a Civil War veteran who came to Powell's camp at Hot Sulphur Springs with the Howlands and continued with them that year and the next.

Powell's over-mountain trek along the almost nonexistent Bridger Trail to the Valley of the White River was more of an adventure than any of them bargained for. The advance party strayed from the trail repeatedly, but worse trouble occurred when one of their members, Gus Lankin, abandoned them, making off with a horse, a mule, and more than his share of the provisions. Even the posse that set out after him got lost and spent a full day wandering around in the mountains before they found their way back to camp. The Major and Mrs. Powell followed in the main party, and although the terrain was rough, they arrived at the site of their winter camp in early October 1868. Located just downstream from the modern town of Meeker, Colorado, Powell Bottoms, as the location is generally called, is a wide, fertile valley that provided protection, hay and grazing for the pack animals, and good hunting.

Powell Bottoms was to be the winter home for the Major's Rocky Mountain Scientific Exploring Expedition. However, a handful of students and several scientists who planned to return east had tagged along. This group of eight hoped to meet the Union Pacific at Green River, Wyoming, which was roughly one hundred and seventy-five miles northwest, across unmapped and unknown lands. Starting out in early November, Powell and O. G. Howland led this group of eight weary explorers to Green River, mostly over parched cactus and sagebrush country, and returned by much the same route. The Major continued his investigations of the White River Valley and surrounding country throughout the winter.

During all this time, Powell was familiarizing himself with the landforms, rivers, and other features of the region, so that when his expedition traveled down the Green and Colorado rivers he would know as much about the surrounding lands as possible and could fill in the river data on his roughly drawn maps. When inclement weather kept him from exploring the region, he turned his attention to the culture and language of the Utes, who shared the valley with his party. The men and their Indian neighbors traded equipment for pottery, beadwork, leggings, and ceremonial garb. Although his interest in Indian culture had begun to grow the previous summer, it flourished during this six months of intimate contact with the Utes. The Major kept copious notes here and in the years to come on all aspects of Indian life and language, notes that would eventually represent an encyclopedic knowledge of various tribes of the Colorado Plateau country.

Living in such close proximity to an Indian tribe was not without its misunderstandings and near disasters, however. On one such occasion, Powell drove a series of stakes into the ground as part of his topographical studies. The Utes, who knew almost nothing about the white man's ways, had seen or heard of surveyors' stakes before, as a first step to white settlements and railroads. Suddenly the kindly Major appeared to be a threat to their territory. Powell and his whole party might well have been scalped then and there had not Jack Sumner come to their rescue. Sumner, it seems, was an old and trusted acquaintance of the Ute chief, Antero. Powell no doubt learned from this humbling experience, for in all his years of western exploring and ethnologic studies, he never again incurred the wrath of an Indian tribe. Powell traveled among the Indians unarmed, except with a sensitivity to their culture. Without realizing it, of course, the White River Utes had both challenged and shared their culture with the man who was eventually to found the Bureau of Ethnology as part of the Smithsonian Institution.

During those winter months, confined to Powell Bottoms and its environs, the party talked more and more about the impending journey, the kind of boats they would need, the number of men, the provisions, and equipment. They had also looked down into the Green River and had some small notion of what it would be like to run the river. With the spring thaw and melt-off, the White

River rose and forced Powell's people from their cabins; it was time to move on. The Powells, Seneca Howland, and Billy Hawkins made a fairly direct route to Green River, and there the Powells caught the train that would take them to Chicago. The other members of the exploration made a more leisurely trip to the rendezvous point, the Union Pacific Bridge on the Green River.

The Major and Mrs. Powell stopped in Chicago to leave specifications for the four boats with a boatbuilder there. The Major's next stop was Washington, where he hoped to obtain financial support through a congressional appropriation such as the Clarence King exploration had enjoyed. But Powell was working against the congressional clock since he wanted to leave from Green River in May. Consequently, he had little time to build support for his planned voyage and fared no better than the previous year. He received another order from the adjutant general, authorizing Powell to draw rations for a dozen men from any western army post, and to commute any unneeded parts of the ration into cash. As with the previous trip, Powell also received scientific instruments, including barometers and sextants, from the Smithsonian Institution, and some more from the Chicago Academy of Sciences. Powell made it clear to the press that his expedition was not government sponsored at all, but under the auspices of the Illinois Natural History Society and the Illinois Industrial University, his sole financial supporters. The Major's one real success in Washington was in obtaining a discharge for George Bradley.

Powell had met Sergeant Bradley during the Major's Colorado explorations and told the sergeant about his planned river trip. Bradley announced that he was both an experienced boatsman and more than anxious to get out of the army. He wrote in his diary that if Powell could get him discharged from the army he "would be willing to explore the River Styx"—and indeed he nearly had to!

George Young Bradley grew up in Newberryport, Massachusetts. He enlisted in the Volunteer Infantry in 1862 and soon afterward saw action in Virginia. During a skirmish near Fredericksberg, Bradley was wounded in the right thigh, a wound that healed slowly and kept him from further combat. Toward the end of the war, he returned to civilian life, worked as a druggist for a time, but found it a lackluster career, and reenlisted in 1867. Bradley's military records reveal that he was five feet nine inches tall, brown haired, dark complected, and weighed 150 pounds. His post-war duty took him west, where he was assigned to a unit responsible for guarding the stage coach lines and constructing the Union Pacific railroad. Bradley proved to be as proficient a boatsman as he claimed, and a proficient diarist as well. According to Sumner's description he was not particularly big but "tough as a badger."

Major Powell and his newly constructed river boats arrived at the Union Pacific station at Green River, Wyoming, on 11 May 1869. Mrs. Powell stayed home in Detroit to await the outcome. Each of the boats contained three watertight compartments large enough to hold food, instruments, and supplies. The three larger boats measured twenty-one feet, carried forty-five hundred pounds each, and were built of oak. The fourth, a sixteen-footer, was Powell's pilot boat, built of pine to keep it light and maneuverable. Despite their several virtues, Powell's other boats were heavy, cumbersome, and often unmaneuverable. Every time the crew was obliged to line down or portage around a bad rapid, they cursed both the Major and his boats.

At practically the last minute, while the boats were being loaded and the crew was getting used to them, Powell signed on two more men. The Major noticed Andy Hall standing about at the Green River campsite, resting on the oars of his homemade boat. The Major talked to Andy for a few minutes and enlisted him on the spot. Andy Hall was but eighteen at the time, but he had five years of experience behind him as a bullwacker, scout, and mule driver. He was a husky, hard-hitting lad who had been involved in Indian skirmishes and had a large capacity for adventure and "raising hell" wherever he went. Powell comments in his journal that Andy was "without known family ties." His cheerfulness and humor amused and lifted the others throughout the trip. As the cook for the expedition, he did the best he could with the limited foods he had and seems to have compensated for the mediocre product with endless pranks. He became known as "the character" of the outfit. The last man to join the expedition was Frank Goodman, a young Englishman who had been wandering about the West seeking adventure and who offered to pay Powell if the Major would take him on. There is no indication as to whether the Major took Goodman's money, but he did take Frank Goodman. The trip was more work than Goodman bargained for and, after he nearly drowned in the wreck at Disaster Falls, he left the expedition, making his way to an Indian agency.

What a strange crew they were for a major expedition: a one-armed ex-major, a psychologically wounded ex-captain, a disillusioned army sergeant, a printer, a bullwacker and scout, an English adventurer, and four mountain men. Only three of the ten had not served in the army during the Civil War. Professor Powell was motivated by his drive for knowledge and his desire to map the unknown region and understand its history. But what drove the other nine men to risk their lives on Powell's exploration? Obviously they were not going along for the wages, since the voyage had received scant financial backing and hardly enough to pay them. Certainly they were drawn by the adventure of it, the magnetism unexplored country holds out to frontiersmen on the brink of any unknown region. But one other word was in their imaginations if not on their tongues and that word was gold. Nearly everyone in the West in the 1860s had heard stories about ledges of pure gold just waiting for prospectors and of gold-laden tributaries to the Colorado that no man had panned. Yet interestingly enough, once the voyage got underway, there is almost no reference to gold in the journals.

During the days immediately preceding the 24th of May, Powell and his nine companions named their boats and loaded them down with provisions sufficient for a ten-month expedition. Powell named his pilot boat for his wife, the *Emma Dean,* and the others were christened *Maid of the Canyon, Kitty Clyde's Sister,* and, somewhat ominously, the *No-Name.* At noon on 24 May, the crew took to their oars and sweeps, and Powell waved his hat to the little crowd assembled to wish them well.

They were fortunate to start out with a stretch of mild water, since most of them were not practiced boatmen. The river turned fast and dangerous soon enough, however, and they discovered how quickly a lapse of attention or a trivial error could lead to a soaking. From his command boat, the Major could survey the rapids before the others were upon them and he signaled to them whether to run each rapid or pull for shore.

Lining is the method Powell devised for letting boats down by rope through a severe rapid. All of the supplies had to be removed beforehand to lighten the boats and then portaged to the lower end. With ropes tied fore and aft, half the crew would slowly line the boat down one side of the rapid. When they could no longer hold on, they would release their rope, hoping the crew on the lower end would be able to pull tight on their ropes and bring the bounding craft to shore. This made for slow, exhausting progress, and Powell's crew would have often preferred to take their chances with the rocks. But the Major was in command and he had no intention of jeopardizing his expedition to the thrill of running rapids.

It may have been just this sort of conflict that caused the loss of one boat, the *No-Name,* at Disaster Falls, on 9 June. In his excitement over the treacherous rapids before him, the Major may have forgotten to signal, or Oramel Howland, tired of portaging, may have decided to run the rapid. Before he could maneuver the *No-Name,* already half-full of water from the previous rapid, it was swept right into the falls. The *No-Name* soon broadsided and broke in two on a boulder. With great difficulty, her crew was rescued from the raging river, but the food, clothing, and some of the equipment stored in the *No-Name* were lost. This first taste of the river's fury brought caution to the crew, but it also caused their later famine, and touched off Powell's smoldering animosity toward Oramel Howland. These two factors contributed to the growing conflict that culminated at Separation Rapids on 28 August.

Despite the continual grumblings of his crew, Powell seems to have been a happy man, making measurements, taking readings, drawing maps and geologic sections. Bradley put it this way in his journal: "If the Major does not do something soon I fear the consequences. . . . If he can only study geology he will be happy without food or shelter. . . ." By contrast, the preoccupied Major records in his journal on the same day: "The men talk as cheerfully as ever. . . ."

Powell's sense of the historic significance of his expedition does seem to have influenced his crew. Not only were they traveling an unknown, unmapped river, its features were also unnamed. Their journals contain notes and sometimes report discussion and debate over the naming of a tributary, a rapid, each new canyon, even the rock strata.

Through every day and hour of their ordeal in the great unknown, Powell seems to have remained a man of granitic will. His determination not to abandon the expedition or the river ultimately proved sound. Powell knew he was engaged in work of major significance and gave himself to the trip with the obsession of both the dedicated scientist and the fanatic. He felt quite certain his discoveries would add his "mite to the great sum of human knowledge." What Powell could not have known then is that the journals he and his men were keeping would form so dramatic a living narrative, one of America's great sagas of adventure and exploration.

A Note on the Text

*The merging of these individual journals and accounts has presented editorial chal-
lenges since some were written during the 1869 expedition (the journals of Bradley,
Hawkins, and Powell), while others were written much later (the accounts of Hawkins, Powell, and Sumner). Although the accounts add valuable later insights and
perspectives they sometimes suffer from loss of memory and immediacy. The entries are
arranged chronologically and alphabetically, the journals for each day appearing
before the accounts. In order to avoid excessive duplication and to aid readability, I
have cut about five percent of the original text, as indicated by ellipses. Since
nonstandard spelling and syntax often help readers capture the flavor of individual
voices, the entries have not been corrected. Occasional footnotes, or notes within the text*
[in brackets], have been added for clarification.

*Readers will probably come to rely on certain voices for the things they do best. Even
though Major Powell's account is often inaccurate as to dates and details, no other
voice gives us his sweep of geography and his wide-angle vision. On the other hand,
Bradley provides the personnel reports, an area in which Powell provides almost
nothing. As if individual soloists in an ensemble, one learns to listen to each voice, to
Bradley, Hawkins, Powell, and Sumner, for its distinctive part in this dramatic work
that touches our human need for adventure, our need to explore unknowns.*

The Journals

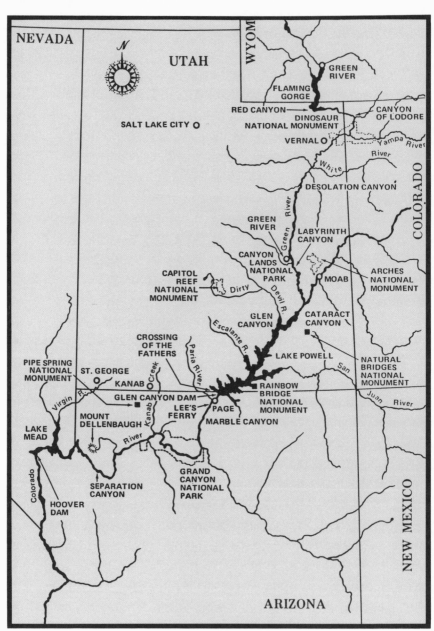

Route of the Powell expedition.

I.   Preparations for Departure

This opening section serves as a prologue to the river voyage and introduces, at length, the two most colorful characters and journal writers of the expedition. Their accounts, unlike the raw and immediate trip journals, were written many years after the adventure. Since even Major Powell did not write about this phase of the expedition, it is fortunate that Hawkins and Sumner recorded their first encounters with and impressions of the Major and his entourage of students and naturalists, between autumn 1867 and 24 May 1869.

Powell and his dream of exploring the Colorado must have had magnetic pull on both men, for Sumner, who ran a trading post, and Hawkins, who had purchased his supplies for a winter of trapping, both decided to join the Major's party. They also made arrangements to sell Powell their supplies and equipment, probably imagining he had greater financial backing than he did. Both men complained, at the end of the voyage, that Powell never adequately compensated them for their equipment and expenses, which may well be the case since he financed the project himself with minimal public support.

Because Sumner's and Hawkins's accounts were written years after the trip, they should be read as the fixed attitudes and settled stories each established regarding Powell and the voyage. One can also see this tendency at work in Powell's account, which starts on 24 May. It was written about five years after the experience, even after the second expedition (1871-72), and published in

1875. In all three accounts, while one misses the directness and immediacy of a journal entry, one can see what the whole experience, including its many subadventures, came to mean to these three narrators. Unlike John Wesley Powell, Hawkins and Sumner did not achieve fame, high position, and a place in history. They were relegated to the position of footnote figures in the exploration of the West, and they knew it. Thus, when asked to write their recollections of the experience, with the hindsight of having read Powell's published account, they had at last some opportunity to tell the tale their way. Consequently, each claims a major role in initiating, planning, and preparing for the voyage, leaving, if we were to take their accounts as fact, almost nothing for Powell to have done except follow orders. Since Powell had enjoyed a distinguished Washington career, some of the criticisms of Sumner and Hawkins, who wrote their accounts a few years after his death in 1902, may have stemmed from bruised egos at having been left behind. Regardless of their motives, the three narrative voices of Powell, Hawkins, and Sumner present an interesting study in contrasts: the parallax of personality and selective memory. Since readers may be as interested in narrative personalities as in accurate historical representation, there is little point in trying to isolate the truth, if indeed there is such a thing, from some colorful journalistic bullwacking by Sumner and Hawkins.

Hot Sulphur Springs, Colorado

Jack Sumner Account of Fall 1867   In the fall of 1867 Major J. W. Powell came to me at my trading post in the Hot Springs in Middle Park, Colorado, bringing letters from Denver parties requesting me to show him the country at large, and give him all the information I could, especially in regard to the natural history of the Park and adjacent country. I saddled up and took him around to about all the points of interest, making daily collections of the various animals at that time inhabiting that part of the Rocky Mountains. They were elk, mule deer, mountain sheep, antelope, and the various fur-bearing animals, three kinds of bear—the grizzly, the cinnamon, and the black— beaver, otter, marten, and mink; the grey wolf and his bastard cousin, the coyote, wolverine, silver cross and red foxes, besides some smaller animals generally classed as vermin by a free trapper, of no value for furs, but of great interest to the naturalist.

In our evening talks around the campfire, I gave the Major some new ideas in regard to the habits of animals, as he had gotten his information from books, and I from personal observation of the animals themselves, in a perfectly wild state. We differed widely, especially so in regard to beaver and how they worked. I had to take him to a beaver village on the sly and let him see for himself before I could get that silly idea out of his head that beaver use their tails as trowels and sleds in building their dams. . . .

After spending two or three weeks wandering in the Park, the Major seemed to get stuck on me for some reason or no reason at all, and wanted me to leave Middle Park, and go with him the following summer to the Bad Lands of Dakota on a geological trip. I declined the proposition and fired back at him the counter-proposition—the exploration of the Colorado River of the West, from the junction of the Green and Grand rivers to the Gulf of California. He at first scouted the idea as foolhardy and impossible. I urged on him the importance of the work, and what a big feature it would be in our hats if we succeeded. After several windy fights around the campfire, I finally outwinded him, and it was agreed that he should come out the following spring and we would make the attempt. I believe Major Powell states in his report that the exploration of the Colorado River had been in his mind for years. He mentioned nothing of the kind to me previous to our discussion and agreement. The ideas was certainly not his own.

Collecting the specimens I had gratuitously gathered for him in the Middle Park region, Major Powell departed for the States, agreeing to be back as soon as the grass started the following spring, and we would then commence the generally supposed foolish and impossible task. Each of us was to bear, share and share alike, all of the expense. I remained in Middle Park that winter collecting for the Smithsonian Institution.

Major Powell appeared on the field at Berthoud Pass the following June (1868), with a gang of twenty-five or thirty college students from fifteen to twenty-five years of age, with no experience whatever. They were good enough in their place, but about as fit for the work supposedly to be ahead of us as I would be behind a dry-goods counter, or hell for a powder house. He then told me he had changed the original plan of attack, as he had secured authority from Congress, through the influence of Senator Trumbull of Illinois, to draw supplies for twelve men at any western army post whenever the supplies were called for, which was a pretty good thing, as supplies were very expensive at all frontier posts.

Sumner Account of Summer 1868   After remaining at Berthoud Pass for two or three weeks, the outfit moved down to Hot Sulphur Springs and made that place headquarters for the remainder of the summer, collecting, mapping the country, and measuring various mountains around the extreme head of Grand Rivers, and made the first ascent of Long's Peak, August 4th, 1868.

William Hawkins Account of Summer 1868   In the summer of 1868, I was camped at Hot Sulphur Springs in Middle Park, Colorado, with my pack train of two mules and two horses. I was at that time trapping. My headquarters camp was 100 miles west, but in the summer I would take the furs I had caught during the winter out to Denver and sell them, and then put in three months packing provisions to my camp for the next season's trapping. I had gone out as soon as the snow was so I could cross the mountain range, and had already made two trips and was on my third and last for that summer when I heard of Major J. W. Powell's proposed expedition.* Returning, I camped at Jack Sumner's place at Hot Sulphur to rest my animals three or four days. I think it was the second day after I got to Sumner's post that Major Powell's pack outfit came in and camped a short distance from where I was. It was the custom of us mountaineers as well as the Indians to find out where strangers were going and what for, since we as well as the Indians respected each other's trapping grounds. Therefore, I went over to Powell's camp to find out what his intentions were.

I found the Major a very pleasant gentleman and very easy to get acquainted with. I asked him his business in that part of the country, and he stated his final object was the exploration of the Grand Canyon of the Colorado.

Next morning Sumner and Major Powell came over to my camp, where Dunn had spent the night with me, and Sumner spoke up and said that the Major would like us (Dunn and me) to join his party for the winter, as well as for the trip down the canyons of the Colorado. I told the Major that Sumner was thinking of selling his trading post, and that he, Dunn, and myself were going to try the canyons as far as Cottonwood Island. I told him that I had already packed my year's supplies in from Denver. The Major replied, "Those things are just what we want, also your mules and horses. I will buy them and pay you just what you can sell them for elsewhere." I told him I would think the matter over and let him know in the evening. In the meantime he and Sumner arranged a trade for Sumner's supplies at his post.

White River Camp to Green River

Sumner Account of Fall 1868 In October we commenced moving everything to the White River country. We had to pack in relays, as there was a lot of stuff of no use whatever. As game was plentiful on the route, we lived well and finally got bag and baggage to the White River and built winter quarters on the north side of the White River at the point afterwards made historical by Nathan

---

*Powell originally contemplated boating down the Grand River. What really changed his mind was the completion of the Transcontinental Railroad to Green River, Wyoming. This meant that boats and supplies could be transported directly to the river by railroad rather than across the Colorado Rockies by wagon.

Meeker, who built an agency there for the Ute Indians.

Later on Meeker and all the men of the agency were killed and all the women kept prisoners for some time, and they would have been killed, too, but for the influence of Chief Ouray of the Uncompahgre band of Utes.* A similar fate was narrowly averted for our party of '69 through the friendship of Chief Antero of the Uinta tribe of Utes and myself. Major Powell had measured off some geological work and set some stakes. The Utes thought that meant farming, and of course they would not have it that way. As we were only ten to about a thousand, our cake would have been dough if they had not been well talked to and the obnoxious stakes pulled up and thrown into the White River.

It has always been a strange thing to me that educated men seldom use common sense in their dealings with wild Indians. Meeker proposed to make the Utes good farmers and highly civilized in a few days. We know the results. Powell had a notion that his name and prestige would carry him anywhere, a common and very often a fatal mistake with army officers. Note the cases of Col. Fetterman and Gen. Custer, I doubt very much if Lewis and Clark could have traveled across the continent but for the cool head and quiet ways of Clark in dealing with the Indians. Fremont would have been stopped at the forks of the Platte but for the cool heads of his guides and scouts.

Hawkins Account of Winter 1868-69   We made our Winter camp on White River, hunting, trapping, and gathering specimens. In the spring of 1869 we moved to Green River City, and waited for the arrival of Major Powell and the boats from the East.

Sumner Account of Fall and Winter 1868-69   We camped on White River from November, 1868, until next March, collecting and exploring the country for a hundred miles around, the snow being too deep for us to make any very extended trips. Major Powell's students had by this time dwindled down to one out of the twenty-five, and he was terribly homesick. March 4th, 1869, we abandoned our winter camp and started through pretty deep snow for Bear

---

*The Meeker Massacre occurred in 1879. It was an interesting case of pure blindness of a "superior" toward an "inferior" culture. The references to Fetterman and Custer are pertinent in that their arrogance assisted in their own destruction. Captain (not Colonel) William Fetterman, based at Fort Phil Kearny, disregarded orders of his superior, Colonel Henry B. Carrington, on 6 December 1866, not to follow the Sioux over Lodge Trail Ridge. Fetterman and 40 cavalrymen were wiped out by Crazy Horse and the Sioux. Custer, of course, showed this same type of arrogance when he and his command were surrounded and killed by thousands of Sioux and Cheyenne on 25 June 1876. Lewis and Clark wisely avoided this type of arrogance, even to the extent of hiring an Indian girl, Sacajawea, as guide.

River, about sixty miles northwest on the old trail to Brown's Hole.* We reached Bear River in three days and found no snow at all, good grass, and plenty of antelope but no other game.

Next day the main party pulled on, Major Powell going back to the States to make preparations for our Colorado River journey. Howland, Dunn, and I remained behind to examine the country adjacent to Bear, Little Snake, and Vermilion rivers. We spent several days in the work and then moved on to Brown's Hole, where we camped for about two weeks and had lots of fun. Deer were very plentiful and the water fowl were in flight, so we had duck soup and roasted ribs about every meal. After we got tired of our camp in Brown's Hole, we proceeded on our way to old Fort Bridger by way of Henry's Fork, seeing nothing of interest but a fight between a large flock of mountain ravens and a mountain lion in the cliffs of a cavernously eroded butte—a form of butte characteristic of that graveyard of prehistoric reptiles. We reached Fort Bridger, and then on to Green River Station on the Union Pacific railroad, where we camped and awaited orders and in the meantime tried to drink all the whiskey there was in town. The result was a failure, as Jake Fields persisted in making it faster than we could drink it.

Green River City, Wyoming

Sumner Account of Spring 1869   About May 12th, '69, Major Powell returned from the States with the four boats which had been built in Chicago from plans I drew at our winter quarters on White River. Three of them were twenty-one feet long, six feet wide and two feet, two inches deep, decked fore and aft about five feet, and with water-tight compartments. The pilot boat, the "Emma Dean," was sixteen feet long, four feet wide, and twenty inches deep. Major Powell brought out a lot of necessary trinkets, and also a young scientific duck who was not at all necessary. However, he did not give us much time to imbibe his wisdom, as he stayed only one day. One good look at the Green River and the gang was enough. He vamoosed the camp that night, and we were left in darkness, mourning bitterly. I then induced Seneca Howland, Frank Goodman, and Andy Hall, the latter a rollicking young Scotch boy, to cast their lot with us. George Bradley, a sergeant from Fort Bridger, also joined us at Green River, he having been discharged by order of Gen. Grant especially to go with us. He was something of a geologist and, in my eyes far more

---

*Brown's Hole (now known as Brown's Park) lies half in Utah and half in Colorado, with the Green River cutting directly through it. Surrounded by mountains, its mild winter climate was well known to both Indians and mountain men. It was named for Baptiste Brown, as ex-Hudsons Bay Company employee, who became the valley's first white settler in 1827.

important, he had been raised in the Maine codfishery school, and was a good boatman, and a brave man, not very strong but as tough as a badger.

The start from Green River Station.

II. Green River City to Flaming Gorge

After nearly a month of final preparations, while encamped just below the transcontinental railroad bridge at Green River City, Wyoming, Powell's party of ten men and four boats was finally set for departure on 24 May. They were ready to test the worthiness of their new boats and their own strength of limb and character. Although the boats proved to be enormously heavy, cumbersome, and, with their long stern sweeps, barely maneuverable, still they were stout, solid craft that withstood tremendous beating.

Even though the entire voyage took only seventy-one days, Powell had no idea what to expect in the great unknown before him and thus took boats big enough to accommodate equipment and food for ten months. Not only were the boats designed to Powell's amateur specifications, he also selected a crew of amateurs. Except for Bradley, they possessed very limited boating and river experience, nor were they trained as naturalists, geographers, cartographers, or geologists.

Joining the voices of Hawkins and Sumner are those of Bradley, whose steady and reliable journal appears on every day of the expedition, and Powell, first his verbose account of the day-to-day experiences and then his clipped journal entries, forming a contrasting medley of voices. The journal voices of Bradley and Sumner give us, in contrast to Powell's descriptive passages, very detailed notes on such practical and mundane considerations as the size of rapids, the difficulties encountered, the number of miles completed. Greater contrast in subject and perspective there could hardly be. Powell's account reveals his search for the best perspective of the river and surrounding region; he climbs while his crew is repairing boats, hunting for supper, or gathering firewood. Here and throughout the narrative, Powell's attention is occasionally drawn to practical matters and the crew's grumbling or concern, but usually he lifts his eyes and his pen to record the wonders of this region.

Bradley, 24 May 1869   Left Green River City, Wyoming, with four boats (The "Emma Dean," "Maid of the Canon," "Kitty Clide's Sister" and "No Name") and 10 men (Prof. Powell and Brother, the Howland brothers, Wm. Dunn, Wm. Rhodes, Andy Hall, Frank Goodman, Jack Sumner and myself) at about one o'clock P.M. for the purpose of exploring the Green and Colorado Rivers. Passed rapidly down with the tide [current] almost without effort for about 8 or 10 miles when we encamped for the night in a cottonwood grove. The night was pleasant with indications of approaching rain. Made geological survey, found nothing worthy of note.

Sumner, 24 May   After much blowing off of gas and the fumes of bad whiskey, we were all ready by two o'clock and pulled out into the swift stream. The Emma Dean, a light four-oared shell, lightly loaded, carrying as crew Professor J. W. Powell, W. H. Dunn, and a trapper,* designed as a scouting party, taking the lead. The "Maid of the Canon" followed close in her wake, manned by Walter H. Powell and George Y. Bradley, carrying two thousand pounds of freight. Next on the way was "Kitty Clyde's Sister," manned by as jolly a brace of boys as ever swung a whip over a lazy ox, W. H. Rhodes, of Missouri, and Andrew Hall, of Fort Laramie, carrying the same amount of freight. The last to leave the miserable adobe village was the "No Name" (piratic craft) manned by O. G. Howland, Seneca Howland, and Frank Goodman. We make a pretty show as we float down the swift, glossy river. As Kitty's crew have been using the whip more of late years than the oars, she ran on a sand-bar in the middle of the river, got off of that, and ran ashore on the east side, near the mouth of Bitter creek, but finally got off and came down to the rest of the fleet in gallant style, her crew swearing she would not "gee" or "haw" a "cuss." We moved down about seven miles and camped for the night on the

---

*Sumner reserves for himself the title of trapper, a profession of high standing from 1824 to 1840 when the mountain men were stripping the fur-bearing animals from the Upper Colorado River basin.

eastern shore where there is a large quantity of cord wood. As it was a cold, raw night, we stole a lot of it to cook with. Proff., Walter, and Bradley spent a couple of hours geologising on the east side. Howland and Dunn went hunting down the river; returned at dark with a small sized rabbit. Rather slim rations for ten hungry men. The balance of the party stopped in camp, and exchanged tough stories at a fearful rate. We turned in early, as most of the men had been up for several proceding nights, taking leave of their many friends, "a la Muscovite." The natural consequence were fog[g]y ideas and snarly hair.

Hawkins Account of 24 May   On the 24th of May, 1869, we started down the Green River with provisions for eight or ten months, according to Major Powell. Our provisions got wet and were lost in different ways, and finally the largest boat-load was lost in Diamond Falls on the Green River. All this reduced our rations. Though we had plenty of fish on Green River, we caught very few on the Colorado and soon found we were up against it for grub. It was not long before we began to lose our hats and clothes. I had a pair of buckskin breeches. They were so wet all the time that they kept stretching and I kept cutting off the lower ends till I had nothing left but the waist band. When this was gone I was left with a pair of pants and two shirts. I took the pants and one shirt and put them in the boat's locker, as I did not know what the law was below as to nakedness. I cut holes in my shirt tail and tied the loose ends around my legs so they would not bother me in the water. Major Powell said he was dressed when he had his life preserver on, and he always had it on when the water was bad.

I can say one thing truthfully about the Major—that no man living was ever thought more of by his men up to the time he wanted to drive Bill Dunn from the party. A description of this you will find below.* I have only written here a few facts on things that happened on the Colorado expedition. There is no revenge in my heart. With the best of feelings towards the Major, I have written this because I think his Report is somewhat lacking. I am willing to do more by him than he ever did by any of us men. I am willing to call him a brave and daring leader, but I do not think the boys who left the party, the Howland brothers and Bill Dunn, under the circumstances herein mentioned, deserve to be branded as cowards. I do not wish to cast any discredit on Major Powell's Report or upon his memory of the Colorado expedition. But in justice to Dunn and the Howland brothers I must say that the account in the Report which accuses them of cowardice is entirely wrong, and that it was made to cover up the real cause of their leaving.

---

*For Hawkins's full commentary on this issue see his account of 28 July.

Powell Account of 24 May   The good people of Green River City turn out to see us start. We raise our little flag, push the boats from shore, and the swift current carries us down.

Our boats are four in number. Three are built of oak; stanch and firm; double-ribbed, with double stem and stern posts, and further strengthened by bulkheads, dividing each into three compartments.

Two of these, the fore and aft, are decked, forming water-tight cabins. It is expected these will buoy the boats should the waves roll over them in rough water. The little vessels are twenty-one feet long, and, taking out the cargoes, can be carried by four men.

The fourth boat is made of pine, very light, but sixteen feet in length, with a sharp cut-water, and every way built for fast rowing, and divided into compartments as the others.

We take with us rations deemed sufficient to last ten months; for we expect, when winter comes on and the river is filled with ice, to lie over at some point until spring arrives; so we take with us abundant supplies of clothing. We have also a large quantity of ammunition and two or three dozen traps. For the purpose of building cabins, repairing boats, and meeting other exigencies, we are supplied with axes, hammers, saws, augers, and other tools, and a quantity of nails and screws. For scientific work, we have two sextants, four chronometers, a number of barometers, thermometers, compasses, and other instruments.

The flour is divided into three equal parts; the meat and all other articles of our rations in the same way. Each of the larger boats has an ax, hammer, saw, auger, and other tools, so that all are loaded alike. We distribute the cargoes in this way, that we may not be entirely destitute of some important article should any one of the boats be lost. In the small boat, we pack a part of the scientific instruments, three guns, and three small bundles of clothing only. In this, I proceed in advance, to explore the channel.

J. C. Sumner and William H. Dunn are my boatmen in the "Emma Dean" then follows "Kitty Clyde's Sister," manned by W. H. Powell and G. Y. Bradley; next, the "No Name," with O. G. Howland, Seneca Howland, and Frank Goodman; the last comes the "Maid of the Cañon," with W. R. Hawkins and Andrew Hall.

Our boats are heavily loaded, and only with the utmost care is it possible to float in the rough river without shipping water.

A mile or two below town, we run on a sand bar. The men jump into the stream, and thus lighten the vessels, so that they drift over; and on we go. In trying to avoid a rock, an oar is broken on one of the boats, and thus crippled, she strikes. The current is swift, and she is sent reeling and rocking into the eddy. In the confusion, two others [oars] are lost overboard and the men seem quite discomfited, much to the amusement of the other members of the party.

Catching the oars and starting again, the boats are once more borne down the stream until we land at a small cottonwood grove on the bank, and camp for noon. . . .

Standing on a high point, I can look off in every direction over a vast landscape, with salient rocks and cliffs glittering in the evening sun. Dark shadows are settling in the valleys and gulches, and the heights are made higher and the depths deeper by the glamour and witchery of light and shade.

Away to the south, the Uinta Mountains stretch in a long line; high peaks thrust into the sky, and snow-fields glittering like lakes of molten silver; and pine forests in somber green; and rosy clouds playing around the borders of huge, black masses; and heights and clouds, and mountains and snowfields, and forests and rocklands, are blended into one grand view. Now the sun goes down, and I return to camp.

Sumner Account of 24 May　We recalked and repainted the boats and, having everything in readiness, on May 24th, 1869, we pulled out into the swift current of the Green River in the following order: the "Emma Dean" with a crew of J. W. Powell, Bill Dunn and Jack Sumner; "Kitty Clyde's Sister," Walter Powell and George Bradley; "No Name," O. G. Howland, and Frank Goodman; "Maid of the Canyon," Bill Hawkins and Andy Hall.

The boats were ordered to keep one hundred yards apart. Flag signals were arranged as follows, always to be given by Major Powell from the pilot boat: flag waved right and left, then down, "Land at once"; waved to right, "Keep to right"; and waved to left, "Keep to left of pilot boat." As Major Powell was the only free-handed man in the outfit, he was supposed always to attend to that part of the business, but I fear he got too badly rattled to attend to it properly on several occasions, notably so at Disaster Falls in Lodore Canyon. As Bradley and I were the only experienced boatmen, there were some ludicrous mishaps for the first few days, running around at the head of sand bars being the principal trouble. Hall, who had once been a bull-whacker, swore that his boat would "neither gee or haw nor whoa worth a damn"—in fact, it "wasn't *broke* at all!"

The first day we ran down about ten miles and camped on an island. It rained most all day and night. We pulled out next morning and rowed nearly all day and arrived at the mouth of Henry's Fork, a famous beaver stream coming in from the northwest, and camped at the head of Flaming Gorge, our first canyon to butt into. The walls are not very high and are of a brilliant, fiery red color. We had no trouble in running the various canyons above Brown's Hole, but had to make a portage at Ashley Falls which kept us busy for nearly a day, as all the large boats were loaded to the safety limit. We carried the supplies over the rocks on the north side about fifty feet above the river. The boats were then let down by lines and rounded in and landed at the foot of the falls. . . .

Passing the falls, we leisurely rowed down and camped in about the middle of Brown's Hole, a fine camp, where we enjoyed ourselves to the limit, fishing, shooting ducks, and geologizing. From the camp we dropped down about ten miles and camped in the head of Lodore Canyon, measured the cliffs and took observations for exact location. We camped there one day and then attacked the worst place on Green River, as we soon found to our sorrow. There is a nest of nearly continuous rapids for twenty miles that is a holy terror. We had some trouble from the start in Lodore Canyon, shipping more or less water at every rapid.

Bradley, 25 May   Started little after 6 o'clock and passed on rapidly as ever until about 9½ A.M., when the leading boat grounded and before the signal of danger could be obeyed two other boats were aground. I had just time to go to the right of the leading boat and passed without touching. Landed and in a few moments all were clear. Only two men were wet by pushing off the boats. Went down a few miles farther and landed at 10½ A.M. to allow the two men to dry clothing. Bill Rhodes caught a young mountain sheep which offered an excellent dinner.

Sumner, 25 May   Pull out early and dropped down to an old cabin, where I stole two bread-pans for the cook's use. Moved about eight miles and camped in the willows, as it was raining hard; stopped two hours; made some coffee, and cooked some villainous bacon to warm us up a little.

Then pulled out again, as it showed some signs of clearing off. Went another five or six mile stretch when we saw five mountain sheep on a cliff; stopped to give chase, but they proved to be too nimble for us. Rhodes, however, found a lamb asleep on the cliff caught it by the heels and threw it off toward camp. The Professor and Bradley climbed a black looking cliff on the west side to see how it was made. All into camp by 3 o'clock, when we had our young sheep for dinner. Packed up the cooking utensils and pulled out again, and moved down through a rather monotonous country for six or eight miles further. Saw several wild geese and four beavers, but failed to get any. While rounding to on the west side, all the boats except Kitty's Sister got fast on a sand bar—the Maid so fast she had to be pried off with oars. Camped on the west side, in the willow brush. While we were gathering drift-wood for camp fires, two mountain sheep ran out of the willows and up the side of the bluff.

Two of the boys followed, but failed to get either of them. Rained all day and most of the night.

Powell Account of 25 May We started early this morning and run along at a good rate until about nine o'clock, when we are brought up on a gravelly bar. All jump out, and help the boats over by main strength. Then a rain comes on, and river and clouds conspire to give us a thorough drenching. Wet, chilled, and tired to exhaustion, we stop at a cottonwood grove on the bank, build a huge fire, make a cup of coffee, and are soon refreshed and quite merry.

Upper Flaming Gorge

Bradley, 26 May Got breakfast and entered boats at 8 A.M. Shortly after it commenced raining and kept it up all day. Stopped for dinner at 12 M. and then passed on, crossed the largest and most difficult rapid yet seen—only one boat grounded and no injury done except *one man took a bath*. The leading boat have shot a Duck and Goose, we went on shore at about 4 P.M., and had an excellent supper. Prepared a bed of willows with great care expecting that as it had rained all day it would be fair at night, but soon after bedtime it commenced to rain and kept it up all night. Got pretty wet but expect to be wetter before we reach our destination.

Sumner, 26 May All afloat early; went about three miles, when we came to our first rapid. It cannot be navigated by any boat with safety, in the main channel, but the river being pretty high, it made a narrow channel, under the overhanging willows on the west shore, so that we were not delayed more than twenty minutes, all the boats but Kitty's Sister getting through easily. She getting on a rock, compelled Rhodes to get overboard and pry her off. About 4 o'clock, came to a meadow of about a thousand acres, lying between Green River and Henry's Fork. Camped for the night on the east shore, about a mile above the mouth of Henry's Fork. Passed the mouth of Black's Fork of the Green River today; it is but little wider at the mouth than at Fort Bridger, but deep. Henry's Fork is a stream about thirty feet wide, and is fed by the snows of the Uinta Mountains, about seventy-five miles northwest of this camp; it has some good pasturage on it, but no farming land, as it is too great an altitude. At the mouth is a good place for one or two ranches. There are about three hundred acres of good land, but is inundated nearly every spring by freshets. There is a large stack of hay standing in the meadow, that has been left over from last year's crop.

Powell Account of 26 May   We glide quietly down the placid stream past the carved cliffs of the *mauvaises terres,** now and then obtaining glimpses of distant mountains. Occasionally, deer are started from the glades among the willows; and several wild geese, after a chase through the water, are shot.

After dinner, we pass through a short, narrow canyon into a braod valley; from this, long, lateral valleys stretch back on either side as far as the eye can reach.

The river is running to the south; the mountains have an easterly and westerly trend directly athwart its course, yet it glides on in a quiet way as if it thought a mountain range no formidable obstruction to its course. It enters the range by a flaring, brilliant, red gorge, that may be seen from the north a score of miles away.

The great mass of mountain ridge through which the gorge is cut is composed of bright vermilion rocks; but they are surmounted by broad bands of mottled buff and gray, and these bands come down with a gentle curve to the water's edge on the nearer slope of the mountain.

This is the head of the first canyon we are about to explore—an introductory one to a series made by the river through this range. We name it Flaming Gorge. The cliffs or walls we find on measurement, to be about one thousand two hundred feet high.

Henry's Fork

Bradley, 27 May   Started late this morning as we intended to go only a few miles down to the first canon at Henries Fork. Landed about two miles below starting point and took in some goods which had been cached since early spring; found everything safe and we passed on and soon passed a ranch at the mouth of Henries Fork now occupied by a Mormon family. Just below this fork we entered the mouth of the first canon and encamped amid the cotton-wood trees surrounded by bluffs 1200 ft. high and on one side nearly perpendicular. It is the grandest scenery I have found in the mountains and I am delighted with it. I went out to see the country this morning and found it grand beyond conception. The river winds like a serpent through between nearly perpendicular cliffs 1200 ft. high but instead of rapids it is deep and calm as a lake. It is the most safe of any part we have yet seen for navigation. Found some marine focils [fossils] in hard limestone—first yet found.

Mauvaises terres refers to badlands, an area of disintegrated Green River shale, sometimes colorful, but usually bleak, that supports little vegetation.

Sumner, 27 May   Raised a cache that we made two months since, and found everything safe; moved down to the head of a canyon and camped on the east side, under a grove of cottonwood trees. Proff., Walter, and Bradley went geologising. Tramped around most of the day in the mud and rain to get a few fossils. Distance from Green River City to mouth of Henry's Fork sixty miles* general course, 30 degrees E. of S; estimated land distance forty miles. Country worthless. Grease wood and alkali on the river bottom; on the hills sparse bunch grass, Artemissia, and a few stunted cedars. At intervals of four or five miles on the river there are a few scrubby cottonwoods, but none large enough for anything but fuel. Rained most of the day.

Powell Account of 27 May   Today it rains, and we employ the time in repairing one of our barometers, which was broken on the way from New York. A new tube has to be put in; that is, a long glass tube has to be filled with mercury four or five inches at a time, and each installment boiled over a spirit lamp. It is a delicate task to do this without breaking the glass; but we have success, and are ready to measure mountains once more.

Upper Flaming Gorge

Bradley, 28 May   Started alone this morning to explore the clift on N.E. side of the river. Went out at 8:20 A.M., and having traveled without being able to find foccils or to get down the clift to the river I got *mad* and resolved to get down if possible, but having climbed and walked until 2½ P.M., gave it up and set out for home, and having walked as fast as possible against a driving rain with an empty stomach until 7¼ P.M., I arrived opposite camp and the boat took me to camp as tired and hungry and mad as a bear.

Sumner, 28 May   Still in camp, Proff. and the "Trapper" repaired a broken barometer. Walter and Bradley went geologizing on the west side. Bradley did not get into camp until night, having lost his way, and had a long, weary tramp through the mud and rain.

Powell Account of 28 May   Today we go to the summit of the cliff on the left and take observations for altitude, and are variously employed in topographic and geological work.

---

*Sumner's estimate of sixty miles was not far off the sixty-eight miles measured by the 1922 survey. According to Frederick Dellenbaugh, Powell's party estimated miles traveled by having two men sight down a stretch of river with prismatic compasses. They then individually put down estimates and compared them, checking occasionally probably with a transit.

Bradley, 29 May   Rained all last night and is still (10:15 A.M.). Can't go out at all but if it rains only till noon shall take a geological section this P.M. The Major is mending two barometers which have become broken—Nothing of importance occured. Rain ceased at night.

Sumner, 29 May   Proff climbed the hill on the east side of the canyon and measured it with a barometer; h[e]ight above the river 1140 feet, not perpendicular. There is a cliff on the west side that is fifty feet higher, and perpendicular. The rock is hard, fiery-red sandstone. It has been named Flaming Gorge.

Powell Account of 29 May   This morning, Bradley and I cross the river, and climb more than a thousand feet to a point where we can see the stream sweeping in a long beautiful curve through the gorge below. Turning and looking to the west, we can see the valley of Henry's Fork, through which, for many miles, the little river flows in a tortuous channel.* Cottonwood groves are planted here and there along its course, and between them are stretches of grassland. The narrow mountain valley is enclosed on either side by sloping walls of naked rock of many bright colors. To the south of the valley are the Uintas, and the peaks of the Wasatch Mountains can be faintly seen in the far west. To the north, desert plains, dotted here and there with curiously carved hills and buttes, extend to the limit of vision.

For many years, this valley has been the home of a number of mountaineers, who were originally hunters and trappers, living with the Indians. Most of them have one or more Indian wives. They no longer roam with the nomadic tribes in pursuit of buckskin or beaver, but have accumulated herds of cattle and horses, and consider themselves quite well-to-do. Some of them have built cabins; others still live in lodges.

James Baker is one of the most famous of these men; and, from our point of view, we can see his lodge three or four miles up the river.**

---

*Henry's Fork could be named for Andrew Henry, partner of William H. Ashley in the early 1820s. Ashley, however, in his journal of his 1825 trip, named it "Randavouze Creek," since it was here that the first Rocky Mountain rendezvous was held. By 1829, however, he referred to it as "Henry Creek." Dale Morgan, in *The West of William H. Ashley,* says that the creek might be named for Henry "Boatswain" Brown, a mountain man killed in 1827 by Mohaves on the lower Colorado River.

**Jim Baker was a well-known former mountain man who lived, not on Henry's Fork, but on the Little Snake River in northwestern Colorado. If Powell could see Baker's lodge from the Green River it indicates only that Baker was on a visit—possibly trading with Indians—and probably living with an Indian woman. Baker lived into the 1880s, telling stories to reporters and others.

Gate of Lodore.

III.   Flaming Gorge through the
Canyon of Lodore to Echo Park

The great adventure that climaxed the first third of the trip was the capsizing and loss of one of the four boats, the *No Name,* at a mile-long rapid they named Disaster Falls. The loss of one of the boats, some of the equipment, one third of the food supplies, and all the clothing for three of the party, was serious enough, but the crash of the *No Name* may have had even more serious impact on the morale of the team. Fortunately, the next day they recovered their barometers, thermometers, and a small keg of "medicinal" whiskey from the waterproof compartment of the still-intact stern section of the boat. Recovery of the instruments was as much a restorative to Powell as was the whiskey to the men. But the crew knew they could have lost lives as well as a boat and equipment, a realization that sobered and cautioned them in their approach to subsequent white water. They also must have realized the mishap could have been averted if the *No Name* had been bailed out faster, had approached the rapid more cautiously, or if the hand signals had been more clearly given. If Hawkins and Sumner recall the episode accurately, Disaster Falls may well have marked the first step in a growing animosity between the two Powells on the one side and George Dunn and the Howland brothers on the other. It is their interpretation that the hard feelings over Disaster Falls started a conflict between the two groups that resulted in the splitting of the expedition at Separation Rapids, just days before the end of the expedition.

Kingfisher Cañon and Beehive Point

Bradley, 30 May   Named the first canon "Flaming Gorge," second "Canon of the Rappid," for we found in it a roaring rapid with a fall of several feet, but there being plenty of water we passed it with little difficulty though we took off boots and coats and prepared for a swim. My boat went over next to the little boat and took in but little water. All passed in safety. Next passed through another canon which we named "Kingfisher Canon," and at the upper end a stream which we called "Kingfisher Fork," for a kingfisher we saw at mouth of Fork. Camped in this canon for the night just above another rapid which I think we can pass with safety if we keep on the other side of the river. The bluff opposite our camp we call "Beehive Point" from its resemblance in shape to a straw beehive. Pleasant all night. Shot two geese and a bever but the latter sunk before we could get it.

Sumner, 30 May   Professor, Bradley, Senica, and Hall went up the river five miles, measuring a geological section. All in camp by three o'clock, when we loaded up and pulled on again into a channel as crooked as a street in Boston. Passed out of Flaming Gorge into Horseshoe Canon, out of Horseshoe Canon into Kingfisher Canon. While rounding a bend, we came on a herd of mountain sheep, that scampered up a steep, rocky side of the canon at an astonishing rate. The crews of the freight boats opened a volley on them that made the wilderness ring, reminding us all of other scenes and times, when we were the scampering party. Passed the mouth of a small stream coming in from the west, which we named King Fisher Creek, as there was a bird of that species perched on the branch of a dead willow, watching the finny tribe with the determination of purpose that we often see exhibited by politicians while watching for the spoils of the office.* Killed two geese, and saw a great number of beavers today, but failed to get any of them. No sooner would we get within gunshot, than down they would go with a plumping noise like dropping a heavy stone into the water. Made seven miles today, and camped for the night on the west bank opposite a huge grayish white sandstone that loomed up a thousand feet from the water's edge, very much the shape of an old-fashioned straw beehive, and we named it "Beehive Point." Saw the tracks of elk, deer and sheep on the sand. Near our camp, Goodman saw one elk, but missed it.

Powell Account of 30 May   This morning we are ready to enter the mysterious canyon, and start with some anxiety. The old mountaineers tell us that it

---

*The stream was later renamed Sheep Creek.

cannot be run; the Indians say, "Water heap catch 'em," but all are eager for the trial, and off we go.

Entering Flaming Gorge, we quickly run through it on a swift current, and emerge into a little park. Half a mile below, the river wheels sharply to the left, and we turned into another canyon cut into the mountain. We enter the narrow passage. On either side, the walls rapidly increase in altitude. On the left are overhanging ledges and cliffs five hundred—a thousand—fifteen hundred feet high.

On the right, the rocks are broken and ragged, and the water fills the channel from cliff to cliff. Now the river turns abruptly around a point to the right, and the waters plunge swiftly down among great rocks; and here we have our first experience with canyon rapids. I stand up on the deck of my boat to seek a way among the wave-beaten rocks. All untried as we are with such waters, the moments are filled with intense anxiety. Soon our boats reach the swift current; a stroke or two, now on this side, now on that, and we thread the narrow passage with exhilarating velocity, mounting the high waves, whose foaming crests dash over us, and plunging into the troughs, until we reach the quiet water below; and then comes a feeling of great relief. Our first rapid is run. Another mile, and we come into the valley again.

Let me explain this canyon. Where the river turns to the left above, it takes a course directly into the mountain, penetrating to its very heart, then wheels back upon itself, and runs out into the valley from which it started only half a mile below the point at which it entered; so the canyon is in the form of an elongated letter U, with the apex in the center of the mountain. We name it Horseshoe Canyon.

Soon we leave the valley, and enter another short canyon, very narrow at first, but widening below as the canyon walls increase in height. Here we discover the mouth of a beautiful little creek, coming down through its narrow water-worn cleft. Just at its entrance there is a park of two or three hundred acres, walled on every side by almost vertical cliffs, hundreds of feet in altitude, with three gateways through the walls—one up, another down the river, and the third passage through which the creek comes in. The river is broad, deep, and quiet, and its waters mirror towering rocks.

Kingfishers are playing about the streams, and so we adopt the names Kingfisher Creek, Kingfisher Park, and Kingfisher Canyon. At night, we camp at the foot of this canyon.

Kingfisher Cañon

Bradley, 31 May   Have been passing rapids all day. Have once had to let the boats down with ropes. Have worked very hard to pass about 10 miles and have encamped in the midst of a very bad rapid which we must pass with ropes in the morning.

Sumner, 31 May   This morning Professor, Bradley, and Dunn went up the river two miles to examine some rocks and look for a lost blank book. Howland and Goodman climbed a high mountain on the west side to get a good view of the country at large, and so draw a good map. All ready by ten o'clock when we pull out and are off like the wind; ran about two miles through a rapid and into still water for half an hour, then to a bad rapid through which no boat can run; full of sunken rocks, and having a fall of about ten feet in two hundred yards. We were compelled to let our boats down along the west side with ropes from men holding the line, two men with oars keeping them off the rocks; made the passage in about two hours, and ran a large number of them in ten miles travel.

About 5 o'clock, we came to the worst place we had seen yet; a narrow gorge full of sunken rock, for 300 yards, through which the water run with a speed that threatened to smash everything to pieces that would get into it.

All the boats were landed as quick as possible on the east side of the river, when we got out to examine the best point to get through, found ourselves on the wrong side of the river, and how to cross was the next question. We all plainly saw that it would be no child's play. Dunn and the trapper finally decided to take the small boats across or smash her to pieces; made the passage safe, unloaded and returned to relieve the freight boats, they taking out half their loads by making two trips with the freight boats and five with the small; we got everything safely across where we wanted it by sunset. Had supper; turned in; and in two minutes all were in dreamland.

Powell Account of 31 May   We start down another canyon and reach rapids made dangerous by high rocks lying in the channel; so we run ashore, and let our boats down with lines. In the afternoon we come to more dangerous rapids, and stop to examine them. I find we must do the same work again, but, being on the wrong side of the river to obtain a foothold, must first cross over—no very easy matter in such a current, with rapids and rocks below. We take the pioneer boat "Emma Dean" over, and unload her on the bank; then she returns and takes another load. Running back and forth, she soon has half our cargo over; then one of the larger boats is manned and taken across, but carried down almost to the rocks in spite of hard rowing. The other boats follow and make the landing, and we go into camp for the night.

At the foot of the cliff on this side, there is a long slope covered with pines; under these we make our beds, and soon after sunset are seeking rest and sleep. The cliffs on either side are of red sandstone, and stretch up toward the heavens 2,500 feet. On this side, the long, pine-clad slope is surmounted by perpendicular cliffs, with pines on their summits. The wall on the other side is bare rock from the water's edge up 2,000 feet, then slopes back, giving footing to pines and cedars. . . .*

Ashley Falls and Red Cañon

Bradley, 1 June   Let the boats down a little way this morning and then got in and went down like lightning for a very long distance until we came again to so bad a place we had to let down again, after which we passed on for many miles, sometimes going like a racehorse until near night when we came upon a place where the red sand-stone from the mountain had fallen into and blocked up the river, making a heavy fall. Have unloaded and taken one boat down with ropes but night coming on we shall wait until morning before we take the rest down the fall. We unload them and attaching a strong rope to each end we let them down without much injury to the boats but we have to carry the rations around on our backs, and as the shore is filled with huge bowlders recently fallen from the mountain, we shall have a hard day's work, to get all around tomorrow for each of the three large boats has over 2000 lbs. baggage. The river looks smooth below and as the mountains begin to slope more, we feel certain that we are getting out of this succession of rappids. Weather has been pleasant for the past two days but threatens rain tonight. Named the falls "Ashley Falls," for we found his name on the rocks beside them.** Named the canon "Red Canon," for it is chiefly red sand-stone.

Sumner, 1 June   After an early breakfast, all hands went to work letting the boats down with ropes, made the passage in three hours, when we jumped aboard again, and off we go like a shot; ran through about a dozen rapids in the course of ten miles, when we came to some signs of the country opening out. The walls were getting lower, and not so rough, and the current gradually slackens till it almost ceases. As the roaring of the rapids dies away above us, a new cause of alarm breaks in upon us from below. We ran along on the still water, with a vague feeling of trouble ahead, for about two miles, when, turning an abrupt corner, we came in sight of the first fall, about three hundred yards below us. Signaled the freight boats to land, when the Emma was run

---

*These mountain cliff heights are, of course, mere estimates based on experienced observation. Powell did have a technique of "laying down," viewing an elevation first with one eye and then the other, thus providing a rough "optical triangulation."

**General Wm. H. Ashley, the famous explorer and fur trader, descended the canyons of the Green in 1825.

down within a rod of the fall, and landed on the east side. Her crew then got out to reconnoitre; found a fall of about ten feet in twenty-five. There is a nearly square rock in the middle of the stream about twenty-five by thirty feet, the top fifteen above the water. There are many smaller ones all the way across, placed in such a manner that the fall is broken into steps, two on the east side, three on the west. We all saw that a portage would have to be made here. Without any loss of time the Emma Dean was unloaded and pushed into the stream, four men holding the line, the remainder of the party stationed on the rocks, each with oar, to keep her from being driven on some sharp corners and smahed to pieces. Got her under the fall in fifteen minutes, when we returned, unloaded Kitty's Sister, had supper and went to sleep on the sand. There is not much of a canyon at the falls. Three hundred yards from the east side there is a cliff about 450 feet high, from whence the rocks have fallen to make the dam.

Powell Account of 1 June   Last spring I had a conversation with an old Indian named Pa-ri-ats, who told me about one of his tribe attempting to run this canyon. "The rocks," he said, holding his hands above his head, his arms vertical, and looking between them to the heavens, "the rocks h-e-a-p, h-e-a-p high; the water go h-oo-woogh, h-oo-woogh; water-pony (boat) h-e-a-p buck; see 'em papoose any more!"* Those who have seen these wild Indians ponies rearing alternately before and behind, or "bucking," as it is called in the vernacular, will appreciate his description.

Little Brown's Hole

Bradley, 2 June   Had the boats all over the fall and loaded by 11 A.M., and were on board and away again immediately after dinner. Have run over 15 miles and camped at 3 P.M. in what hunters call "Little Brown's Hole."** The camp is green and grassy and our beds are made beneath two noble pines. The hills around seem low after passing such huge mountains as we have had for several days. The rapids have been more noisy today than yesterday but the bowlders have not been so thick as usual and a general improvement in the

---

*Powell spent the winter of 1868–69 in a cabin at the White River Ute Agency (present-day Meeker, Colorado), from which he made short overland forays to the Uinta Basin, Brown's Hole, and Green River, Wyoming. He was in almost daily contact with Ute Indians, including Pa-ri-ats, and many others.

**Renamed "Brown's Park" by Major Powell.

water as the hills grow lower. The men are out hunting and have not yet come in but if they have their usual luck *we shall have bacon for breakfast.* I am too tired to go out for specimens today. Think the hills are too much covered with earth to be good ground for foccils.* The hunters have come in as usual without game, but the Major has brought in two grouse which will make a nice breakfast. The sky is clear—weather warm and delightful.

Sumner, 2 June All out early to breakfast; dispatched it, and let Kitty's Sister over the falls as we did the small boat. Then came the real hard work, carrying the freight a hundred yards or more over a mass of loose rocks, tumbled together like the ruins of some old fortress. Not a very good road to pack seven thousand pounds of freight. Got the loads of the two boats over, loaded them, and moved down three hundred yards to still water; tied up and returned to the other boats, to serve them the same; got everything around in still water by 11 o'clock; had dinner and smoked all round; distance from Bee-Hive Point unknown; course east of south; continuous canyon of red sand-stone; estimated height of one thousand feet; three highest perpendicular walls estimated at two thousand two hundred feet: named Red Canyon; on a rock the east side there is the name and date—"Ashley, 1825"—scratched on evidently by some trapper's knife; all aboard, and off we go down the river; beautiful river, that increases its speed as we leave the fall, till it gets a perfect rapid all the way, but clear of sunken rocks; so we run through the waves at express speed; made seventeen miles through Red Stone canyon in less than an hour running time, the boats bounding through the waves like a school pony. We plunge along singing, yelling, like drunken sailors, all feeling that such rides do not come every day. It was like sparking a black-eyed girl—just dangerous enough to be exciting. About three o'clock we came suddenly out to a beautiful valley about two by five miles in extent. Camped about the middle of it, on the west side, under two large pine trees; spread our bedding out to dry, while we rested in the shade. Two of the party came in at sunset, empty handed except the Professor, he being fortunate enough to get a brace of grouse. Spread our blankets on the clean, green grass, with no roof but the old pines above us, through which we could see the sentinel stars shining from the deep blue pure sky, like happy spirits looking out through the blue eyes of a pure hearted woman.

As we are guided on this voyage by the star in the blue; so may it be on the next, by the spirit in the blue.

---

*They sought any kind of small, transportable fossil, such as trilobites, leaves, and fish.

Powell Account of 2 June*   On a high rock by which the trail passes we find the inscription: "Ashley 18—5." The third figure is obscure—some of the party reading it 1835, some 1855.

James Baker, an old time mountaineer, once told me about a party of men starting down the river, and Ashley was named as one. The story runs that the boat was swamped, and some of the party drowned in one of the canyons below.** The word "Ashley" is a warning to us, and we resolve on great caution. Ashley Falls is the name we give to the cataract.

The river is very narrow; the right wall vertical for two or three hundred feet, the left towering to a great height, with a vast pile of broken rocks lying between the foot of the cliff and the water. Some of the rocks broken down from the ledge above have tumbled into the channel and caused this fall. One great cubical block, thirty or forty feet high, stands in the middle of the stream, and the waters, parting to either side, plunge down about twelve feet, and are broken again by the smaller rocks into a rapid below.

Bradley, 3 June   After eating a hearty breakfast of fried grouse and hot biscuit went out to hunt for game and foccils. Found neither but found the country just as I expected, too much covered with trees and earth to be an interesting place to study geology. Think it will not be many years before these green hills will be covered with cattle and dotted here and there with the homes of ranchmen, for the hillsides are green and watered with little mountain torrents that seem to leap and laugh down the hillsides in wild delight. Can stand on almost any eminence and overlook thousands on thousands of acres of most excellent grazing land and we have lowered our altitude and lattitude until it is warm enough to raise almost any kind of veretables that will grow in Northern New England. Think it would pay well to buy cattle in Texas and bring them here to fatten and then send them to market but it would not pay to raise horses for the Indians (Utes) would steal too many of them to make it profitable. Have not yet seen any Indians on our journey and if we do they will be Utes, and they are friendly and we are prepared to trade with them. I returned to camp at 12 M., and found all the hunters in before me except one who is still out. Hope he may have better luck than the rest for they, like me, could see no game though the hills and the ravines are covered with tracks of

---

*Powell's Account, as occasionally happens throughout the voyage, is a day behind the journals of Bradley and Sumner.

**William H. Ashley was appointed governor of Missouri in 1820. He and his exploring party descended the river, in bullboats, all the way through Brown's Hole, the Uinta Mountain canyons, and the Uinta Basin. Ashley descended the Green to about Nine Mile Creek, where he and his men left the river. Powell's account is highly inaccurate.

deer and mountain sheep, and yesterday just before we reached the place we saw three mountain sheep and fired at them from the boats, but the shot had no effect except to frighten them and they ran up the almost perpendicular clifts as fast as a deer would run on level ground. They will scale any crag, however broken or giddy, and seem to feel no fear except the single one of being shot. Have just been fishing and have caught 12 of the finest whitefish I ever saw. The cook [Billy Hawkins] has just taken them from my boat and it is about all he wants to carry. Some of them will weight 4 lbs. They have been biting very fast while a shower has been coming on, but it is over now and they seem to have left the ground. On account of showers we have pitched the tents. There was a beautiful rainbow about sunset and it looks now like fair weather tomorrow. The last hunter is in and if we are dependent on them for subsistance we should be as fat as "Job's turkey" in a few weeks, for they didn't bring in enough game to make a grease spot.

Sumner, 3 June   Laid over to-day to dry out, and take observations. Several of the party hunting, but killed nothing. In the evening, some of the boys got out the fishing tackle and soon had the bank covered with queer mongrel of mackerel, sucker and whitefish; the other an afflicted cross of white fish and lake trout. Take a piece of raw pork and paper of pins, and make a sandwich, and you have the mongrels. Take out the pork and you have a fair sample of the edible qualities of the other kinds. From this camp to Bee-Hive Point is called by the Professor, Red Canyon, not very appropriately, as there are two distinct and separate canyons. This park is the best land we have seen, so far; good land; season long enough to raise rye, barley and potatoes, and all kinds of vegetables that would mature in four months. Irrigation not necessary, but if it should be, there is a beautiful clear trout stream running through the middle of it that can be thrown on almost any part of if at comparatively little cost. Counting agriculture out, there is money for whoever goes in there and settles and raises stock. It is known by the frontiersmen as "Little Brown's Hole." Altitude is 6,000 feet. Game in abundance in the mountains south of the park; good trail to Green River City, and there could be a good wagon road made without a great outlay of money. All turn in early, as we want an early start in the morning.

Powell Account of 3 June   This morning we spread our rations, clothes, etc., on the ground to dry, and several of the party go out for a hunt. I take a walk of five or six miles up to a pine-grove park, its grassy carpet bedecked with crimson, velvet flowers, set in groups on the stems of pear-shaped cactus plants; patches of painted cups are seen here and there, with yellow blossoms protruding through scarlet bracts; little blue-eyed flowers are peeping through the grass; and the air is filled with fragrance from the white blossoms of a spiraea. A mountain brook runs through the midst, ponded below by beaver dams. It is a quiet place for retirement from the raging waters of the canyon.

It will be remembered that the course of the river, from Flaming Gorge to Beehive Point, is in a southerly direction, and at right angles to the Uinta Mountains, and cuts into the range until it reaches a point within five miles of the crest, where it turns to the east, and pursues a course not quite parallel to the trend of the range, but crosses the axis slowly in a direction a little south of east. Thus there is a triangular tract between the river and the axis of the mountain, with its acute angle extending eastward. I climb a mountain over-looking this country. To the east, the peaks are not very high, and already most of the snow has melted; but little patches lie here and there under the lee of ledges of rock. To the west, the peaks grow higher and the snow fields larger. Between the brink of the canyon and the foot of these peaks, there is a high bench. A number of creeks have their sources in the snow banks to the south, and run north into the canyon, tumbling down from 3,000 to 5,000 feet in a distance of five or six miles. Along their upper courses, they run through grassy valleys; but, as they approach Red Canyon, they rapidly disappear under the general surface of the country, and emerge into the canyon below in deep, dark gorges of their own. Each of these short lateral canyons is marked by a succession of cascades and a wild confusion of rocks and trees and fallen timber and thick undergrowth.

The little valleys above are beautiful parks; between the parks are stately pine forests, half hiding ledges of red sandstone. Mule deer and elk abound; grizzly bears, too, are abundant; wild cats, wolverines, and mountain lions are here at home. The forest aisles are filled with the music of birds, and the parks are decked with flowers. Noisy brooks meander through them; ledges of moss-covered rocks are seen; and gleaming in the distance are the snow fields, and the mountain tops are away in the clouds.

Brown's Hole and Swallow Canyon

Bradley, 4 June   Made an early start and have run rapidly up to this time (12 M.), when stopped for dinner. Have had a very pleasant run of it, only few rapids and mostly deep water. Got wet once where the river was full of islands and all the boats grounded but all were got off without injury. We find that the two men who started in a boat from same point we did only a few days before us, have passed through safe and their boat lies where we are now lying. They are prospectors. The weather has been very fine this A.M., but it now threatens a shower. The light boat signals to move on so must stop writing until we camp for the night—Camped about two miles below the point at which we stopped for dinner and the Major made an ineffectual attempt to get an observation. Camped for the night.

Sumner, 4 June   All afloat early, feeling ready for anything after our rest. Had another splendid ride, of six or eight miles and came to the mouth of Red Fork, a most disgusting looking stream, coming in from the east, off of the "Bitter Creek Desert." It is about ten feet wide, red as blood, smells horrible and tastes worse. Passed on through five miles more of canyon and came to "Brown's Hole"* a large valley, about twenty miles long and five wide— splended grass on it. Passed on about the middle of the valley and camped at the mouth of a small trout stream, coming in from the east, named on Fremont's map, "Tom Big Creek."** Had dinner and moved down about two miles, and camped on the west side of Green River, under a great cottonwood tree that would furnish shade and shelter for a camp of two hundred men. Hall killed several ducks in a lake near camp, and in the evening, Bradley, Howland and Hall caught a large number of fish.

Powell Account of 4 June   We start early and run through to Brown's Park. Halfway down the valley, a spur of a red mountain stretches across the river, which cuts a canyon through it. Here the walls are comparatively low, but vertical. A vast number of swallows have built their adobe houses on the face of the cliffs, on either side of the river. The waters are deep and quiet, but the swallows are swift and noisy enough, sweeping by in their curved paths through the air, or chattering from the rocks. The young birds stretch their little heads on naked necks through the doorways of their mud houses, clamoring for food. They are a noisy people. We call this Swallow Canyon.

Still down the river we glide, until an early hour in the afternoon, when we go into camp under a giant cottonwood, standing on the right bank, a little way back from the stream. They party had succeeded in killing a fine lot of wild ducks, and during the afternoon a mess of fish is taken.

Bradley, 5 June   Remained at same point all day but as usual could get no observations on account of clouds and rainy weather. Went across the river with two men to carry the line and measured out to the bluffs, a distance of

---

*Brown's Hole, now known as Brown's Park, is named for its first resident, Baptiste Brown, who arrived there in 1827.

**Lt. John C. Fremont and his party passed through Brown's Park, headed east, in 1844. A check of Fremont's map shows no "Tom Big Creek."

3½ miles, and it extends along the river for 15 or 20 miles affording excellent grazing land if anyone wished to raise cattle here. Shot a rattlesnake but did not stop to count the rattles as the men were in haste to return. Saw many trout in a small brook about 3 miles from the river. Shot at them with my pistol but did not kill any. Returned to camp about noon and after dinner courted "Tired nature's sweet restorer" for a few hours and then went out and caught whitefish enough for supper and breakfast.

Sumner, 5 June   This morning we were all awakened by the wild birds singing in the old tree above our heads. The sweet songs of birds, the fragrant odor of wild roses, the low, sweet rippling of the ever murmuring river at sunrise in the wilderness made everything as lovely as a poet's dream. I was just wandering into paradise; could see the dim shadow of the dark-eyed houris, when I was startled by the cry, "Roll out; bulls in the corral; chain up the gaps"—our usual call the breakfast. The hour is vanished, and I rolled out to fried fish and hot coffee. The Professor and Dunn climbed the hill south of camp, two miles from the river-h[e]ight, 2200 feet; Howland spent the day dressing up his maps; Bradley, Seneca and Hall crossed to eastside and measured off a geological section. The remainder of the party spent the day as best suited them. Measured the old tree; circumference, 5 feet from the ground, 23½ feet.

Powell Account of 5 June   With one of the men, I climb a mountain, off on the right. A long spur, with broken ledges of rock, puts down to the river; and along its course, or up the "hog-back," as it is called, I make the ascent. Dunn, who is climbing to the same point, is coming up the gulch. Two hours' hard work has brought us to the summit. These mountains are all verdure clad; pine and cedar forests are set on green terraces; snowclad mountains are seen in the distance, to the west; the plains of the upper Green stretch out before us, to the north, until they are lost in the blue heavens; but half of the river-cleft range intervenes, and the river itself is at our feet.

This half range, beyond the river, is composed of long ridges, nearly parallel with the valley. On the farther ridge, to the north, four creeks have their sources. These cut through the intervening ridges, one of which is much higher than that on which they head, by canyon gorges; then they run, with gentle curves, across the valley, their banks set with willows, boxelders, and cottonwood groves.

To the east, we look up the valley of the Vermilion, through which Fremont found his path on his way to the great parks of Colorado.*

---

*John C. Fremont, known as the "Pathfinder," lead five expeditions across the Colorado Basin between 1842 and 1853, in part to explore the southwestern boundary of the Louisiana Purchase for the U.S. government. His primary goal was to open up the West to settlement and to locate railroad routes.

The reading of the barometer taken, we start down in company, and reach camp tired and hungry, which does not abate one bit our enthusiasm, as we tell of the day's work, with its glory of landscape.

Brown's Hole

Bradley, 6 June   Started early this morning but have made only 15 miles. The river is so broad and still and the wind contrary that we have had to row all the way and I feel quite weary tonight. Would rather have rappids than still water but think I shall be accommodated, for we have now reached the canon at the lower end of Brown's Hole, and have camped tonight at the mouth of the Canon. It looks like a rough one for the walls are very high and straight and the sides are of sand-stone much broken with seams but at the mouth nearly perpendicular; in such the worst bowlders have been found and I expect them below here.

Sumner, 6 June   Took our time in getting off, as we had but a short journey before us for the day; but it proved a pretty hard one before we got done with it. No sooner had we started than a strong head-wind sprung up directly in our faces. Rowed about twenty-five miles against it—no easy task, as the river is a hundred and fifty yards wide, with hardly any current. Saw thousands of ducks of various kinds; killed a few, and one goose. Camped at the head of a canyon, at the southern end of the valley, on the east side of the river under a grove of box elder trees. The Professor and Hall caught another mess of fish.

Powell Account of 6 June   At daybreak, I am awakened by a chorus of birds. It seems as if all the feathered songsters of the region have come to the old tree. Several species of warblers, woodpeckers, and flickers above, meadow larks in the grass, and wild geese in the river. I recline on my elbow, and watch a lark near by, and then awaken my bed fellow, to listen to my Jenny Lind. A morning concert for me; none of your "matinees."

Our cook has been an ox-driver, or "bull-whacker," on the plains, in one of those long trains now no longer seen, and he hasn't forgotten his old ways. In the midst of the concert, his voice breaks in: "Roll out! roll out! bulls in the corral: chain up the gaps! Roll out! roll out! roll out!" And this is our breakfast bell.

Today we pass through the park, and camp at the head of another canyon.

Bradley, 7 June   Have been lying in camp all day just where we came last night. Have climbed the mountain and find it exactly 2085 ft. above the level of the river. The scenery from the summit is grand. We could see the river part of the way for 6 or 7 miles. It is very rapid and noisy but we hope not dangerous.

Shall probably try it tomorrow. Nothing of interest has transpired.

Sumner, 7 June   Still in camp, Professor and Dunn measured the wall of the canyon on the east side; Bradley geologising; Howland and Goodman sketching; Rhodes brushing up Kitty's Sister, swearing all the time that she can stand more thumps than Kitty ever could. Professor and Dunn came in at noon and reported the wall 2086 feet. All the party in camp the rest of the day; wind and rain in the evening. Distance from the mouth of Henry's Fork 90 miles; general course of the river 25 degrees south of east.* The valley called Brown's Hole is a pretty good piece of land; would make a splendid place to raise stock; it has been used for several years as a winter herding ground for the cattle trains. Last winter there were about 4000 head of oxen pastured in it without an ounce of hay. I saw them in March and am willing to swear that half of them were in good enough order for beef.

Powell Account of 7 June   Today, two or three of us climb to the summit of the cliff, on the left, and find its altitude, above camp, to be 2,086 feet. The rocks are split with fissures, deep and narrow, sometimes a hundred feet, or more, to the bottom. Lofty pines find root in the fissures that are filled with loose earth and decayed vegetation. On a rock we find a pool of clear, cold water, caught from yesterday evening's shower. After a good drink, we walk out to the brink of the canyon, and look down to the water below. I can do this now, but it has taken several years of mountain climbing to cool my nerves, so that I can sit, with my feet over the edge, and calmly look down a precipice 2,000 feet. And yet I cannot look on and see another do the same. I must either bid him come away, or turn my head.

The canyon walls are buttressed on a grand scale, with deep alcoves intervening; columned crags crown the cliffs, and the river is rolling below.

When we return to camp, at noon, the sun shines in splendor on vermilion walls, shaded into green and gray, where the rocks are lichened over; the river fills the channel from wall to wall, and the canyon opens, like a beautiful portal, to a region of glory.

This evening, as I write, the sun is going down, and the shadows are settling in the canyon. The vermilion gleams and roseate hutes, blending with the green and gray tints, are slowly changing to somber brown above, and black shadows are creeping over them below; and now it is a dark portal to a region of gloom—the gateway through which we are to enter on our voyage of exploration tomorrow. What shall we find?

---

*Sumner's estimate was sixteen miles too much.

Lodore Canyon and Disaster Falls

Bradley, 8 June Started quite early this morning and find that what seemed comparatively easy rapids from the top of the mountains are quite bad ones, and as we advanced they grew worse until we came to the wildest rapid yet seen. I succeeded in making a landing in an eddy just above where the dangerous part began. So did one other of the heavy boats, but one (the "No Name") with three men in it [the Howland brothers and Frank Goodman] with one-third of our provisions, half of our mess-kit and all three of the barometers went over the rapids and though the men escaped with their lives yet they lost all of their clothing, bedding and everything except shirt and drawers, the uniform in which we all pass rapids. It is a serious loss to us and we are rather low spirited tonight for we must camp right at the head of a roaring rapid more than a mile in length and in which we have already lost one of our boats and nearly lost three of our number. Yet I trust the sun of another day will bring better cheer. "All's well that ends well," but the end is not yet.

Sumner, 8 June Pulled out early and entered into as hard a day's work as I ever wish to see. Went about a half a mile when we came to a terrible rapid, and had to let our boats down with ropes. Passed about a dozen bad rapids in the forenoon. Camped for dinner on the east side at the foot of a perpendicular rose-colored wall, about fifteen hundred feet; pulled out again at one o-clock; had proceeded about half a mile when the scouting boat came to a place where we could see nothing but spray and foam. She was pulled ashore on the east side and the freight boats instantly signaled to land with us.

The Maid and Kitty's Sister did so but the No Name being too far out in the current and having shipped a quantity of water in the rapid above, could not be landed, though her crew did their best in trying to pull ashore at the head of the rapid, she struck a rock and swung into the waves sideways and instantly swamped. Her crew held to her while she drifted down with the speed of the wind; went perhaps 200 yards, when she struck another rock that stove her bow in; swung around again and drifted toward a small island in the middle of the river; here was a chance for her crew, though a very slim one. Goodman made a spring and disappeared; Howland followed next, and made the best leap I even saw made by a two-legged animal, and landed in the water where he could touch the rocks on the bottom; a few vigorous strokes carried him safe to the island. Seneca was the last rat to leave the sinking ship, and made the leap for life barely in time; had he stayed aboard another second we would have lost as good and true a man as can be found in any place. Howland got a pole that happened to be handy, reached one end to him and hauled him on the isle. Had they drifted thirty feet further down nothing could have saved them, as the river was turned into a perfect hell of waters that nothing could enter and live. The boat drifted into it and was instantly smashed to pieces. In half a second there was nothing but a dense foam, with a cloud of spray above it, to mark the spot. The small boat was then unloaded and let down with ropes opposite the wrecked men on the island. The trapper crossed over and brought them safely to shore to the east side. She was then let down about a half a mile further, where we could see part of the stern cuddy of the wrecked boat on a rocky shoal in the middle of the river. Two of the boys proposed to take the small boat over and see how much of the lost notes could be recovered. The Professor looked ruefully across the foaming river, but forbade the attempt. All hands returned to the head of the rapids, feeling glad enough that there were no lives lost, a little sore at the loss of the boat and cargo of 2,000 pounds of provisions and ammunition, all the personal outfit of the crew, three rifles, one revolver, all the maps and most of the notes and many of the instruments, that cannot be replaced in time to carry on the work this year, and do it right, ate supper of bread and bacon, and went to sleep under the scrubby cedars.

Powell Account of 8[9] June*   One of the party suggests that we call this the Canyon of Lodore, and the name is adopted.** Very slowly we make our way, often climbing on the rocks at the edge of the water for a few hundred yards, to examine the channel before running it.

During the afternoon, we come to a place where it is necessary to make a portage. The little boat is landed, and the others are signaled to come up.

When these rapids or broken falls occur, usually the channel is suddenly narrowed by rocks which have been tumbled from the cliffs or have been washed in by lateral streams. Immediately above the narrow, rocky channel, on one or both sides, there is often a bay of quiet water, in which we can land with ease. Sometimes the water descends with a smooth, unruffled surface, from the broad, quiet spread above, into the narrow, angry channel below, by a semicircular sag. Great care must be taken not to pass over the brink into this deceptive pit, but above it we can row with safety. I walk along the bank to examine the ground, leaving one of my men with a flag to guide the other boats to the landing-place. I soon see one of the boats make shore all right and feel no more

---

*Powell's accounts run consistently one day behind between 8 June and 19 June; they have been repositioned to correspond with the more accurate journals of Bradley and Sumner. The date in brackets is the date indicated by Powell to be the correct one, but in fact, it is not.

**A reference to English romantic poet Robert Southey's poem "The Cataract of Lodore": ". . . And so never ending, but always/descending, Sounds and motions for ever and ever/are blending,/All at once and all o'er, with a mighty/uproar-/And this way the water comes down/at Lodore."

concern; but a minute after, I hear a shout, and looking around, see one of the boats shooting down the center of the sag. It is the "No Name," with Captain Howland, his brother, and Goodman. I feel that its going over is inevitable, and run to save the third boat. A minute more, and she turns the point and heads for the shore. Then I turn downstream again, and scramble along to look for the boat that has gone over. The first fall is not great, only ten or twelve feet, and we often run such; but below, the river tumbles down again for forty or fifty feet, in a channel filled with dangerous rocks that break the waves into whirlpools and beat them into foam. I pass around a great crag just in time to see the boat strike a rock, and, rebounding from the shock, careen and fill the open compartment with water. Two of the men lose their oars; she swings around, and is carried down at a rapid rate, broadside on, for a few yards, and strikes amidships on another rock with great force, is broken quite in two, and the men are thrown into the river; the larger part of the boat floating buoyantly, they soon seize it, and down the river they drift, past the rocks for a few hundred yards to a second rapid, filled with huge boulders, where the boat strikes again, and is dashed to pieces, and the men and fragments are soon carried beyond my sight. Running along, I turn a bend, and see a man's head above the water, washed about in a whirlpool below a great rock.

It is Frank Goodman, climbing to it with a grip upon which life depends. Coming opposite, I see Howland trying to go to his aid from an island on which he has been washed. Soon, he comes near enough to reach Frank with a pole, which he extends toward him. The latter lets go the rock, grasps the pole, and is pulled ashore. Seneca Howland is washed further down the island, and is caught by some rocks, and, though somewhat bruised, manages to get ashore in safety. This seems a long time, as I tell it, but it is quickly done.

And now the three men on an island, with a swift, dangerous river on either side, and a fall below. The "Emma Dean" is soon brought down, and Sumner, starting above as far as possible, pushes out. Right skillfully he plies the oars, and a few strokes set him on the island at the proper point. Then they all pull the boat upstream, as far as they are able, until they stand in water up to their necks. One sits on a rock, and holds the boat until the others are ready to pull, then gives the boat a push, clings to it with his hands, and climbs in as they pull for mainland, which they reach in safety. We are as glad to shake hands with them as though they had been on a voyage around the world, and wrecked on a distant coast.

Down the river half a mile we find that the after cabin of the wrecked boat, with a part of the bottom, ragged and splintered, has floated against a rock and stranded. There are valuable articles in the cabin; but, on examination, we determine that life should not be risked to save them. Of course, the cargo of rations, instruments, and clothing is gone.

We return to the boats, and make camp for the night. No sleep comes to me in all those dark hours. The rations, instruments, and clothing have been divided among the boats, anticipating such an accident as this; and we started with duplicates of everything that was deemed necessary to success. But, in the distribution, there was one exception to this precaution, and the barometers were all placed on one boat, and they are lost. There is a possibility that they are in the cabin lodged against the rock, for that is where they were kept. But, then, how to reach them! The river is rising. Will they be there tomorrow? Can I go out to Salt Lake City, and obtain barometers from New York?

Sumner Account of 8[9]* June   About ten miles from the head of Lodore Canyon we encountered what was afterwards named Disaster Falls, a very bad rapid, or rather four very bad rapids. As I was always in the lead, I stood up on the forward deck and saw at once our danger, and immediately landed on the left bank. Two of the other boats following did the same, but the "No Name," in charge of O. G. Howland, failed to make a landing. It was drawn into the rapids and ground to pieces on the rocks below. The three men escaped by a scratch on a small sand bar island near the right bank. To get the men off was a conundrum for sure. The channel was not wide, but the river ran with the speed of a race horse, with a fall and a cataract below that meant certain death to anyone carried into it.

The three men were finally rescued by a man [Sumner] who took the "Emma Dean" across the channel, making a landing only by a scratch. The boat was then pulled up to the extreme head of the island and the men taken aboard. Major Powell, in describing the rescue, makes a mistake in saying all hands pulled on the oars for dear life. The man who took the boat over would not allow any oars in the boat but the oars he used. When all were on board he compelled the three men to lie down flat in the bottom of the boat, and he rowed the boat back alone, as he did not care to risk certain destruction to all by a false stroke. The trip was made all right and the men rescued, none the worse for it except for a good ducking. But a good boat was gone and a full load of supplies.

This wreck marked the beginning of the many quarrels between Major Powell and O. G. Howland and Bill Dunn. As soon as Howland got out of the boat after the rescue Major Powell angrily demanded of him why he did not land. Howland told him he saw no signals to do anything, and could not see the other boats that had landed until he was drawn into the rapid, when it was too late. I asked Hawkins and Bradley in charge of the other boats if they saw

---

*Sumner's date is off probably because he had read Powell's published account of the trip (1875) before he wrote his own account, thus perpetuating Powell's dating errors.

signals to land, and they said no signals were given, but as they saw me turn in they suspected something wrong and followed suit at once.

Disaster Falls

Bradley, 9 June Have lowered our boats and brought part of the baggage down with great labor, having first to clear an imperfect road through the broken rocks and stunted mountain cedars and have had better luck with the wrecked boat than we anticipated, for two of the men [Jack Sumner and Andy Hall] with great risk have succeeded in getting a boat out to an island on which they found a small part of the boat and the barometers. They are what we cared the most about after the men's outfit, for without them we should have to make the trip and never know the height of the mountains which we pass through. We have plenty of rations left, much more than a mile long. The scenery at this point is sublime. The red sand-stone rises on either side more than 2000 ft., shutting out the sun for much of the day while at our feet the river, lashed to foam, rushes on with indescribably fury. O how great is He who holds it in the hollow of His hand, and what pygmies we who strive against it. It will take us nearly or quite another day before we can start in again. Major and brother are gone ahead *to see what comes next.* Hope for a favorable report but can't rely on anything but actual tryal with the boats, for a man can't travel so far in a whole day [of walking] in these canyon as we go in a single hour.

Sumner, 9 June All up by sunrise and at work unloading the boats, ready for letting down the ropes. Got the boats and remaining cooking utensils over and opposite the wreck on the shore. Had dinner, when Hall bantered one of the men to go over to the wreck and see what there was left. Away they went and got to it safely, after a few thumps on the rocks, and fished out three barometers, two thermometers, some spare barometer tubes, a pair of old boots, some sole leather, and a ten gallon cask of whisky that had never been tapped. Not a sign of anything else. How to get back was the next question, it being impossible to go back over the route they came. A narrow, rocky race offered a chance to get through the island into the man channel. After an hour's floundering in the water among the rocks, they got through to the main channel, and dashing through some pretty rough passes, they reached the shore, where the rest of the party stood ready to catch the lines, their arms extended, like children reaching for their mother's apron strings. The Professor was so much pleased about the recovery of the barometers, that he looked as happy as a young girl with her first beau; tried to say something to raise a laugh, but couldn't. After taking a good drink of whisky all around, we concluded to spend the rest of the day as best suited. Some packed freight for future use; the rest slept under the shade of the scrubby cedars.

Powell Account of 9[10] June I have determined to get the barometers from the wreck, if they are there. After breakfast, while the men make the portage, I go down again for another examination. There the cabin lies, only carried fifty or sixty feet farther on.

Carefully looking over the ground, I am satisfied that it can be reached with safety, and return to tell the men my conclusion. Sumner and Dunn volunteer to take the little boat and make the attempt. They start, reach it, and out come the barometers; and now the boys set up a shout, and I join them, pleased that they should be as glad to save the instruments as myself. When [the] boat lands on our side, I find that the only things saved from the wreck were the barometers, a package of thermometers, and a three-gallon keg of whiskey, which is what the men were shouting about. They had taken it aboard, unknown to me, and now I am glad they did, for they think it will do them good, as they are drenched everyday by the melting snow, which runs down from the summits of the Rocky Mountains.

Now we come to our work at the portage. We find that it is necessary to carry our rations over the rocks for nearly a mile, and let our boats down with lines, except at a few points, where they also must be carried.

Between the river and the eastern wall of the canyon there is an immense talus of broken rocks. These have tumbled down from the cliffs above, and constitute a vast pile of huge angular fragments. On these we build a path for a quarter of a mile, to a small sand beach covered with driftwood, through which we clear a way for several hundred yards, then continue the trail on over another pile of rocks, nearly half a mile farther down, to a little bay. The greater part of the day is spent in this work. Then we carry our cargoes down to the beach and camp for the night.

While the men are building the campfire, we discover an iron bake oven, several tin plates, a part of a boat, and many other fragments, which denote that this is the place where Ashley's party was wrecked.

Lodore Canyon

Bradley, 11 June Have been working like galley-slaves all day. Have lowered the boats all the way with ropes and once unloaded and carried the goods around one very bad place. The rapid is still continuous and not improving. Where we are tonight it roars and foams like a wild beast. The Major as usual has chosen the worst camping-ground possible. If I had a dog that would like where my bed is made tonight I would kill him and burn his collar and swear I never owned him. Have been wet all day and the water flies into the boats so badly that it is impossible to keep anything dry. The clothes in my valise are all wet and I have nothing dry to put on, but fortunately it is not cold for though I have only shirt and drawers on and they only half dry, yet I am not cold though the sun does not reach us more than 5 or 6 hours in the [day]. I fell today while trying to save my boat from a rock and have a bad cut over the left eye which I fear will make an ugly scar. But what odds, it can't disfigure my ugly mug and it may improve it, who knows?

Sumner, 11 June Rapids and portages all day. By hard work we made three miles. Passed the mouth of a small trout stream coming in from the west. Hall shot an osprey on her nest in the top of a dead pine, near the mouth of the creek. Camped for the night on the west side, under an overhanging cliff.

Powell Account of 11[12] June Today we take the boats down to the bay. While at this work, we discover three sacks of flour from the wrecked boat, that have lodged in the rocks. We carry them above high-water mark, and leave them, as our cargoes are already too heavy for the three remaining boats. We also find two or three oars, which we place with them.

As Ashley and his party were wrecked here, and as we have lost one of our boats at the same place, we adopt the name Disaster Falls for the scene of so much peril and loss.

Though some of his companions were drowned, Ashley and one other survived the wreck, climbed the canyon wall, and found their way across the Wasatch Mountains to Salt Lake City, living chiefly on berries, as they wandered through almost destitude of clothing, and nearly starved. The Mormon people gave them food and clothing, and employed them to work on the foundation of the Temple, until they had earned sufficient to enable them to leave the country. Of their subsequent history, I have no knowledge. It is possible they returned to the scene of the disaster, as a little creek entering the river below is known as Ashley's Creek, and it is reported that he built a cabin and trapped on this river for one or two winters; but this may have been before the disaster.

Sumner Account of 11[12] June We finally worked our way through Lodore Canyon and reached the mouth of Bear River (Yampah), the largest stream joining the Green in its whole length. We camped there two days, repaired everything and took observations. We caught fish wholesale, some of them pretty big fellows. They are called Colorado Salmon, but do not resemble a salmon any more than I resemble a dude, and are about as edible as a paper of pins cooked in lard oil.*

---

*The Colorado "salmon" is now called a squawfish. Due to changes in its habitat, caused by water depletion in the river and by dams, this fish is now on the list of rare and endangered species.

I believe Major Powell speaks in his report of finding a bake-oven and a lot of tin plates at the foot of Disaster Falls, and concludes they were the relics of Ashley's party. The could not have been, for several reasons. I have been among different trapping parties, and I never saw a bake-oven in any of them, they being too cumbersome to carry. Old "Cut Rocks" Brown, as he was called, trapped that section of the country pretty thoroughly many years ago, but he was never known to have any cooking utensils but a battered brass kettle holding probably a gallon, so they could not have been his. Brown was a queer old cuss, always wanting to get off alone in some canyon, "cut rocks," as he called them, to conceal himself from the red-bellies. Brown's Hole is named for him, but he certainly left nothing there except possibly, some half-breed Ute children. The camp utensils were probably left by some of the bullwhackers who made Brown's Hole a wintering place for the many work cattle used in transporting supplies for Johnston's Army during the Utah war . . .*

Bradley, 12 June   Today has been the repetition of yesterday only more of it. We have carried the goods around two bad places and run several others. One run of nearly or quite a mile is the largest for 4 days. We camp tonight in a fine spot on the east side of the cañon, but below us about a stone's throw is another furious rapid near a mile long, past which we must take the goods tomorrow and if possible get out boats over, though the prospects of success are not bright. I put out all my clothing, papers, etc., and have got 2 hour's sun on them which in this pure air will dry almost anything. My eye is very black today and if it is not very *useful* it is very ornamental.

Sumner, 12 June   More rapids that are impossible to run. Excessively hard work. Made three miles. Camped on the east side of the river in a grove of elder trees, at the head of a long rapid. Will have to make another half mile cartage.

Powell Account of 12[13] June   Still rocks, rapids, and portages. We camp tonight at the foot of the left wall on a little patch of flood plain covered with a dense growth of box-elders, stopping early in order to spread the clothing and rations to dry. Everything is wet and spoiling.

---

*"Johnston's Army" refers to the Utah Expedition of 1857–58, in which 2,500 U.S. troops were sent west to quell the "insurrection" in Utah. After Mormons ambushed and burned the army supply wagons, Johnston was forced to spend the winter near Fort Bridger. The crisis was settled peaceably in 1858.

Bradley, 13 June   We remain in camp today for we are tired out from the effects of constant hard labor and constant wetting. It is Sunday and the first one we have paid any attention to and whether this is accident or design I can't tell, but I am inclined to believe it accidental for I don't think anyone in the party except myself keeps any record of time or events.* The sun reached our camp at 10 A.M., and will afford us another excellent opportunity to dry clothing, etc. Our rations are getting very sour from constant wetting and exposure to a hot sun. I imagine we shall be sorry before the trip is up that we took no better care of them. It is none of my business, yet if we fail it will be want of judgment that will defeat it and if we succeed it will be *dumb luck,* not good judgment that will do it. The men have all come in from hunting, as ever without game. We frequently see mountain sheep as we pass along, and if we kept *still* we might kill them but as soon as we land the men begin to shoot and make a great noise and the game for miles around is allarmed and takes back from the river. This makes one think that these are not *hunters* and I believe that if left to maintain themselves with their rifles they would fare worse than Job's turkey. They seem more like school-boys on a holiday than like men accustomed to live by the chase, but as I am no hunter myself I must not criticize others. Still as usual I have my opinion.

Sumner, 13 June   Rested today, as we all need it very much. Three of the boys went hunting, but there is nothing in this part of the country but a few mountain sheep, and they stay where a squirrel could hardly climb. We are looking for better traveling pretty soon, as we have got to the point where the white sandstone caps the hard red, 2000 feet above our heads.

Bradley, 14 June   Up to this hour (1 o'clock P.M.) we remain in camp. Have landed the provisions on the rocks above the rapid and spread them to dry.... Some of the men are making moccasins, some playing cards or reading, others mending clothing or sleeping, while I am lying flat on my back with a geology for a desk, writing. Major's brother lies beside me singing "John Anderson, My Jo."** The Major and Howland are fixing up as well as possible the map of the river over which we have passed, for all was lost in the lost boat and must be made again as correct as possible from memory. I have been fixing my boat and calking the cubfins to keep my clothing dry while in the waves.

---

*Curiously, the Major did not know that Bradley was keeping a diary either.

**"John Anderson My Jo" was probably a vocal rendition of the Robert Burns poem of that time.

Below each rapid there is a heavy sea and one would actually fancy himself in a gale at sea if he could not see the land so near him.

Sumner, 14 June   Still in camp; repaired a broken barometer and started our plunder over the Portage; Professor and Howland have been busy for two days restoring the lost maps.

Hell's Half-Mile

Bradley, 15 June   Another day finds us past that rapid and at another five times as bad as the last. We have made a trail along the mountainside and think that from that point we can run it. We encamped for the night after making the trail. My boat was sunk while being lowered over the rapid this morning and all my books and papers soaked with water, and I fear both my albums and most of my photographs and tintypes spoiled. Some of them I value very highly for I can never replace them. My notes were soaked but I have dried them and since that have carried them in my *hat*. My clothing is of course all wet again but aside from the trouble of drying it, it is no matter for I need only shirt and drawers in this warm weather and lately have seldom worn anything else.

Sumner, 15 June   Made the Portage and ran a bad rapid at the lower end of the Portage and through half a mile of smooth water, when we came to another impassable rapid; unloaded boats and camped on the east side, under some scrubby cedars. Rain at dark. Made a trail and turned in for the night.

Powell Account of 15[16] June   On the east side of the canyon, a vast amphitheater has been cut, with massive buttresses, and deep, dark alcoves, in which grow beautiful mosses and delicate ferns, while springs burst out from the further recesses, and wind, in silver threads, over floors of sand rock. Here we have three falls in close succession. At the first, the water is compressed into a very narrow channel, against the right-hand cliff, and falls fifteen feet in ten yards; at the second, we have a broad sheet of water, tumbling down twenty feet over a group of rocks that thrust their dark heads through the foaming waters. The third is a broken fall, or short, abrupt rapid, where the water makes a descent of more than twenty feet among huge, fallen fragments of the cliff. We name the group Triplet falls.

We make a portage around the first; past the second and third we let down with lines.

During the afternoon, Dunn and Howland, having returned from their climb, we run down, three-quarters of a mile, on quiet water, and land at the head of another fall. On examination, we find that there is an abrupt plunge of a few feet, and then the river tumbles, for half a mile, with a descent of a hundred feet, in a channel beset with great numbers of huge boulders. This stretch of the river is named Hell's Half-Mile.

Lodore Canyon

Bradley, 16 June We labored hard all day and got all down. We shortened the distance somewhat by loading the boats and hauling them through a large eddy and then carrying the goods again across a point. We sank one boat today and another got away from us but we recovered both without serious damage.

Sumner, 16 June Pulled out early and went to work with a will. While letting the Maid down with ropes she got crossways with the waves and broke loose from the five men holding the line, and was off like a frightened horse. In drifting down she struck a rock that knocked her stern part to pieces. Rhodes and the trapper jumped in the small boat and gave chase; caught her half a mile below. Got everything over by sunset and camped on the east side on a sand bar. Pulled out at seven o'clock, and ran a bad rapid the first half mile. The freight boats went through in good style, but the Emma, in running too near the east shore, got into a bad place and had a close collision, filling half full, but finally got out, all safe, baled out, and ran two miles through smooth water, when we came to another bad rapid and had to let down with ropes; tied up while we repaired the Maid; passed the rapid and on through two miles of smooth water, when we came to another rapid that has a fall of about twelve feet in a hundred and fifty, but clear of rock; the Emma ran through without shipping a drop, followed close by the Maid, she making the passage without shipping much, but poor Kitty's Sister ran on a rock near the east side and loosened her head block and came down to the other boats leaking badly. She was run ashore when Rhodes caulked her with some oakum that would serve to keep her afloat for a while; when we pulled out again, run half a mile with the Emma and got into a complete nest of whirlpools, and got out of them by extreme hard work; decided that it was unsafe for the freight boats to attempt it; so we were compelled to let them down with ropes on the east side through a narrow channel. Jumped aboard again and pulled down two miles further through smooth water, and camped for the night on the east side at the head of a rapid. While we were cooking supper a whirlwind came up the canyon, and in an instant the fire was running everywhere; threw what happened to be out on board again as quickly as possible, and pulled out and ran the rapid and on down two miles further and camped again on the east side, and commenced anew our preparations for supper; had supper, and laughed for an hour over the ludicrous scene at the fire. Went to bed and were lulled to sleep by the rain pattering on the tent.

Fire in Camp

Bradley, 17 June   Have had a little better running today. Have made over 5 miles. Ran many little rapids. Several times let down with ropes and once made a short portage. Have passed 5 or 6 whirlpools today, one so bad we had to take the boats around it with ropes. It whirled them around so fast we couldn't row them through it. One rapid we ran today was full of rocks and we all struck our boats and tonight they are leaking badly, but we can repair them with pitch from the mountain pine. We camped for this night on a little point where the mountain pine and sage-brush was very thick and the cook built his fire and had supper on the way when the fire spread to the pines. At first we took little notice of it but soon a whirlwind swept through the cañon and in a moment the whole point was one sheet of flames. We seized whatever we could and rushed for the boats and amid the rush of wind and flames we pushed out and dropped down the river a few rods. My handkerchief was burned that I had tied around my neck, and my ears and face badly scorched. We had hardly landed before the fire was again upon us and we were forced to run a bad rapid to escape it. We got through safe, however, and are all right tonight except that we lost most of our mess-kit.

Powell Account of 17[16] June   Late in the afternoon we make a short run to the mouth of another little creek, coming down from the left into an alcove filled with luxuriant vegetation. Here camp is made with a group of cedars on one side and a dense mass of box-elders and dead willows on the other.

I go up to explore the alcove. While away a whirlwind comes, scattering the fire among the dead willows and cedarspray, and soon there is a conflagration. The men rush for the boats, leaving all they cannot readily seize at the moment, and even then they have their clothing burned and hair singed, and Bradley has his ears scorched. The cook fills his arms with the mess kit, and, jumping into a boat, stumbles and falls, and away go our cooking utensils into the river. Our plates are gone; our spoons are gone; our knives and forks are gone. "Water catch 'em; h-e-a-p catch 'em."

When on the boats, the men are compelled to cut loose, as the flames, running out on the overhanging willows, are scorching them. Loose on the stream, they must go down, for the water is too swift to make headway against it. Just below is a rapid, filled with rocks. On they shoot, no channel explored, no signal to guide them. Just at this juncture I chance to see them, but have not yet discovered the fire, and the strange movements of the men fill me with astonishment. Down the rocks I clamber, and run to the bank. When I arrive, they have landed. Then we all go back to the late camp to see if anything left behind can be saved. Some of the clothing and bedding taken out of the boats is found, also a few tin cups, basins, and a camp kettle, and this is all the mess kit we now have.

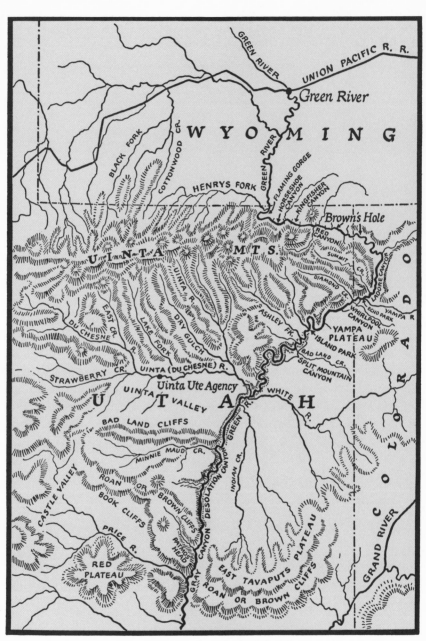

Green River to the mouth of the Uinta.

IV.   Echo Park to the Mouth
of the Uinta River

Each major river intersection during the long and torturous voyage became an important marker of the party's progress, giving both a location fix and a psychological boost. After Disaster Falls and the prolonged ordeal of Lodore Canyon, Bradley predicted that they had experienced *"the worst we shall ever meet."* Little could he anticipate the size and difficulty of the rapids that still awaited them.

The most significant event of this next section, which takes the expedition to the broad Uinta Valley where the White and Uinta rivers join the Green, was their return to familiar territory and brief contact with the outside world. This location, at the mouth of the Uinta and just across from the mouth of the White River, became an agreeable and needed eight-day resting place from 28 June through 5 July. It was familiar territory, as Powell and some of his group had followed the White River to this spot and camped here the previous winter. Since the Uinta Indian Agency was located but forty miles west on the Uinta River, four of the eight days were taken up in transit to the agency for mail and resupply. Powell did what he could, given his meager supply of cash, to replace the food lost in the sinking of the *No Name* at Disaster Falls. He was able to buy three hundred pounds of flour, an amount barely enough to keep his men from starvation.

The writers among the crew also sent letters and brought their journals up to date. Oddly enough, Bradley, who was the loner of the group, kept his journal so thoroughly secret none of the others knew he kept one, even at the end of the voyage. Ironically, his secret journal is the most consistent and accurate day-to-day record of the trip, and the best source for verifying dates and events. Powell's accounts, as mentioned earlier, are at times off by a day or more, especially during this part of the trip; the reader has also to rely on Bradley's entries for most of the personnel reports. In this section, for example, we learn from Bradley that Powell was sick for two days (23 June entry), and that Sumner was also ill (25 June entry).

Mouth of the Yampa

Bradley, 18 June   After a run of almost railroad speed for 5 miles we came to Bear River [the Yampa] which comes into the Green from the east, and at this season of the year has almost or quite as much water. What its effect on the future stream will be is uncertain. I predict that the river will improve from this point, for the more water there is the wider channel it will make for itself and the less liability will there be of its falling in and blocking up clear across, and if there is one side clear we can run it or at least have one good side to let down the boats with ropes. I commenced fishing soon after we arrived but the fish were so large they broke four hooks and three lines for me; in a few moments I could haul them to the top of the water, great fellows some of them quite a yard long, but the moment they saw me they were off and the hook or line must break. At last by twisting four silk lines together and putting on a hook two inches long I managed to secure one that weighted 10 lbs., and will make a fine breakfast for all hands. We intend to stay here several days and take a set of observations. Have named the canon above this point "Lodore Canon," for as the banks here are not above 400 ft. high the Major thinks we had better commence a new canon at this point, but the canon is really continuous and has now reached 25 miles. It has been the worst by far and I predict *the worst we shall ever meet.*

Sumner, 18 June   Repaired Kitty's Sister and pulled out again, and had a splended ride of six miles, and came to the mouth of Bear River a stream one hundred and twenty yards wide and ten feet deep; camped on a point of land between the two rivers, under some box elder trees. All hands went to work fishing, and soon had a good number of them. Bradley was much provoked by one large one that carried off three of his best hooks, but finally got him with a strong line got up for his special benefit. He proved to be about thirty inches long and fifteen pounds weight. Opposite the mouth of Bear River there is the prettiest wall I have ever seen. It is about three miles long and five hundred feet high, composed of white sandstone, perpendicular and smooth, as if built by man. It has been christened Echo Rock as it sends back the slightest and most varying sounds that we can produce.*

Powell Account of 18[17] June   We run down to the mouth of Yampa River. This has been a chapter of disasters and toils, notwithstanding which the Canyon of Lodore was not devoid of scenic interest, even beyond the power of pen to tell. The roar of its waters was heard unceasingly from the hour we entered it until we landed here. No quiet in all that time. But its walls and cliffs, its peaks and crags, its amphitheaters and alcoves, tell a story of beauty and grandeur that I hear yet—and shall hear.

The Yampa enters the Green from the east. At a point opposite its mouth, the Green runs to the south, and a foot of a rock, about seven hundred feet high and a mile long, and then turns sharply around it to the right, and runs back in a northerly course, parallel to its former direction, for nearly another mile, thus having the opposite sides of a long, narrow rock for its bank. The tongue of rock so formed is a peninsular precipice, with a mural escarpment along its whole course on the east, but broken down at places on the west. . . .

We have named the long peninsular rock on the other side Echo Rock. Desiring to climb it, Bradley and I take the little boat and pull upstream as far as possible, for it cannot be climbed directly opposite. We land on a talus of rocks at the upper end, to reach a place where it seems practicable to make the ascent; but we must go still farther up the river. So we scramble along, until we reach a place where the river sweeps against the wall. Here we find a shelf, along which we can pass, and now are ready for the climb.

We start up a gulch; then pass to the left, on a bench, along the wall; then up again, over broken rocks; then we reach more benches, along which we walk, until we find more broken rocks and crevices, but which we climb, still up, until we have ascended six or eight hundred feet; then we are met by a sheer precipice.

Looking about, we find a place where it seems possible to climb. I go ahead; Bradley hands the barometer to me, and follows. So we proceed, stage by stage, until we are nearly to the summit. Here, by making a spring, I gain a foothold in a little crevice, and grasp an angle of the rock overhead. I find I can get up no farther, and cannot step back, for I dare not let go with my hand, and cannot reach foothold below without. I call to Bradley for help. He finds a way by which he can get to the top of the rock over my head, but cannot reach me. Then he looks around for some stick or limb of a tree, but finds none. Then he suggests that he had better help me with the barometer case; but I fear I cannot

---

*Echo Rock is also known as The Blade and Steamboat Rock.

hold on to it. The moment is critical. Standing on my toes, my muscles begin to tremble. It is sixty or eighty feet to the foot of the precipice. If I lost my hold I shall fall to the bottom, and then perhaps roll over the bench, and tumble still farther down the cliff. At this instant it occurs to Bradley to take off his drawers, which he does, and swings them down to me. I hug close to the rock, let go with my hand, seize the dangling legs, and with his assistance, I am enabled to gain the top.

Then we walk out on a peninsular rock, make the necessary observations for determining its altitude above camp, and return, finding an easy way down.

Bradley, 19 June   Went out this morning to climb the rocks on the west side to ascertain the exact height but as it is quite perpendicular we went up the river a mile or two where the red and white sand-stone meet and thought to climb the red and then work our way back onto the White and then onto the top of what we call "Echo Clift" opposite our camp, but what was our surprise to find on climbing a little over 800 ft., to come out right over the river. The crag on which we were, fairly overhangs the water on the other side so much does the river fold back on itself. I could see two rappids but think we can run them both. The river looks much larger below than above Bear [Yampa] River and though it is quite noisy yet I think the increase of water will permit us to go safely.

Sumner, 19 June   Still in camp. Professor, Bradley and Hall climbed the northern end of Echo Wall. The remainder of the men in camp, fishing, washing, etc.

Powell Account of 19 June   Today, Howland, Bradley, and I take the "Emma Dean," and start up the Yampa River. The stream is much swollen, the current swift, and we are able to make but slow progress against it. The canyon in this part of the course of the Yampa is cut through light gray sandstone. The river is very winding, and the swifter water is usually found on the outside of the curve, sweeping against vertical cliffs, often a thousand feet high. In the center of these curves, in many places, the rock above overhangs the river. On the opposite side, the walls are broken, craggy, and sloping, and occasionally side canyons enter. When we have rowed until we are quite tired we stop, and take advantage of one of these broken places to climb out of the canyon. When above, we can look up the Yampa for a distance of several miles.

From the summit of the immediate walls of the canyon the rocks rise gently back for a distance of a mile or two, having the appearance of a valley, with an irregular, rounded sandstone floor, and in the center of the valley a deep gorge, which is the canyon. The rim of this valley on the north is from two thousand five hundred to three thousand feet above the river; on the south, it is not so high. A number of peaks stand on this northern rim, the highest of which was received the name Mount Dawes.*

Late in the afternoon we descend to our boat, and return to camp in Echo Park, gliding down in twenty minutes on the rapid river a distance of four or five miles, which was only made upstream by several hours' hard rowing in the morning.

Bradley, 20 June   Sunday again and we remain in camp. What is going to happen? I have kept my tintype album shut trying to save it whole but should have been more wise to have opened it at once for it fell to pieces anyway, and by lying wet so long shut up some of the pictures are spoiled. It is "painfully pleasing" to see what freaks the water has cut with the tintypes. Those on the first page are spoiled. Mother has but one eye while all that is left of Aunt Marsh is just *the top of her head.* Eddie has his chin untouched while Henry loses nearly all his face. . . .**

Sumner, 20 June   All hands in today, taking a general rest. Wrote our names on Echo rocks opposite the camp. The entire distance from the southern end of the valley called Brown's Hole to the mouth of the Bear river is a canyon, except at two creeks on the west side, where there is a gorge cut through by the water of each. It has been named Ladore canyon by the Professor, but the idea of diving into musty trash to find names for new discoveries on a new continent is un-American, to say the least. Distance through it, 25 miles†; general course, 25 degrees west of south; average h[e]ight on both sides about 1700 feet; highest cliff measured (Black Tail Cliff) 2307 feet. There are many still higher but having enough other work on our hands to keep us busy, we did not attempt to measure them.

---

*Named after Henry L. Dawes, republican from Massachusetts, who served a thirty-six-year congressional term. He sponsored the bill establishing Yellowstone National Park and the controversial Dawes Severalty Act of 1887, regarding Indian rights.

**The emulsion on tintypes is easily destroyed by water, particularly if it is allowed to remain for any length of time.

†The Canyon of Lodore was measured as eighteen and one-half miles by the 1922 survey.

Powell Account of 20 June   This morning two of the men take me up the Yampa for a short distance, and I go out to climb. Having reached the top of the canyon, I walk over long stretches of naked sandstone, crossing gulches now and then, and by noon reach the summit of Mount Dawes. From this point I can look away to the north, and see in the dim distance the Sweetwater and Wind River Mountains, more than a hundred miles away. To the northwest, the Wasatch Mountains are in view and peaks of the Uinta. To the east, I can see the western slopes of the Rocky Mountains, more than a hundred and fifty miles distant.

. . . Late in the afternoon I stand on this elevated point, and discover a monument that has evidently been built by human hands. A few plants are growing in the joints between the rocks, and all are lichened over to a greater or less extent, showing evidences that the pile was built a long time ago. This line of peaks, the eastern extension of the Uinta Mountains, has received the name of Sierra Escalanti, in honor of a Spanish priest, who traveled in this region of country nearly a century ago; and, perchance, the reverend father built this monument. . . .

Whirlpool Cañon

Bradley, 21 June   Have made a good run today but have been obliged to make two portages on account of bad rappids. We could have run the last but for a whirlpool below which brought the small boat nearly back again into the worst of the waves. We camp tonight in a fine grove of cottonwoods through which a creek comes in clear and cold from the mountains full of fine trout. The boys are catching them while I write but I am too tired or too lazy to do anything except what I can't help. The river is very rappid but not dangerously so except in some short places. We are now out of the old red sand-stone but I fear if we run west much farther we shall strike it again. Our first portage today was past a rapid in red sand-stone. The second was in white but not so bad and but for a whirlpool below it we should have run it. The men (Andy and Howland) have just come with 20 fine trout which will make a fine breakfast.

Sumner, 21 June   Off at seven o'clock and row down for one mile and a half along the base of Echo Wall, a nearly south course; passed the point of it, turned and ran due north for about five miles; back into the hard red sandstone again, through a narrow, dangerous canyon full of whirlpools, through which it is very hard to keep a boat from being driven on the rock; if a boat should be wrecked in it her crew would have a rather slim chance to get out, as the walls are perpendicular on both sides and from 50 to 500 feet high. Made a portage at the lower end of it; had dinner and pulled out again, and went five miles further, making one short portage on the way; camped for the night on the west side, at the mouth of a clear, beautiful trout stream. Mr. Howland dropped his maps and pencils, rigged a line, and soon had a score of large trout, the first we have been able to catch so far. Made fifteen miles to-day; continuous canyon named "White Pool Canyon [whirlpool?]"; trout stream named Brush Creek.*

Powell Account of 21 June We float around the long rock, and enter another canyon. The walls are high and vertical; the canyon is narrow; and the river fills the whole space below, so that there is no landing-place at the foot of the cliff. The Green is greatly increased by the Yampa, and we now have a much larger river. . . . It is the merry mood of the river to dance through this deep, dark gorge; and right gaily do we join in the sport.

Soon our revel is interrupted by a cataract; its roaring command is heeded by all our power at the oars, and we pull against the whirling current. The "Emma Dean" is brought up against a cliff, about fifty feet above the brink of the fall. By vigorously plying the oars on the side opposite the wall, as if to pull upstream, we can hold her against the rock. The boats behind are signaled to land where they can. The "Maid of the Cañon" is pulled to the left wall, and, by constant rowing, they can hold her also, the "Sister" is run into an alcove on the right, where an eddy is in a dance, and in this she joins. Now my little boat is held against the wall only by the utmost exertion, and it is impossible to make headway against the current. On examination, I find a horizontal crevice in the rock, about ten feet above the water, and a boat's length below us, so we let her down to that point. One of the men clambers into the crevice, in which he can just crawl; we toss him the line, which he makes fast in the rocks, and now our boat is tied up. Then I follow into the crevice, and we crawl along a distance of fifty feet, or more, upstream, and find a broken place, where we can climb about fifty feet higher. Here we stand on a shelf, that passes along downstream to a point above the falls, where it is broken down, and a pile of rocks, over which we can descend to the river, is lying against the foot of the cliff.

It has been mentioned that one of the boats is on the other side. I signal for the men to pull her up alongside of the wall, but it cannot be done; then to cross. This they do, gaining the wall on our side just above where the "Emma Dean" is tied.

The third boat is out of sight, whirling in the eddy of a recess. Looking about, I find another horizontal crevice, along which I crawl to a point just over the water, where this boat is lying, and, calling loud and long, I finally succeed in making the crew understand that I want them to bring the boat

---

*Known as Jones Hole Creek now. Brush creek enters the Green farther downstream.

down, hugging the wall. This they accomplish, by taking advantage of every crevice and knob on the face of the cliff, so that we have the three boats together at a point a few yards above the falls. Now, by passing a line up on the shelf, the boats can be let down to the broken rocks below. This we do, and, making a short portage, our troubles here are over. . . .

At night we camp at the mouth of a small creek, which affords us a good supper of trout. In camp, tonight, we discuss the propriety of several different names for this canyon. At the falls, encountered at noon, its characteristics change suddenly. Above, it is very narrow, and the walls are almost vertical; below, the canyon is much wider, and more flaring; and, high up on the sides, crags, pinnacles, and towers are seen. A number of wild, narrow side canyons enter, and the walls are much broken. After many suggestions, our choice rests between two names, Whirlpool Canyon and Craggy Canyon, neither of which is strictly appropriate for both parts of it; but we leave the discussion at this point, with the understanding that it is best, before finally deciding on a name, to wait until we see what the canyon is below.

Island Park

Bradley, 22 June   Made a short and rapid run of about 5 miles and camped to allow the men to hunt. They *hunted* with their usual success. At 1 P.M., started again and after a run of about 5 miles more we came out into an exceedingly beautiful valley full of islands covered with grass and cottonwood. After passing so many days in the dark cañons where there is little but bare rocks we feel very much pleased when for a few days we enjoy the valley. I have found a lot of currants and have picked about four quarts which will make a fine mess for all hands. We intend to lay here tomorrow and allow the men a chance to *hunt*. Have spread the rations to dry, and find one sack of rice spoiled. We are glad to get rid of it for our boat is too much loaded to ride the waves nicely but is all the time growing lighter as we eat the provisions.

Sumner, 22 June   After a good breakfast on fried trout, we pulled out and made a splendid run of six miles through a continuous rapid and stopped to have a hunt, as we saw many tracks of deer and sheep on the sand. All ready by one o'clock, when the Emma started down a long rapid, which has a fall of about thirty feet per mile. Went along in splendid style till she got to the lower end, where there is a place about a hundred yards long that had a dozen waves in it fully ten feet high. As she could not be pulled out of there her crew kept her straight on her course and let her ride it out. Went trough them safe, but shipped nearly full, and pulled ashore looking like drowned rats. Decided it unsafe for the freight boats to try it, so we were compelled to make a short portage and let down with ropes. Jumped aboard again and pulled out into more rapids, every one of which would thoroughly drench us and leave an extra barrel or two in the boats; but we kept bailing out without any unnecessary stoppages. Dancing over the waves that had never before been distrubed by any keel, the walls getting gradually lower, till about four o'clock, when we came suddenly out into a splendid park; the river widened out into a stream as large as the Missouri, with a number of islands in it covered with cottonwood trees. Camped on the first one we came to, and rolled out on the grass in the shade to rest. Distance from mouth of Bear river 26 miles.* General course 20 degrees south of west from Brown's Hole to this point. The whole country is utterly worthless to anybody for any purpose whatever, unless it should be the artist in search of wildly grand scenery, or the geologist, as there is a great open book for him all the way.

Powell Account of 22 June   Still making short portages and letting down with lines. While we are waiting for dinner today, I climb a point that gives me a good view of the river for two or three miles below, and I think we can make a long run. After dinner, we start; the large boats are to follow in fifteen minutes, and look out for the signal to land. Into the middle of the stream we row, and down the rapid river we glide, only making strokes enough with the oars to guide the boat. What a headlong ride it is! shooting past rocks and islands! I am soon filled with exhilaration only experienced before in riding a fleet horse over the outstretched prairie. One, two, three, four miles we go, rearing and plunging with the waves, until we wheel to the right into a beautiful park, and land on an island, where we go into camp.

An hour or two before sunset, I cross to the mainland, and climb a point of rocks where I can overlook the park and its surroundings. On the east it is bounded by a high mountain ridge. A semicircle of naked hills bounds it on the north, west, and south. The broad, deep river meanders through the park, interrupted by many wooded islands; so I name it Island Park, and decided to call the canyon above Whirlpool Canyon.

Island Park and Mount Hawkins

Bradley, 23 June   The men went hunting and wonderful to relate they have been successful for Bill R. [Hawkins] has brought in a deer. It is a fine large buck and is as fat as beef. He shot it on a mountain over 2000 feet above the river, and brought in both hind quarters himself. Frank brought in one forequarter but they left the other hanging on a tree and as we are much in need

---

*Bear River to Island Park is eleven miles.

of fresh provisions we have moved our camp around to the foot of this mountain, going 5 miles by the river but if we could go straight it is less than one. The Major has been sick for two days and if he is well enough tomorrow we shall go up to the top of the mountain and take observations and I will bring in the deer. The men are on tiptoe and each swears by everything he can name that some *little innocent* deer must die by his hand tomorrow. We shall see.

Sumner, 23 June   Unloaded the boats and spread our plunder out to dry. Rhodes, Dunn, Hawkins[?], Goodman, and Howland sketching; the others, in common, repairing boats and washing. Hunter came in about noon with a fine buck that Rhodes had killed, when we loaded up and moved down about five miles, and camped on the east side, at the lower end of a splendid island covered with a heavy growth of cottonwood. Our camp is within half a mile of the last one above, the river making an almost complete circle.

Hawkins Account of 23 June   Breaking camp at the mouth of Bear River and pulling round the beautiful cliffs of Echo Rocks, we worked our way down to a fine circular park called by the trappers Kelly's Hole, after a hunter of the American Fur Company. I believe it is now called Island Park. I don't remember any portages on the way, but all hands were ducked. Kelley's Hole was an ideal winter camp, swarming with beaver and, in the winter, thousands of mule deer and some mountain sheep. We camped in the middle of the park and had fine sport shooting half-grown wild geese with our pistols. Hawkins killed a fine mule deer. We were amazed at Hall trying to kill a loon. After firing a dozen shots at it, he blurted out, "Damn you! If I could not kill you, I filled you so full of lead you had to sink and drown!"

It is generally supposed that this wary bird, the loon, can dodge a bullet. This is not the case. They sit so low in the water that the hunter overshoots them, nine times out of ten.

I presume Kelly's Hole is now ruined by sheep-herders, who have overrun every place they can get their sheep into, which soon destroy every green thing, root and branch. It seems there is no place left in its primitive beauty. Go where you will, you will find a sheep-herder or the cattle baron who claims the valley and all the surrounding country, and who always objects to a prospector's or trapper's picketing his horse.

Breaking camp in Kelly's Hole, we worked our way down through a low canyon and entered the large and beautiful Uinta Valley and had a fine time for the next three days floating on the wide, gentle current of Green River, shooting many water fowl of all kinds, and shooting *at* antelope and that nuisance of the world, the coyote, which frequently came trooping down to the bank to view the strange things going down the river.

Powell Account of 23 June   We remain in camp today to repair our boats, which have had hard knocks, and are leaking. Two of the men go out with the barometer to climb the cliff at the foot of Whirlpool Canyon and measure the walls; another goes on the mountain to hunt; and Bradley and I spend the day among the rocks, studying an interesting geological fold and collecting fossils. Late in the afternoon, the hunter returns, and brings with him a fine, fat deer, so we give his name to the mountain—Mount Hawkins. Just before night we move camp to the lower end of the park, floating down the river about four miles.

Island Park

Bradley, 24 June   Major is much better today but as he fancied that he wanted to explore the mountain to the south of here, I left him to go his way and I went mine up to the top of the cliff after the quarter of deer for I have no faith in the men finding another today and it will not do to leave a fine quarter of deer to the wolves while we live on bacon. I ascended without much difficulty and found the meat untouched by wolves. I suppose they do not often climb quite so high for I found by the barometer that it is 2800 ft. above the river but I am so used to climbing them now that I hardly notice it—yet it came very hard at first. The river about four miles below here cuts this same mountain chain in two and comes out on the other side into delightful valleys like the one in which we now lie and which we have named "Island Park." The river is very rapid and we can see from the mountain that we must work to get through and shall go at it with a will for we can see for 50 or 60 miles that it is all valley and island covered with cottonwood groves and the cañon cannot be very long.*

Sumner, 24 June   The Professor and Howland climbed the mountain on the east side, with barometer and drawing materials; spent the greater part of the day sketching the park, which they have named "Island Park"; rain in the evening.

Powell Account of 24 June   Bradley and I start early to climb the mountain ridge to the east; find its summit to be nearly three thousand feet above camp, and it has required some labor to scale it; but on its top, what a view! There is a long spur running out from the Uinta Mountains toward the south, and the river runs lengthwise through it. Coming down Lodore and Whirlpool Canyons, we cut through the southern slope of the Uinta Mountains; and the

---

*Note the discrepancy between the Bradley and Powell entries for 24 June.

lower end of this latter canyon runs into the spur, but, instead of splitting it the whole length, the river wheels to the right at the foot of Whirlpool Canyon, in a great curve to the northwest, through Island Park. At the lower end of the park, the river turns again to the southeast, and cuts into the mountain to its center, and then makes a detour to the southwest, splitting the mountain ridge for a distance of six miles nearly to its foot, and then turns out of it to the left. All this we can see where we stand on the summit of Mount Hawkins, and so we name the gorge below Split Mountain Canyon.

We are standing three thousand feet above its waters, which are troubled with billows, and white with foam. Its walls are set with crags and peaks, and buttressed towers, and overhanging domes. Turning to the right, the park is below us, with its island groves reflected by the deep, quiet waters. Rich meadows stretch out on either hand, to the verge of a sloping plain, that comes down from the distant mountains. These plains are of almost naked rock, in strange contrast to the meadows; blue and lilac colored rocks, buff and pink, vermilion and brown, and all these colors clear and bright.

Split Mountain Cañon

Bradley, 25 June   Started this morning with the hope that we might get through the cañon today and possibly we could have done it, but one of the men* was taken sick and as we came to a place about 11 A.M., where we had to make a portage we concluded to wait until tomorrow and let Jack have a chance to rest and sleep as he will take no medicine. We have carried the loads around and lowered the boats so that we have only to load up and start. We shall have any easy run to get through tomorrow if we have no portages to make. Jack is better tonight and we shall probably start early in the morning.

Sumner, 25 June   Pulled out at seven and moved down four miles, to the head of another canyon . . . and into more rapids; made two portages and camped on the west side, at the head of another impassable rapid to loaded boats; one of the men sick.

Powell Account of 25 June   This morning, we enter Split Mountain Canyon, sailing in through a broad, flaring, brilliant gateway. We run two or three rapids after they have been carefully examined. Then we have a series of six or eight, over which we are compelled to pass by letting the boats down with lines. This occupies the entire day, and we camp at night at the mouth of a great cave.

---

*Sumner was the sick man.

The cave is at the foot of one of these rapids, and the waves dash in nearly to its very end. We can pass along a little shelf at the side until we reach the back part. Swallows have built their nests in the ceiling, and they wheel in, chattering and scolding at our intrusion; but their clamor is almost drowned by the noise of the waters. Looking out of the cave, we can see, far up the river, a line of crags standing sentinel on either side, and Mount Hawkins in the distance.

Bradley, 26 June Have made a pleasant run today of 30 miles. Made a short portage and have run a succession of rappids through the cañon which lengthened out beyond our expectation. We have reached the valley this A.M. Found great numbers of geese; brought in 10 tonight but they are very poor at this season. Passed several old lodges where the Indians live at certain seasons of the year. There are none living in them now. Jack is much better tonight and we anticipate a fine run tomorrow. Found a fine lot of foccils in the last cañon and have added three new varieties to our number and found them in great abundance.

Sumner, 26 June Made the portage and went a short distance when we came to another one, and had to make it in the rain; while the men were at work the Professor climbed up the side-hills looking for fossils; spent two hours to find one, and came back to find a peck that the men had picked up on the bank of the river; all ready by three o'clock, when we pulled out again; ran four miles at a rapid rate through the canyon, when all at once the Great Uinta Valley spread out before us as far as the eye could reach. It was a welcome sight to us after two weeks of the hardest kind of work, in a canyon where we could not see half a mile, very often, in any direction except straight up. All hands pulled with a will, except the Professor and Mr. Howland. The Professor being a one-armed man, he was set to watching the geese, while Howland was perched on a sack of flour in the middle of one of the large boats, mapping the river as we rowed along. Our sentinel soon signaled a flock of geese ahead, when we gave chase, and soon had ten of them in the boats. Summed up the log, found we had run 23 miles since leaving the canyon, and camped for the night on the east side, under three large cottonwoods. Rested, eat supper, and turned in to be serenaded by the wolves, which kept up their howling until we dropped asleep, and I don't know how much longer, as I heard them next morning at daybreak.

Powell Account of 26 June . . . Down the river we are carried by the swift waters at great speed, sheering around a rock now and then with a timely stroke or two of the oars. At one point, the river turns from left to right, in a direction at right angles to the canyon, in a long chute, and strikes the right, where its waters are heaped up in great billows, that tumble back in breakers. We glide into the chute before we see the danger, and it is too late to stop. Two or three hard strokes are given on the right, and we pause for an instant, expecting to be dashed against the rock. The bow of the boat leaps high on a great wave; the rebounding waters hurl us back, and the peril is past. The next moment, the other boats are hurriedly signaled to land on the left. Accomplishing this, the men walk along the shore, holding the boats near the bank, and let them drift around. Starting again, we soon debouch into a beautiful valley, and glide down its length for ten miles, and camp under a grand old cottonwood. This is evidently a frequent resort for Indians. Tent poles are lying about, and the dead embers of late campfires are seen. On the plains, to the left, antelopes are feeding. Now and then a wolf is seen, and after dark they make the air resound with their howling.

Bradley, 27 June We have had a hard day's work. Have run 63 miles and as the tide is not rapid we have to row a little which comes harder to us than running rappids. It is the same beautiful valley filled with green islands and contrasting strangely but pleasantly with the dry and barren bluffs which back them and which sometimes come down to the water's edge and entirely crowd out the valley for a short distance. Our camp tonight is alive with the meanest pest that pesters man—mosquitoes. Yet they will be as quiet as death in an hour or so for the night wind is too cool for them and they take shelter in the grove. We must be very near the Uinta River which everybody said we could never reach, but everybody will be mistaken for we are nearing it so fast and so easily that we are certain of success.

Sumner, 27 June Off again at seven, down a river that cannot be surpassed for wild beauty of scenery, sweeping in great curves through magnificent groves of cottonwood. It has an average width of two hundred yards and depth enough to float a New Orleans packet. Our easy stroke of eight miles an hour conveys us just fast enough to enjoy the scenery, as the view changes with kaleidoscopic rapidity. Made sixty three miles today, and camped on the west side, at the mouth of a small, dirty creek. Killed eight wild geese on the way.

Powell Account of 27 June Now our way is along a gently flowing river, beset with many islands; groves are seen on either side, and natural meadows, where herds of antelope are feeding. Here and there we have views of the distant mountains on the right. . . .

Mouth of the Uinta

Bradley, 28 June   Reached the desired point at last and have camped close
to the mouth of the Uinta River. The White River comes in about a mile below
on the other side. Now for letters from home and friends, for we shall here have
an opportunity to send and receive those that have been forwarded through
John Heard. Hope to receive a good lot and think I shall. The musical little
mosquitoes bite so badly that I can write no longer.

Sumner, 28 June   Same character of country as yesterday. Saw four antelope, but failed to get any. Forty-eight miles brought us to the mouth of Uinta
river, which place reached about three o'clock, and camped on the west side of
Green river, under a large cottonwood, at the crossing of the Denver City and
Salt Lake wagon road, as it was located in 1865. There is not much of a road
now, if any, as it has never been traveled since unless by wolves, antelope, and
perhaps a straggling Indian at long intervals. Distance from the head of the
valley by river, one hundred and thirty miles; by land about fifty miles.*
General course of the river 10° west of south. This part of the country has been
written up so often by abler pens, that I hesitate in adding anything more. As an
agricultural valley it does not amount to much, as it is too dry on the uplands,
and there are but few meadows on the river bottom, and they as a general rule
are small—from fifty to two hundred acres in size and overflows, though very
seldom. At present it is clothed with a thick growth of grass, waist high. On the
uplands there is the common bunch grass of the west—short but very rich. No
part of the country that we have seen can be irrigated, except the river bottoms,
as the uplands are rolling and cut up by ditches in almost every direction. But
for a stock country it would be hard to excel, as almost all kinds would do well
on the bunch grass throughout the entire year. There is plenty of timber for
building purposes and fuel, and enough farming land to produce all that a
large settlement would require for home consumption. But there is one thing
in the way. According to the treaty of 1868 between Gov. Hunt, of Colorado,
and the Ute Indians, most, if not the whole of this valley belongs to the
reservation, selected by the Indians themselves. Most likely they will, as one
band of them have a permanently settled thing of it, and have a winter agency
twenty-five miles from this point on Uinta river. So far we have accomplished
what we set out for. We were told by the frontiersmen while at Green River that
we could not get to the mouth of White river. One man that filled the

---

*The river miles from Craggy Canyon, now known as Split Mountain, to the mouth of the Uinta
are 71½.

important office of policeman in Pgitmont had the assurance to tell me that no boat could get as far down as Brown's Hole. We expect to remain here for a week to meet Col. Mead, and send off some specimens and all the notes and maps, to make sure of that much. Total distance run 356 miles; estimated distance to junction and Grand rivers 300 miles by river.*

Powell Account of 28 June   Today, the scenery on either side of the river is much the same as that of yesterday, except that two or three lakes are discovered, lying in the valley to the west. After dinner, we run but a few minutes, when we discovered the mouth of the Uinta, a river coming in from the west. Up the valley of this stream, about forty miles, the reservation of the Uinta Indians is situated. We propose to go there, and see if we can replenish our mess kit, and perhaps, send letters to friends. We also desire to establish an astronomic station here; and hence this will be our stopping place for several days. . . .**

Bradley, 29 June   Have written a lot of letters and commenced to copy my notes but find the latter so great a job fear unless Major makes some change in his present design to go to the Agency day after tomorrow, shan't be able to copy them. If not I will send originals, though it would puzzle a Philadelphia lawyer to read them. Camp is very quiet for all are busy writing home. Built a huge fire last night to attract the attention of any Indians that might be straggling in the bluffs, that they might either come in themselves or report it to the Agency, but no one has come in today and fear it was not seen. Weather showery with hot sun when it can get a chance to shine. Saw two pelican on the lake tonight but they are on the opposite side out of reach of our rifles.

Powell Account of 29 June   A mile and three quarters from here is the junction of the White River with the Green. The White has its source far to the east, in the Rocky Mountains. This morning, I cross the Green, and go over into the valley of the White, and extend my walk several miles along its winding way, until, at last, I come in sight of the strangely carved rocks, named by General Hughes, in his journal, "Goblin City. . ."

---

*They had traveled 258½ miles and had 245 miles more to the junction with the Grand River.

**An astronomic station is simply a location from which an accurately predicted celestial event from a published almanac can be timed and measured to determine latitude and longitude.

Camp at Mouth of Uinta
June 29, 1869*

Mr. Edwards: My dear sir:

The party has reached this point in safety and having run 4 cañons of about 25 miles in length each, the walls of which were from 2,000 to 2,800 feet high. We have found falls and dangerous rapids when we were compelled to make portages of rations, and let the boats down with lines. Wrecked one of our boats and lost instruments. The instruments were duplicates, but the loss of the rations will compel us to shorten the time for the work. You will perceive an account of our trip in detail in the *Chicago Tribune*, as I shall send some letters to it for publication.

In the wreck I lost my papers, and have to use plant dryers for my letter paper.

Have not made large general collections, but have some fine fossils, a good geological section and a good map.

Short walk to the Uinta Indian Agency, about 25 or 30 miles from camp where I shall mail this letter, and hope to get letters and some news.

The boats seem to be a success, although filled with water by the waves many times, they never sink; the light cabins at each end acting well as buoys. . .

We shall rest here for 8 or 10 days—make repairs and dry our rations which have been wet so many times that they are almost in a spoiling condition. In fact we have lost nearly half now by one mishap or another.

Personally I have enjoyed myself much, the scenery being wild and beautiful beyond description. All in good health—all to the Grand and Green as I am very anxious to make observations on the 7th of August eclipse.

With earnest wishes for your continued success and prosperity at Normal.

I am, with great respect,
Yours cordially,
J.W. POWELL.

Bradley, 30 June   Major has changed his mind and sent his brother and Andy [Hall] to the Agency. Will go himself in two days. Have kept my letters and note to send by him for I hope to get my mail before he goes. We carried

---

*Letter to Dr. Richard Edwards, President of Illinois Normal University, reprinted in the *Chicago Tribune*, 20 July 1869.

the small boat about 100 yds. overland to the lake tonight but the pelicans are too shy. They hid in the tall reeds beside the water. Shot great quantities of geese and ducks. They can be counted by hundreds as they float on the lake or fly over our camp to their favorite feeding places—the mouths of the Uinta and White rivers below.

Powell Account of 30 June   We have a row up the Uinta today, but are not able to make much headway against the swift current, and hence concluded we must walk all the way to the agency.*

Bradley, 1 July   Went out today with Major to find foccils which were reported to abound about three miles up White River. Think we were on the wrong side of the stream. They were found by an officer sent out by the government with two companies of cavalry to lay out a stage road from Denver to Salt Lake City via White River in 1865. He had a train of 70 wagons camped just where we now lie. He built a ferry here and crossed over. According to the officer's notes which Major has, they sunk the ferry-boat under the tree where our boats are now lying but we have not sounded to see if she still remains. Presume she does. Across the river is a splendid meadow of the finest grass I ever saw growing naturally. It is without exception the finest mowing land I ever saw, as smooth and level as a floor and no rocks. It would average two tons to the acre for four miles square. Talk of grazing land—that beats even far-famed Texas.

Powell Account of 1 July   Two days have been employed in obtaining the local time, taking observations for latitude and longitude, and making excursions into the adjacent country. This morning, with two of the men, I start for the agency. It is a toilsome walk, twenty miles of the distance being across a sand desert. Occasionally, we have to wade the river, crossing it back and forth. Toward evening, we cross several beautiful streams, which are tributaries of the Uinta, and we pass through pine groves and meadows, arriving just at dusk at

---

*The Uinta Indian Agency was located on the Whiterocks River, a tributary of the Duchesne. (Note that in Powell's day, the main stream was the Uinta—now it is the Duchesne.) The agency was established by President Lincoln in 1861, but not funded until 1865. By 1869, it still had only a few wooden buildings for the superintendent and perhaps 8 or 10 employees. No troops were stationed there. Its main function was to serve as a gathering point for displaced Utes who had no other place to go. The treaty that would have given the Utes up to $25,000 per year in compensation was rejected by the U.S. Senate. Therefore, in 1869, the agency was still trying to attract Utes to move to the reservation.

the Reservation. Captain Dodds, the agent, is away, having gone to Salt Lake City, but his assistants receive us very kindly. It is rather pleasant to see a house once more, and some evidence of civlization, even if it is on an Indian reservation, several days' ride from the nearest home of the white man.

Letter from O. G. Howland to the *Rocky Mountain News*

Camp Near Mouths of Uinta and White Rivers.
On the Green, July 1, 1869*

Dear News:—My last letter gave you a hasty sketch of our trip from Green River City to the mouth of the Bear, and up to the eighteenth of June. I forgot to mention then a little incident in which the two elements—fire and water— played prominent parts. We had run in on smooth water, just above some falls, to camp for the night on a bench about fifty yards wide by a quarter mile in length, thickly overgrown with willows, cedar, sage and grass, so much so it was almost impossible to get through it; built a fire to cook grub by, and were unloading the boats to dry out things a little, when a heavy wind came sweeping up the river, scattering the fire in all directions over our small camp, and fanning into a blaze a hundred different places the dry drift underneath the bushes. To beat a retreat to the rear was impossible, as the walls of the cañon rose perpendicular hundreds of feet above. Something must be done quickly— the boats were the only alternative—and a run over the falls. So tumbling in what little on shore could be reached, the boats were pulled out into the center of the river above the falls, the crew of each just having time to snatch off some of their clothing which was on fire, and smother the rest before the use of their oars was needed to engineer the boats down the fall. Luckily all three of the boats came in safe and sound. One of the crew came in hatless, another shirtless, a third without his pants, and a hole burned in the posterior portion of his drawers; another with nothing but drawers and shirt, and still another had to pull off his handkerchief from his neck, which was all ablaze. With the loss of his eyelashes and brows, and a favorite moustache, and scorching of his ears, no other harm was done. One of the party had gathered up our mess kit and started hastily for the boat, the smoke and heat was so blinding that in his attempt to spring from the shore to the boat he lost his footing and fell, mess kit and all, in about ten feet of water, that put him out (I mean the fire in his clothes) and he crawled over the side of the boat as she was being pushed off, not worse, but better, if possible, for his ducking. Our mess kit, however, was lost, as also a number of other things, of which we felt the need quite often. We

---

*Reprinted from the Denver *Rocky Mountain News,* 18 August 1869.

have since managed to raise up a sufficient number of bailing dishes to furnish one for every two of us, from which to drink our tea and coffee. The sum total of our mess kit for ten men, at present time, is as follows:

One gold pan, used for making bread
One bake-oven, with broken lid
One camp-kettle, for making tea or coffee
One frying-pan
One large spoon and two tea spoons
Three tin plates and five bailing cups
One pick-ax and one shovel

The last two articles we do not use on ordinary occasions, but when a pot of beans, which by the way is a luxury, is boiled in place of tea or coffee, our cook sometimes uses the latter article for a spoon, and the former to clean his teeth after our repast is over.

Another incident of interest I forgot to mention in my last letter, occurred on the sixteenth of June. Two of us had started out to climb Blacktail Cliff, for the purpose of measuring its hight by barometer, and to get the surrounding topography, while the rest made portage of provisions and let down boats. When we returned to camp it was deserted, and only one large boat was to be found. Soon, however, all appeared at camp and all were made aware of what had happened. After making the portage of provisions and letting down the little boat, they attempted to let down one of the large ones; but by paying out too much line to drop her around big boulders, her nose got turned into the main current, into which she instantly shot so far that the combined strength of five men was unable to resist the action of the water, and she pulled away from them, shooting clear across the breakers to the opposite shore, into smoother water about a half mile below. The little boat was immediately manned and sent in pursuit. They overhauled her before she got into the next rapids, and tied her fast for the night. The next morning, taking her cargo and crew in the two boats, we ran down and across, loaded up and manned her with her usual cargo and crew, and went our way rejoicing that we had not lost her entirely. She got one pretty severe thump in her stern, which stove a hole and made her leak badly; but at noon we repaired that, and she is now as good as ever. . . .

. . . In my last letter to you I mentioned that the river appeared to run without any design. I have partially rejected that idea since leaving the mouth of Bear River. In Whirlpool Cañon, and also in this (Cleft Mountain Cañon) the river seems to go for the highest points within the range of vision, disemboweling first one and striking for the next and serving it the same, and so on, indefinitely. Here it turns short and sharp into the very center at the upper end of a long mountain, then turns again as sharply, and goes tearing down through it to almost the lower end, and shoots out to the left again into the prairie, whirling, splashing and foaming as if in fury to think so tiny an obstacle should tower 3,000 feet above it to check its progress. This makes me think it has designs on all mountains of any pretensions. Small ones are not considered worthy its notice, it seems. . . .

. . . This valley, as also the valleys of the White and Uinta for twenty-five or thirty miles, has the appearance of being very fine for agricultural purposes and for grazing. The Indians on Uinta Agency have fine looking crops of corn, wheat and potatoes, which they put in this spring, on the sod. They have also garden vegetables of all kinds, and are cultivating the red currant. Everything is said to look well. Most of the Indians are now from the Agency to see the railroad, while the rest stay to attend to their stock and keep their cattle from getting in and eating up their crops.

We have been nearly eaten up by mosquitoes since lying in camp here, our principal amusement having been fighting and smoking the pests.

Two of the Utes living at the Agency are here to take up our mail and some fossils we have collected, and will leave this morning. They are the only Indians we have seen since starting. It is scarcely sunrise yet, but anticipating an early start this morning I got up early to finish this letter, and having done so will dry up. When or where you will hear from us again is hard to tell. Mr. Goodman, one of the wrecked party, leaves us here, being unable to raise a personal outfit for the remainder of the trip, so we now number only nine to finish up our work.

O. G. HOWLAND.

Bradley, 2 July   Major, Bill R., and Frank started for the Agency early this morning. Sent letters, etc. Have had a very lazy day for there are but five of us left in camp and we feel lonesome. Since we came here I got enough currants for all hands and they were so good that I resolved to have some more and as the mosquitoes drove me away before, I thought I would get ahead of them this time so I put a piece of mosquito bar over my hat and fastened it around my waist and with gloves to protect my hands and a pair of boots coming to the knee to protect me from rattlesnakes, I set out and after hunting along the side of the Uinta River for more than a mile I succeeded in finding just one bush which I broke down and brought off in triumph. The mosquitoes are perfectly frightful. As I went through the rank grass and wild sunflower sometimes higher than my head they would fairly *scream* around me. I think I never saw them thicker even in Florida than in this place. I got more than three quarts of currants off the bush I brought in and had an excellent supper of them. Our camp is on the little bluff only about ten or fifteen ft. above the river between the lake and mouth of the Uinta, and strange to say the mosquitoes trouble us but little compared to what they do if we leave our camp. I keep a little smoke in front of my tent nearly all the time and that keeps them very quiet. One of the men says that while out on the shore of the lake a mosquito asked him for his pipe, knife and tobacco and told him to hunt his old clothes for a match while he loaded the pipe. . . .

Beginning of Major Powell's Journal, 2 July   With Rhodes [Hawkins] and Frank [Goodman] I started for the Uinta Indian Agency.* At noon met Hall coming for me with pony. Had a long trip crossing and recrossing the river many times. Wrote letters at night.

Bradley, 3 July   Another day of quiet rest. Have been cleaning rifle and pistols for constant wetting gets them in bad condition. Our cook being up to the Agency we have had a great time cooking today. I cooked some beans. Put on what I thought we could eat and set them to boiling. They boiled and swelled and I kept putting in hot water until I had a large bread-pan that will hold ten or twelve quarts solid full of beans. Cooked them as well as I could but their being so many they scorched a little for the pan wouldn't hold enough water to prevent burning. The rest took a boat and went up to Uinta River and got some ducks and currants for tomorrow. We shall have a poor 4 of July anyway and we must make the best of it.

Powell, 3 July   Went with Lake** to visit Tsau-wi-et† and see the fields. This former chief is very old. His skin lies in wrinkles and deep folds on his limbs and body wherever naked. Each Indian has ½ acres . . . (the head of a lodge) of wheat, then turnips, beets, potatoes, etc., all doing well. Irrigation done by white men and some of the sowing the same. The Indians are learning fast, [to] plough, sow, etc. Will not build houses—Superstitious. Their uncleaniness probably a reason for it. I purchased certain articles. Beautiful place for reservation. Kindness of the people. Bishop, wife of Tsau-wi-et a great talker. Has much influence. Sits in the Council. Often harangues the people. Indians gone to see the R.R.***

---

*The agency was located at what is now called Whiterocks.

**An assistant at the Indian Agency. The agent, Captain Pardyn Dodds, was away at the time.

†Sowiette, as he is known in Utah annals, a famous friend of the Mormons in 1850 and thereafter.

***The Union Pacific Railroad, which had just been completed 10 May 1869.

Powell Account of 3[2] July   I go, this morning, to visit *Tsau-wi-at*. This old chief is but the wreck of a man, and no longer has influence. Looking at him, you can scarcely realize that he is a man. His skin is shrunken, wrinkled, and dry, and seems to cover no more than a form of bones. He is said to be more than a hundred years old. I talk a little with him, but his conversation is inchoherent, though he seems to take pride in showing me some medals that must have been given him many years ago. He has a pipe which, he says, he has used a long time. I offer to exchange with him, and he seems to be glad to accept; so I add another to my collection of pipes. His wife, "The Bishop," as she is called, is a very garrulous old woman; she exerts a great influence, and is much revered. She is the only Indian woman I have known to occupy a place in the council ring. She seems very much younger than her husband, and, though wrinkled and ugly, is still vigorous. She has much to say to me concerning the condition of the people, and seems very anxious that they should learn to cultivate the soil, own farms, and live like white men. After talking a couple of hours with these old people, I go to see the farms. They are situated in a very beautiful district, where many fine streams of water meander across alluvial plains and meadows. These creeks have quite a fall, and it is very easy to take their waters out above, and, with them, overflow the lands.

It will be remembered that irrigation is neccessary, in this dry climate, to [do] successful farming.*   Quite a number of Indians have each a patch of ground, of two or three acres, on which they are raising wheat, potatoes, turnips, pumpkins, melons, and other vegetables. Most of the crops are looking well, and it is rather surprising with what pride they show us that they are able to cultivate crops like white men. They are still occupying lodges, and refuse to build houses, assigning as a reason that when any one dies in a lodge it is always abandoned, and very often burned with all the effects of the deceased, and when houses have been built for them they have been treated in the same way. . . .

Bradley, 4 July   No one has returned from the Agency and we begin to feel some anxiety lest something has happened or they have failed to find it. Hope for the best. Have set our flag on the old flag and as we look upon it our thoughts wander back to other scenes and other days. Three successive 4ths I have been in the wilderness. Two years ago I was on Lodge Pole Creek between

---

*Powell is already making the kinds of observations about farming, irrigation, and water rights that led to his concept of workable settlement in the arid West and to his book, *Report on the Lands of the Arid Region* (1878).

Ft. Sedgwick and Ft. Sanders.* Last year I was in the Uinta Mountains whose snow-clad peaks loom up to the west and north of our present camp. Where shall I be next 4th of July? Took a long walk tonight alone beside the lake and thought of home, contrasted its comforts and privileges with the privations we suffer here and asked myself why am I here? But those green flowery graves on the hillside far away seem to answer for me, and with moistened eyes I seek again my tent where engaged with my own thoughts, I pass hours with my friends at home, sometimes laughing, sometimes weeping until sleep comes and dreams bring me into the apparent presence of those I love.

Powell, 4 July   Wrote letters. Lake went to City.

Bradley, 5 July   All returned today. Bill R., Andy and two Indians with pack ponies came in this morning and Major and brother came in at night. The Indians are remarkably clean looking for Indians. They will take back a lot of stuff which the Major has traded off at the Agency. He has got 300 lbs. flour which will make our rations last a little longer. Frank Goodman left while at the Agency, which will make our party one less. He is one of those that lost everything in the wreck.

Powell, 5 July   Wrote until 10:00 A.M., then came to camp with Walter [Powell].

Powell Account of 5 July   The last two days have been spent in studying the language of the Indians, and making collections of articles illustrating the state of arts among them.

Frank Goodman informs me, this morning, that he has concluded not to go on with the party, saying that he has seen danger enough. It will be remembered that he was one of the crew on the "No Name," when she was wrecked. As our boats are rather heavily loaded, I am content that he should leave, although he has been a faithful man.

We start early on our return to the boats, taking horses with us from the reservation, and two Indians, who are to bring the animals back.

---

*Fort Sedgwick, a small cavalry post established to protect the Overland Stage Line, was located in northeastern Colorado, about where Julesburg now stands. Fort Sanders was established in 1866, 3 miles south of present Laramie, Wyoming, to protect the Overland Trail and the Union Pacific Railroad. Lodgepole Creek runs from the Cheyenne area through southwestern Nebraska.

Sumner Account of 5 July   Major Powell and his brother, Hall, and Frank Goodman left camp and hoofed it up to old Fort Roubidoux, or as it was then called, Fort Winter, a trading post at Disaster Falls. The Howland brothers, Dunn, Bradley, Hawkins, and I remained in camp and amused ourselves by taking astronomical observations, shooting ducks, and fishing. Major Powell was gone five days, and brought back a shirttail full of supplies. I thought at the time it was a damned stingy, foolish scheme, as there was plenty of supplies to be had, to bring back such a meagre mess for nine to make a thousand-mile voyage through an unknown canyon, but as I wasn't boss I suppose I ought to keep still about it.* Goodman, having had all the experience his health called for, stopped at the post. He had had several close calls, and possibly ran out of nerve. He was a fine singer of sea songs, and we missed him around the evening camp.

---

*Although Sumner probably didn't realize it, Powell spent nearly all his remaining cash on the food resupply.

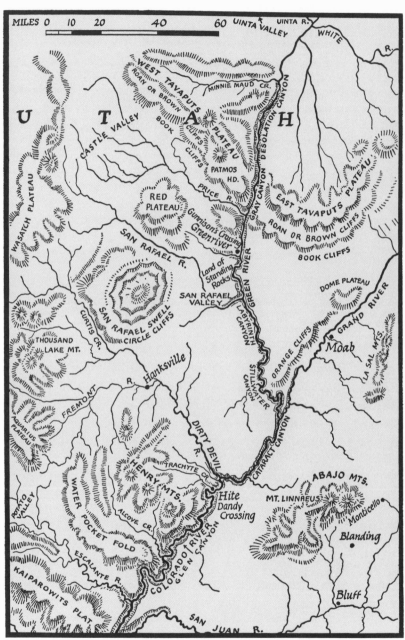

Mouth of the Uinta through Glen Canyon.

V. The Mouth of the Uinta River to the Junction of the Grand and Green

Leaving the friendly Uinta Valley behind, with its Indian Agency and their last contact with civilization, Powell and his crew entered a land of great aridity and desolation. In this barren land of pinnacles and buttes, they found little shelter from the canyon winds and temperatures of 100 degrees. With the swamping of Powell's boat, the *Emma Dean,* the list of near, as well as actual, losses added to their general concern: one boat, one man (Goodman), 3 rifles, barometers, watches, bedding, clothing, cooking equipment, mess kits, and rations. Despite their losses, the forbidding landscape, interpersonal tensions, and a canyon that felt "like an oven," Bradley expressed the collective mood (on 14 July) as a "cool determination to persevere that possessed every man of the party. . . ."

Johnson's Island

Bradley, 6 July   Started about 10 A.M., and moved down the river once more. Was exceedingly glad to get away for I want to keep going. Don't like long stopping. Passed the mouth of White River about two miles below Uinta. Just above its mouth in Green River we passed a large island on which a man who used to be interpreter at Uinta has a garden. We had read that "stolen fruit is sweet" and thought we would try it, so got beets, carrots, turnips and potatoes, all too small to eat the bottoms so we did the next best thing for Andy having cooked all together, we ate them as greens. I tried them but the potato tops tasted so badly I threw them away, very fortunate for me for all the rest except Howland ate them and have been very sick all the P.M. All are vomiting freely now and begin to feel better though think we shan't eat any more potato-tops this season. Made about 35 miles today. River smooth but valley narrow.

Sumner, 6 July   After 7 days of weary, useless waiting we are at last ready to cut loose from the last sign of civilization for many hundred miles—The "Emma Dean," now as before taking the lead, followed close by "Kitty's Sister" manned by Rhodes, Hall and Howland. The "Maid" leaving last, manned by Bradley, Walter Powell and Seneca Howland. Goodman being fonder of "bullwhacking" than rowing, left the party at the Agency. . . .

Powell, 6 July   Started down river again. Got mess of greens on head of island. Made all hands sick. Camped on left bank of river. Cottonwood Grove. Camp No. 1.

Powell Account of 6 July   Start early this morning. A short distance below the mouth of the Uinta, we come to the head of a long island. Last winter, a man named Johnson, a hunter and Indian trader, visited us at our camp in White River Valley.* This man has an Indian wife, and, having no fixed home, usually travels with one of the Ute bands. He informed me it was his intention to plant some corn, potatoes, and other vegetables on this island in the spring, and knowing that we would pass it, invited us to stop and help ourselves, even if he should not be there; so we land and go out on the island. Looking about, we soon discover his garden, but it is in a sad condition, having received no care since it was planted. It is yet too early in the season for corn, but Hall suggests that potato tops are good greens, and, anxious for some change from our salt-meat fare, we gather a quantity and take them aboard. At noon we stop and cook our greens for dinner; but soon, one after another of the party is taken sick; nausea first, and then severe vomiting, and we tumble around under the trees, groaning with pain, and I feel a little alarmed, lest our poisoning be severe. Emetics are administered to those who are willing to take them, and about the middle of the afternoon we are all rid of the pain. Jack Sumner records in his diary that "potato tops are not good greens on the sixth day of July."

———————————

*This is probably "squaw man" Johnson, although there was also a "mountain man" Johnson. Note the discrepancy between Powell's "invitation," vs. Bradley's and Sumner's "stolen" vegetables.

This evening we enter another canyon, almost imperceptibly, as the walls rise very gently.

Sumner Account of 6 July   The next morning, July 6th, after the arrival of the rest of the party, we pulled out and went down the river about ten miles to Johnston's Island, where a squaw-man had planted a garden. Having landed, Hawkins and Hall started to investigate, and as they could not find anything else, they proposed to have a mess of greens. They proceeded to filch turnip tops, beet tops, potato tops, and God knows what else. They brought a backload of the beastly stuff, dumped it into the boat, and we ran down the river a few miles and landed again for dinner. Hawkins cooked a kettle of his plunder, poured it into a gold pan and yelled, "Grub pile!"

We proceeded to devour it to show our appreciation of his ability as a first-class cook. We had not gone a mile after dinner until all hands, the cook included, wished Johnston and his garden in the middle kettle of a lower world. Such a gang of sick men I never saw before or since. Whew! It seems I can feel it yet. I remarked to Hall that I didn't think potato tops made a good greens for the sixth day of July. He ripped out an oath or two, and swore he had coughed up a potato vine a foot long, with a potato on it as big as a goose egg.

Desolation Canyon

Bradley, 7 July   Have had a pretty little run this morning but the hills beginning to get near and higher, we landed about 9 A.M. to measure them. I found on the one I climbed a pile of rocks placed as children call cobhouse (They were long, slatey sand-stone rocks). I repiled them and added a long rock, over seven feet, which I placed on end and made very secure. I also put my name on a flat stone with name of expedition and date and fastened it up very strong. Think it will stand many years. It is the first time I have left my name in this country for we have been in a part where white men may have been before but we are now below their line of travel and we shall not probably see any more evidences of them until we get to the White River No. 2 below here. Major and Dunn found the mountain they climbed about 1000 ft. above the river. The hills close in to the river and we begin to call it a cañon though it was nearly one yesterday with its banks set back from the river. In the A.M. we began to find rappids. Run several good ones. Run all day 40 miles.

Sumner, 7 July   Off again at 7 o'clock. Rowed down 10 miles when we came to a cañon and stopped to measure the walls. Height 1050 ft. Pulled out again at 10 o'clock and rowed until 6 o'clock through a channel that has no more current than a canal. It is cut through a sandstone plateau about 1500 ft.

deep; there are also side cañons coming in every quarter of a mile, making the top of the plateau look like a vast field of honeycomb. Passed 2 rapids today; killed 2 otter and 4 wild geese; made 34 miles and camped on the east side. A few stunted cedars on the side of the cliffs, no timber on the river.

Powell Account of 7 July   We find quiet water today, the river sweeping in great and beautiful curves, the canyon walls steadily increasing in altitude. The escarpment formed by the cut edges of the rock are often vertical, sometimes terraced, and in some places the treads of the terraces are sloping. In these quiet curves vast amphitheaters are formed, now in vertical rocks, now in steps.

The salient point of rock within the curve is usually broken down in a steep slope, and we stop occasionally to climb up, at such a place, where, on looking down, we can see the river sweeping the foot of the opposite cliff, in a great, easy curve, with a perpendicular or terraced wall rising from the water's edge many hundreds of feet. One of these we find very symetrical, and name it Sumner's Amphitheater. . . .*

Bradley, 8 July   Have made run of 12 miles. Didn't start until 1 o'clock P.M. Climbed the mountain this morning, found it very hard one to ascend but we succeeded at last. In one place Major haveing but one arm couldn't get up so I took off my drawers and they made an excellent substitute for rope and with that assistance he got up safe. Found the mountain 1000 ft. above the river. The scenery from its summit is wild and desolate. A succession of craggy peaks like the one we were on was all we could see near us. We seemed to be in about the center of the range as we could look backwards and forewards and they looked about the same in extent, so judge we have got half way through the cañon but not the worst half for since we started today we have had a succession of bad rapids, but have run them all, though one I think was the worst we ever run. Every boat was half full of water when we got through. It is a wild exciting game, and aside from the danger of losing our provisions and having to walk out to civilization I should like to run them all for the danger to life is only trifling. . . .

Sumner, 8 July   Professor, Bradley, and Walter climbed the west wall with

---

*Powell names several natural features after members of the expedition. Besides Sumner's Amphitheater, he named a mountain after Hawkins, a cliff in Lodore Canyon after Dunn, and a mountain after Frederick Dellenbaugh (from the second expedition). He later wanted to rename Navaho mountain after the Howlands, but Thompson and Dellenbaugh persuaded him not to.

barometer; height 1598 ft. Pulled out at one o'clock and ran down 12½ miles, passing 9 rapids. Camped on the east side on a sandbar. Small valley near camp covered with sage and greasewood.

Powell Account of 8 July   This morning, Bradley and I go out to climb, and gain an altitude of more than two thousand feet above the river, but still do not reach the summit of the wall. . . .

The walls are almost without vegetation; a few dwarf bushes are seen here and there, clinging to the rocks, and cedars grow from the crevices—not like the cedars of a land refreshed with rains, great cones bedecked with spray, but ugly clumps, like clubs, beset with spines. We are minded to call this the Canyon of Desolation. . . .

Bradley, 9 July   A terrible gale of dry hot wind swept our camp and roared Through the cañon mingling its sound with the hollow roar of the cataract making music fit for the infernal regions. We needed only a few flashes of lightning to meet Milton's most vivid conceptions of Hell. The sand from the beach buried our beds while that from an island below filled the air until the cañon was no comfortable place for repose as one had to cover his head to get his breath. The barometer fell over 290°. It moderated to an ordinary gale this morning and we started on the wildest day's run of the trip thus far. A succession of rappids or rather a continuous rapid with a succession of cataracts for 20 miles kept our nerves drawn up to their greatest tension. We would dash through one with the speed of the wind, round two in the eddy and pull for shore sometimes with little water on board but frequently half full, bail out and having looked a moment to see the best channel through the next, repeat the same thing, dashing and dancing like so many furies. Twice we let down with ropes but we could have run them all if it had become a necessity to do so. We are quite careful now of our provisions as the hot blasts that sweep through these rocky gorges admonish us that a walk out to civilization is almost certain death, so better go a little slow and safe.

Sumner, 9 July   Made a portage to begin our day's work, then ran 20 miles with that number of rapids, some of them very bad, and 2 that compelled us to let down past them with ropes. Passed the mouth of a small stream coming in from the west. Country worthless, though imposing, as there is some fine timber growing on the tops of the mountains. Camped on the east side in a cotton wood grove.

Powell Account of 9 July   Our run today is through a canyon, with ragged, broken walls, many lateral gulches or canyons entering on either side. The river is rough, and occasionally it becomes necessary to use lines in passing rocky places. During the afternoon, we come to a rather open canyon valley, stretching up toward the west, its farther end lost in the mountains. From a point to which we climb, we obtain a good view of its course, until its angular walls are lost in the vista.

Bradley, 10 July   Major, Dunn and Howland are gone out to climb the mountains. Didn't go as I want to do some washing and copy my notes. It is too much of a job to copy them all at once and I want to have them ready if any unexpected opportunity should offer, so as far as possible I shall copy whenever I get a sheet full. . . . Andy is singing for his own amusement and my edification a song that will no doubt some day rank with America and other national anthems. All I can make out as he tears it out with a voice like a crosscut saw is the chorus: "When he put his arm around her she *bustified* like a forty pounder, look away, look away, look away in Dixie's land."

Sumner, 10 July   In camp taking observation, repairing boats. Professor and Howland measure the east side of the cañon; height 4000 ft.

Powell Account of 10 July   Sumner, who is a fine mechanist, is learning to take observations for time with the sextant. Today, he remains in camp to practice.

Howland and myself determine to climb out, and start up a lateral canyon, taking a barometer with us, for the purpose of measuring the thickness of the strata over which we pass. The readings of a barometer below are recorded every half hour, and our observations must be simultaneous. Where the beds, which we desire to measure, are very thick, we must climb with the utmost speed, to reach their summits in time. Again, where there are thinner beds, we wait for the moment to arrive; and so, by hard and easy stages, we make our way to the top of the canyon wall, and reach the plateau above about two o'clock.*

---

*Powell is describing a method of measuring the thickness of strata. The barometer "below" becomes the control instrument used to record atmospheric pressure changes. These slight changes could later be used to adjust Powell's readings obtained on the cliff. Since he wanted to measure both the bottom and the top of each strata, he had to be at those points exactly on the half-hour, when the control barometer on the canyon floor was also read. Powell does not seem to have named the strata, some of which were already named. Most of the nineteenth-century names have since been changed.

Howland, who has his gun with him, sees deer feeding a mile or two back, and goes off for a hunt. I go to a peak, which seems to be the highest one in this region, and about half a mile distant, and climb, for the purpose of tracing the topography of the adjacent country. From this point, a fine view is obtained. A long plateau stretches across the river, in an easterly and westerly direction, the summit covered by pine forests, with intervening elevated valleys and gulches…

Swamping the Emma Dean

Bradley, 11 July   Sunday again and Major has got his match, for in attempting to run a rapid his boat swamped, lost all his bedding, one barometer and two valuable rifles which we can ill afford to lose as it leaves but 7 rifles in the outfit and we may meet Indians who think our rations worth a fight, though if they try it they will find them deer rations. The rapid is not so bad as some we have run but they shipped a heavy sea at the start which made their boat unmanageable and she rowled over and over, turning everything out. Major had to leave the boat and swim to land as he has but one arm and her constant turning over made it impossible for him to hold onto her with one hand, but the other two (Jack and Dunn) brought the boat in below with the losses stated and the loss of the oars. We will have to make some oars so Major is compelled to keep Sunday though against his will. Weather windy. Run ½ mile.

Sumner, 11 July   Pulled out early and ran ¾ mile; swamped the *"Emma Dean."* Lost $300 worth of arms, all the bedding of the crew and ruined $800 worth of watches. Got the boat ashore by vigorous kicking and camped on the east side to make oars and dry out. Rain in the afternoon.

Powell Account of 11 July   A short distance below camp we run a rapid, and, in doing so, break an oar, and then lost another, both belonging to the *"Emma Dean."* So the pioneer boat has but two oars.

We see nothing of which oars can be made, so we conclude to run on to some point, where it seems possible to climb out to the forest on the plateau, and there we will procure suitable timber from which to make new ones.

We soon approach another rapid. Standing on deck, I think it can be run, and on we go. Coming nearer, I see that at the foot it has a short turn to the left, where the waters pile up against the cliff. Here we try to land, but quickly discover that, being in swift water, above the fall, we cannot reach shore, crippled, as we are, by the loss of two oars; so the bow of the boat is turned downstream. We shoot by a big rock; a reflex wave rolls over our little boat and fills her. I see the place is dangerous, and quickly signal to the other boats to land where they can. This is scarcely completed when another wave rolls our boat over, and I am thrown some distance into the water. I soon find that swimming is very easy, and I cannot sink.* It is only necessary to ply strokes sufficient to keep my head out of the water, though now and then, when a breaker rolls over me, I close my mouth, and am carried through it. The boat is drifting ahead of me twenty or thirty feet, and, when the great waves are passed, I overtake it, and find Sumner and Dunn clinging to her. As soon as we reach quiet water, we all swim to one side and turn her over. In doing this, Dunn loses his hold and goes under; when he comes up, he is caught by Sumner and pulled to the boat. In the meantime we have drifted downstream some distance, and see another rapid below. How bad it may be we cannot tell, so we swim toward shore, pulling our boat with us, with all the vigor possible, but are carried down much faster than distance toward shore is gained. At last we reach a huge pile of driftwood. Our rolls of blankets, two guns, and a barometer were in the open compartment of the boat, and, when it went over, these were thrown out. The guns and barometer were lost, but I succeeded in catching one of the rolls of blankets, as it drifted by, when we were swimming to shore; the other two are lost, and sometimes hereafter we may sleep cold.

A huge fire is built on the bank, our clothing is spread to dry, and then from the drift logs we select one from which we think oars can be made, and the remainder of the day is spent in sawing them out.

Sumner Account of 11 July   Next morning we soon got into a nest of rapids in Desolation Canyon. There was none so very bad, but bad enough to duck us every hour. In the worst rapid the "Emma Dean" was swamped and instantly capsized, two fine rifles being lost, along with some bedding. We broke many oars and most of the Ten Commandments. Major Powell said he lost three hundred dollars in bills. I lost my temper and at least a year's growth—didn't have anything else to lose. . . . The whole river for thirty miles seemed to be swarming with beaver. We shot several with our pistols as they bobbed up near our boats. I had the good fortune to get two otter out of a bunch of five as they swam past puffing and spitting like a whole nest of tom cats. Part of the beaver we cooked and ate, but as they had been living on willows they were not very palatable. There were plenty of wild geese, but so very wild that we got but few to eke out our scanty rations.

Bradley, 12 July   Got a good start this morning and run several fine rapids with little difficulty when we had just begun to think all the worst ones were over, when we came suddenly upon an old roarer and in attempting to run it my

---

*Major Powell neglects mentioning the life preserver he wore, which probably saved his life on several occasions. It is now owned by, and on display at the Smithsonian Museum of American History.

boat was swamped. The little boat run it by shipping considerable water but the first big wave swept right over our stern, knocking me over the side so that I held the boat by one hand and filling the boat. Before we could recover from the shock we had shipped several seas and all we could do was to cling to the boat and keep her from turning over. In this we were successful and having collected our oars from the water as soon as we got below the rapid, we got the boat on shore without any loss or inconvenience except a glorious ducking and a slight cut on one of my legs which I got when I was knocked overboard.

Sumner, 12 July   Pulled out at 7 o'clock and ran 16 miles; passed 10 bad rapids and 20 portages, one very bad portage made under an overhanging cliff on the east side. Let the boats down by stages, the last man swimming after the boats had passed. Saw a herd of sheep, but failed to get any. Walls of the canon getting lower and more broken. Camped on the east side on a sandbar.

Powell Account of 12 July   This morning, the new oars are finished, and we start once more. We pass several bad rapids, making a short portage at one, and before noon we come to a long, bad fall, where the channel is filled with rocks on the left, turning the waters to the right, where they pass under an overhanging rock. On examination, we determine to run it, keeping as close to the left-hand rocks as safety will permit, in order to avoid the overhanging cliff. The little boat runs over all right; another follows, but the men are not able to keep her near enough to the left bank, and she is carried, by a swift chute, into great waves to the right, where she is tossed about, and Bradley is knocked over the side, but his foot catching under the seat, he is dragged along in the water, with his head down; making great exertion, he seizes the gunwale with his left hand, and can lift his head above water now and then. To us who are below, it seems impossible to keep the boat from going under the overhanging cliff; but Powell, for a moment, heedless of Bradley's mishap, pulls with all his power for half a dozen strokes, when the danger is past; then he seizes Bradley, and pulls him in. The men in the boat above, seeing this, land, and she is let down by lines.

Just here we emerge from the Canyon of Desolation, as we have named it, into a more open country, which extends for a distance of nearly a mile, when we enter another canyon, cut through gray sandstone. . . .

Coal or Gray Canyon

Bradley, 13 July   We have had a fine run of 18 miles this A.M., and have run 19 roaring rapids without any accident. Have now come out "Coal Canyon"*

---

*Coal Canyon was renamed "Lignite Canyon" in 1871 and "Gray Canyon" in 1872. It is now known as Gray Canyon.

(the name given to the last part of Canon of Desolation because we found some coal beds) into a valley which seems very extensive, that is it seems to be long, but on each side is a barren parched dessert. The winds that sweep it are hot and sultry indicating that it is quite wide. It is so smoky that we can't see many miles but we are confident that the mountains are quite distant. We have come several miles in the valley and the water continues quite rapid and I hope it will for I am anxious to run down our altitude before we leave Green River so that we may have an easier time in the Colorado. We are prepared, however, to take it as it comes.

Sumner, 13 July   Pulled out early and had an exciting ride of 18 miles, passing 19 rapids, when we came out to an open valley and camped for dinner; passed the mouth of the "Little White River" (a stream 2 rods wide and a foot deep coming in from the west) 7 miles above noon camp. Pulled out about 1 o'clock and ran down about 2 miles when we came to the old Spanish Crossing of Green River; at the ford the river is about 250 yards and very shallow. Saw a vast pile of Satin spar on the east side 10 miles below the ford. Came in sight of "Uncompahgre Mts."; they are a beautiful cluster of snow-capped cones in western Colorado, south of Green River.* Made 40 miles and camped on the east side, near the head of another canon. The valley, or rather desert, first passed is of little use to anyone; the upland is burned to death and on the river there are a few cottonwood trees, but not large enough for any purpose but fuel.

Powell Account of 13 July   This morning, we have an exhilarating ride. The river is swift, and there are many smooth rapids. I stand on deck, keeping careful watch ahead, and we glide along, mile after mile, plying strokes now on the right, and then on the left, just sufficient to guide our boats past the rocks into smooth water. At noon we emerge from Gray Canyon, as we have [since] named it, and camp, for dinner, under a cottonwood tree, standing on the left bank.

Extensive sand plains extend back from the immediate river valley, as far as we can see, on either side. These naked, drifitng sands gleam brilliantly in the midday sun of July. The reflected heat from the glaring surface produces a curious motion of the atmosphere; little currents are generated and the whole seems to be trembling and moving about in many directions, or, failing to see that the movement is in the atmosphere, it gives the impression of an unstable land. Plains, and hills, and cliffs, and distant mountains seem vaguely to be floating about in a trembling, wave-rocked sea, and patches of landscape will

---

*The "Uncompahgre Mountains" he refers to are actually the La Sal Mountains, just east of Moab, Utah.

seem to float away, and be lost, and then reappear.

. . . About two hours from noon camp, we discover an Indian crossing, where a number of rafts, rudely constructed of logs and bound together by withes, are floating against the bank. On landing, we see evidences that a party of Indians have crossed within a very few days. This is the place where the lamented Gunnison crossed, in the year 1853, when making an exploration for a railroad route to the Pacific Coast.*

Mouth of the San Rafael and Labyrinth Canyon

Bradley, 14 July   Have run 33½ miles today. Had to row much of the time for the river is very still. Canon commenced again this A.M., and continues. The walls are perpendicular most of the way *on one side,* seldom on both. A man could leave the canon in many places if it should become necessary to do so but with such still water there could be no necessity for doing so. The whole country is inconceivably desolate, as we float along on a muddy stream walled in by huge sand-stone bluffs that echo back the slightest sound. Hardly a bird save the ill-omened raven or an occasional eagle screaming over us; one feels a sense of loneliness as he looks on the little party, only three boats and nine men, hundreds of miles from civilization, bound on an errand the issue of which everybody declares must be disastrous. Yet if he could enter our camp at night or our boats by day he could read the cool deliberate determination to persevere that posses every man of the party and would at once predict that the issue of all would be success. As we get farther south the weather gets hotter and the sun shining on the sand-stone heats the whole canon like an oven. We are nearly suffocated tonight and but for a breeze that occasionally draws in upon us it would be intolerable. We expect it very hot when we come to the Colorado.

Sumner, 14 July   Pulled out early and ran 33 miles through as desolate a country as anyone need wish to see. The walls over the canon about ¼ mile apart, composed of a bluff sandstone destitute of any strata. On the river there is in some places a small table that affords a footing for a few willows. At intervals of 4 or 5 miles there are also clumps of scrubby cottonwood trees. River about 125 yards wide with a current of 1½ miles per hour.

Powell Account of 14 July   This morning, we pass some curious black bluffs on the right, then two or three short canyons, and then we discover the mouth of the San Rafael, a stream which comes down from the distant mountains in

---

*Captain Gunnison of the U.S. Army crossed here in 1853, surveying for the Pacific Railroad. He was killed a few days later by Gosi-Utes.

the west. Here we stop for an hour or two, and take a short walk up the valley, and find it is a frequent resort for Indians. Arrowheads are scattered about, many of them very beautiful. Flint chips are seen strewn over the ground in great profusion, and the trails are well worn.

Starting after dinner, we pass some beautiful buttes on the left, many of which are very symmetrical. They are chiefly composed of gypsum of many hues, from light gray to slate color; then pink, purple, and brown beds. . . .

Sumner Account of 14 July   Another chapter of the Powell-Howland squabble was commenced as we left the camp near the San Rafael—a sad, bitter business. I wish I had put a stop to it long before I did. Things might have ended differently.*

Stillwater Canyon

Bradley, 15 July   Made another hard run, for the sun was so hot we could scarcely endure it and much of the time the canon was so closely walled in that the breeze could not reach us. We have worked as hard as we could to get only 25 miles and the river has been so crooked that in going 20 miles we have actually advanced less than 11 miles. We have almost lost our trees. We stopped for dinner today in the open sun with the thermometer over 100° close to the water, It is more comfortable to be out on the stream than to be on the land for we can get a better breeze. The water is calm as a lake—hardly moves at all in some places. Camp tonight in a snug little niche in the rocks but without any trees, yet at this time of day the sun is so low that the walls of canon afford ample shade. Most of us have been unwell today from eating sour beans for supper last night.

Sumner, 15 July   Off again at 7 o'clock and a repetition of yesterday's work. Passed the mouth of San Rafael 5 miles below camp. It is another dirty stream, 8 rods wide and a foot deep; comes in from the west. River very crooked. Saw several beaver but got only one. Got one goose out of a flock that we have driven before us for 3 days. Walls of canon 350 ft. perpendicular on both sides, except at side canons. Made 25¾ miles today by hard rowing. Camp on west side. Pulled dead willows to cook our scanty "grub."

Powell Account of 15 July   Our camp is in a great bend of the canyon. The perimeter of the curve is to the west, and we are on the east side of the river. Just

---

*Sumner may be referring to Powell's unhappiness over the loss of Howland's boat, the *No Name*, at Disaster Falls.

opposite, a little stream comes down through a narrow side canyon. We cross, and go up to explore it. Just at its mouth, another lateral canyon enters, in the angle between the former and the main canyon below and the side canyon first mentioned, so that three side canyons enter at the same point. These canyons are very tortuous, almost closed in from view, and, seen from the opposite side of the river, they appear like three alcoves; and we name this the Trin-Alcove Bend.

Going up the little stream, in the central cove, we pass between high walls of sandstone, and wind about in glens. Springs gush from the rocks at the foot of the walls; narrow passages in the rocks are threaded, caves are entered, and many side canyons are observed.

. . . On we go, after dinner, with quiet water, still compelled to row, in order to make fair progress. The canyon is yet very tortuous.

About six miles below noon camp, we go around a great bend to the right, five miles in length, and come back to a point within a quarter of a mile of where we started. Then we sweep around another great bend to the left, making a circut of nine miles, and come back to a point within six hundred yards of the beginning of the bend. In the two circuits, we describe almost the figure 8. The men call it a bow-knot of river; so we name it Bow-Knot Bend. The line of the figure is fourteen miles in length.

There is an exquisite charm in our ride today down this beautiful canyon. It gradually grows deeper with every mile of travel; the walls are symmetrically curved, and grandly arched; of a beautiful color, and reflected in the quiet waters in many places, so as to almost deceive the eye, and suggest the thought, to the beholder, that he is looking into profound depths. We are all in fine spirits, feel very gay, and the bandiage of the men is echoed from wall to wall. Now and then we whistle, or shout, or discharge a pistol, to listen to the reverberations among the cliffs.

At night we camp on the south side of the great Bow-knot, and, as we eat our supper, which is spread on the beach, we name this Labyrinth Canyon.

Junction of the Grand and Green

Bradley, 16 July   Hurra! Hurra! Hurra! Grand River came upon us or rather we came upon that very suddenly and to me unexpectedly 5½ P.M. Had been running all day through higher walls, mostly vertical, but the river was smooth though in some places more rapid than for two days. The cañon looked dark and threatening but at last without warning, no valley or even opening unusual, in broke the Grand with a calm strong tide very different from what it has been represented. We were led to expect that it was a rushing, roaring mountain torrent which when united with the Green would give us a grand promenade across the mountains. The rock is the same old sand-stone underlaid for the last 20 miles with limestone containing marine foccils and at the junction of the two rivers, strangely curved and broken. The river Colorado formed by the junction of these two is as we can see it (1000 yds.) calm and wide and very much unlike the impossible unpassable succession of foaming and raging water falls and cataracts which have been attributed to it. It is possible we are allured into a dangerous and disastrous cañon of death by the placid waters of this cañon which may be no fair specimen of the whole, but this is what has been represented as inaccessible by any means yet devised and one adventurer actually offered to explore it with a balloon* if Congress would furnish the needful greenbacks, and here we float in upon the scene never before beheld by white men and by all regarded as dangerous of approach from any quarter and especially so by water. And the last 75 miles of our journey through a dark calm cañon which a child might sail in perfect safety. Surely men do get frightened wonderfully at chained lyons. Trees have been very scarce all through this cañon (Green River Cañon) and at last failed altogether. We stopped at noon in a notch of the wall where the melting snow and rain have worn away the rocks until we could climb, but Major did so but could not see anything at any distance. We were so fortunate as to get two beaver today and they will afford us fresh meat which we need very much. They are quite decent eating and the tails make excellent coup. After eating bacon for some time we find any kind of fresh meat palatable even the poor old geese, so poor they can't fly and just off the nest, so good to us when long fed on bacon.

Sumner, 16 July   Off at 7 o'clock again, and ran for 29 miles through a terrible desolate cañon with nearly continuous vertical walls on both sides. At 4:45 we came to the mouth of the Grand River, pride of Colorado. Camped on the point of land between Green and Grand. Distance from the mouth of Uintah River 344 miles. General course west of south. Number of rapids ran 65, portages 4. . . .

Our enterprising edition** went so far as to claim that he had laid out a town and called it Junction City. Where he had his burgh is more than I can say, as it is an apparently endless cañon in 3 directions—up the Grand, up the Green, and down the Colorado; the walls 1250 ft. high, not timber enough within 10 miles to supply one family 6 months. There are a few scrubby hackberry trees on both sides of the Colorado for half a mile below the junction and 3 small ones on the point between the 2 branches. The Green is about 70 to

---

*Probably John Wise, the American aeronaut, who also wanted to cross the Atlantic by balloon.

**Possibly should read "One enterprising editor. . ."

80 yards wide and 10 ft. deep; Grand about 125 yards wide, same depth and flow, but a clear stream and 6° cooler than the Green. There is apparently an annual rise of 25 or 30 ft. at the junction.

Powell Account of 16 July *   Still we go down, on our winding way. We pass tower cliffs, then we find the river widens out for several miles, and meadows are seen on either side, between the river and the walls. We name this expansion of the river Tower Park.

At two o'clock we emerge from Labyrinth Canyon, and go into camp.

Bradley, 17 July   Rained considerably last evening. A real southern thunder shower roared through the cañons lighting them for a while with fearful briliancy and shaking the old cliffs with peals of thunder that seemed as if commissioned to make doubly desolate this regeon set apart for desolation but it cleared off about 10 P.M., and we had a lovely night for sleep. Have been overhauling the rations and find the flour in a very bad condition. Have sifted it all through a misquito bar, taking out the lumps and washed the sacks and put it up again. We have only about 600 lbs. left and shall be obliged to go on soon for we cannot think of being caught in a bad cañon short of provisions. It was the intention to remain at this point until Aug. 7 to observe the eclipse† but shall not probably remain more than three or four days, just long enough to get latitude and longitude as the junction of these rivers has never been surely known within one hundred miles.

Sumner, 17, 18, 19, and 20 July   In Camp taking observations and repairing outfit. Examined our stores and found we were getting very short, as we were compelled to throw away 200 lbs. of flour that had got wet so often it was completely spoiled.

Powell Account of 17 July   At once, this morning, we enter another canyon. The water fills the entire channel, so that nowhere is there room to land. The walls are low, but vertical, and, as we proceed, they gradaully increase in

---

*Powell's account is still describing Labyrinth and Stillwater canyons where both Bradley and Sumner report arriving at the junction of the Grand and Green rivers. Since the Major's account was not written until several years afterward, I assume Bradley and Sumner are accurate here.

†The newspapers of the day carried illustrated features and long accounts in anticipation of the phenomenon. Powell had made elaborate plans for careful observations, but clouds obscured the eclipse.

altitude. Running a couple of miles, the river changes its course many degrees, toward the east. Just here, a little stream comes in on the right, and the wall is broken down; so we land, and go out to take a view of the surrounding country. We are now down among the buttes, and in a region, the surface of which is naked, solid rock—a beautiful red sandstone, forming a smooth, undulating pavement. The Indians call this the *"Toom-pin Tu-weap,"* or "Rock Land," and sometimes *"Toom-pin wu-near Tu-weap,"* or "Land of Standing Rock."

Off to the south, we see a butte, in the form of a fallen cross. It is several miles away, still it presents no inconspicuous figure on the landscape, and must be many hundreds of feet high, probably more than two thousand. We note its position on our map, and name it The Butte of the Cross.

We continue our journey. In many places the walls, which rise from the water's edge, are overhanging on either side. The stream is still quiet, and we glide along, through a strange, weird, grand region. The landscape everywhere, away from the river, is of rock—cliffs of rock; tables of rock; plateaus of rock; terraces of rock; crags of rock—ten thousand strangely carved forms. Rocks everywhere, and no vegetation; no soil; no sand. In long, gentle curves, the river winds about these rocks.

When speaking of these rocks, we must not conceive of piles of boulders, or heaps of fragments, but a whole land of naked rock, with giant forms carved on it; cathedral-shaped buttes, towering hundreds or thousands of feet; cliffs that cannot be scaled, and canyon walls that shrink the river into insignificance, with vast, hollow domes, and tall pinnacles, and shafts set on the verge overhead, and all highly colored—buff, gray, red, brown, and chocolate; never lichened; never moss-covered; but bare, and often polished.

. . . Late in the afternoon, the water becomes swift, and our boats make great speed. An hour of this rapid running brings us to the junction of the Grand and Green, the foot of Stillwater Canyon, as we have named it. . . .

These streams unite in solemn depths more than one thousand two hundred feet below the general surface of the country. The walls of the lower end of Stillwater Canyon are very beautifully curved, as the river sweeps in its meandering course. The lower end of the canyon through which the Grand comes down, is also regular, but much more direct, and we look up this stream, and out into the country beyond, and obtain glimpses of snowclad peaks, the summits of a group of mountains known as the Sierra La Sal. Down the Colorado, the canyon walls are much broken.

We row around into the Grand, and camp on its northwest bank; and here we propose to stay several days, for the purpose of determining the latitude and longitude, and the altitude of the walls. Much of the night is spent in making observations with the sextant.

Noon-day rest in Marble Canyon.

VI.   The Junction of the Grand and Green to the Mouth of the Little Colorado

With each completed rapid and canyon, Powell and his men grew ever more skillful at boatmanship, at running, lining, and portaging rapids, and at repairing their leaky and battered boats. Despite their determination to cope with and survive their river ordeal, several factors worked powerfully against their resolve, as this section and the last make clear. For one, their dwindling food supply of coffee, dried apples, and by now, musty flour proved to be an increasingly crucial factor for everyone except Powell. In addition, as the canyon walls grew in height and steepness, the opportunity to augment their near-starvation rations by fishing and hunting altogether disappeared, probably causing all of them to imagine the possibility of death by starvation in the depths of the great unknown. While the crew grew restless and ever anxious to press on, Powell continued to stop for side explorations, measurements, and observations.

Another factor at work may have been growing conflict within the group. It is impossible to know how much interpersonal friction developed during this leg of the trip, but if Hawkins's journal is anything less than complete fabrication, there must have been mounting tension between the Powells, the Howlands, and Dunn. As early as 28 July, Hawkins writes about the growing conflict between the Major and George Dunn, a conflict that apparently erupted over a watch Dunn dropped that became water-soaked. As Hawkins put it, ". . . there was a different feeling to the whole party at this time." Even the imperturbable Bradley showed some annoyance with Powell toward the end of this section, grumbling that the Major would stop of a day of observations, but not for the sabbath, and that he put the importance of his work above the prudence of finishing the voyage as soon as possible. Bradley may also have captured the mood of the crew when he wrote in his journal, "If he [Powell] can study geology he will be happy without food or shelter. . . ."

Bradley, 18 July   Sunday again and though a thousand spires point heaven-ward all around us yet not one sends forth the welcome peal of bells to wake the echoes of these ancient cliffs and remind us of happier if not grander scenes. All has been quiet in camp today, no work, no firing of guns, no noise of any kind. Each seeks the shade of the stinted bushes that skirt the bank and engaged with his own thoughts or in conversation spends the time as suits him best. I with blanket spread on a little bench of sand shaded by overhanging willows have been sleeping off the effects of beavertail soup. And now I sit upon the same bench and write. Our camp is pitched in the angle formed by the two rivers on a sand bank washed down from both of them. To our right when looking south comes the Green with a rapid muddy stream for it has been rising since we ar-rived and now sweeps the Grand back well towards the left bank, but when we came the Grand was master of the field, and I think that is generally the case for now that it is at quite low water and is clear almost as the Merrimac* yet it moves with a strong deep tide and is wider than the Green, though with its pres-ent swift current the latter probably pours the most water. The Grand flows in from the left and its course is not so much changed by the union as the course of the Green, in fact it is properly the Colorado and the Green is its tributary. . . .

Powell Account of 18 July   The day is spent in obtaining the time, and spreading our rations, which, we find, are badly injured. The flour has been wet and dried so many times that it is all musty, and full of hard lumps. We make a sieve of misquito netting, and run our flour through it, losing more than two hundred pounds by the process. Our losses, by the wrecking of the "No Name," and by various mishaps since, together with the amount thrown away today, leave us little more than two months' supplies, and, to make them last thus long, we must be fortunate enough to lose no more.

We drag our boats on shore, and turn them over to recalk and pitch them, and Sumner is engaged in repairing barometers. While we are here, for a day or two, resting, we propose to put everything in the best shape for a vigorous campaign.

---

*The Merrimac River of northeastern Massachusetts and New Hampshire, which Bradley knew so well.

Sumner Account of 18, 19, 20 July ...We camped there at the junction three days—July 18th, 19th, and 20th—and overhauled our boats, supplies, and instruments. I refilled the barometer tubes and boiled the mercury in a little wikiup which I constructed of cedar boughs, using an open fire of dried willow twigs.* I cleaned the chronometer, trued up the sextant, and made all snug in that line. Then I repaired the boats. But when I came to the commissary I was up a stump. We had about five hundred pounds of flour and a little bacon and dried apples. After examining the flour I found it a miserable mess of green fermentation. There was nothing left to do with it but to sift it through a misquito netting onto a wagon sheet and let it dry. After Howland and I had sifted it we had but two sacks, presumably two hundred pounds, a not very liberal supply, considering out position and numbers at that date. But as there was no help for it, we looked the subject square in the face. There was only a dim hope of replenishing the commissary by finding some deer or mountain sheep on the way.

Bradley, 19 July Washing-day with us. Almost all of us have had a turn at it today, getting ready for what comes below. Grand River has been quite muddy today, indicating rain in the mountains above. Hot weather continues and with our scanty shade our camp is not a very pleasant one. Since we left Uinta we have hardly seen a mosquito so hot, dry and desolate is it that it won't produce even that little pest, but the constant and not unwelcome churping of the large black cricket is never silent except where the cañon walls are so vertical as to utterly forbid him a foot-hold. We sometimes hear the harsh shriek of the locust but only in occasional localities. Have heard but few since we came to this point.

Powell Account of 19 July Bradley and I start this morning to climb the left wall below the junction. The way we have selected is up a gulch. Climbing for an hour over and among the rocks, we find ourselves in a vast amphitheater, and our way cut off. We clamber around to the right, and discover a narrow shelf, nearly half a mile long. In some places, this is so wide that we pass along with ease; in others, it is so narrow and sloping that we are compelled to lie down and crawl. We can look over the edge of the shelf, down eight hundred feet, and see the river rolling and plunging among the rocks. Looking up five hundred feet, to the brink of the cliff, it seems to blend with the sky. We

---

*Wickiup is a western Indian name for a hut constructed of a frame covered with brushwood or other material.

continue along, until we come to a point where the wall is again broken down. Up we climb. On the right, there is a narrow, mural point of rocks, extending toward the river, two or three hundred feet high, and six or eight hundred feet long. We come back to where this sets in, and find it cut off from the main wall by a great crevice. Into this we pass. And now, a long, narrow rock is between us and the river. The rock itself is split longitudinally and transversely; and the rains on the surface above have run down through the crevices, and gathered into channels below, and then run off into the river. The crevices are usually narrow above, and by erosion of the streams, wider below, forming a network of caves; but each cave having a narrow, winding skylight up through the rocks. We wander among these corridors for an hour or two, but find no place where the rocks are broken down so that we can climb up. At last, we determine to attempt a passage by a crevice, and select one which we think is wide enough to admit of the passage of our bodies, and yet narrow enough to climb out by pressing our hands and feet against the walls. So we climb as men would out of a well. Bradley climbs first; I hand him the barometer, then climb over his head, and he hands me the barometer. So we pass each other alternately, until we emerge from the fissure, out on the summit of the rock. And what a world of grandeur is spread before us! Below is the canyon, through which the Colorado runs. We can trace its course for miles, and at points catch glimpses of the river. From the northwest comes the Green, in a narrow, winding gorge. From the northeast comes the Grand, through a canyon that seems bottomless from where we stand. Away to the west are lines of cliffs and ledges of rock—not such ledges as you may have seen where the quarry-man splits his blocks, but ledges from which the gods might quarry mountains, that, rolled out on the plain below, would stand a lofty range; and not such cliffs as you may have seen where the swallow builds its nest, but cliffs where the soaring eagle is lost to view ere he reached the summit. Between us and the distant cliffs are the strangely carved and pinnacled rocks of the *Toom-pin wu-near Tu-weap*. * On the summit of the opposite wall of the canyon are rock forms that we do not understand. Away to the east a group of eruptive mountains are seen—the Sierra La Sal. Their slopes are covered with pines, and deep gulches are flanked with great crags, and snow fields are seen near the summits. So the Mountains are in uniform, green, gray, and silver. Wherever we look there is but a wilderness of rocks; deep gorges, where the rivers are lost below cliffs and towers and pinnacles; and ten thousand strangely carved forms in every direction; and beyond them, mountains blending with the clouds.

Now we return to camp. While we are eating supper, we very naturally

---

*Powell translates *Toom pin wo-near Tu-weap* as the Land of Standing Rocks. Today it is generally known as the Doll House, Canyonlands National Park.

speak of better fare, as musty bread and spoiled bacon are not pleasant. Soon I seen Hawkins down by the boat, taking up the sextant, rather a strange proceeding for him, and I question him concerning it. He replies that he is trying to find the latitude and longitude of the nearest pie.

Cave Cliff

Bradley, 20 July   Started to climb the mountains on the east at noon. Thermometer at 95° in the shade. Climbed three hours and at last succeeded in reaching the top of the tallest cliff. The rocks were heated by the sun until the top which is usually the coolest was hotter than the canon for the thermometer indicated 99° at the summit. The cliff is a strange one for the soft sandstone on top has worn out in caves and the top is all like honeycomb with them. We paced one of them 75 yds. in a straight line so high we could walk anywhere in it and many thousand men could be sheltered in that single cliff.

Powell, 20 July   Climbed "Cave Cliff" with Bradley. Summit of cliff full of caves, hence name. Pinnacles in the red sandstone. The terraces, the monuments of the stages of erosion. Found a cool spring in gulch on our way up. One cave 75 paces long, dome, skylight at each end connected by fissure 6 or 8 inches wide, from 10 to 40 ft. wide, 5½ ft. high.

Powell Account of 20 July   This morning, Captain Powell and I go out to climb the west wall of the canyon, for the purpose of examining the strange rocks seen yesterday from the other side. Two hours brings us to the top, at a point between the Green and Colorado, overlooking the junction of the rivers. A long neck of rock extends toward the mouth of the Grand. Out on this we walk, crossing a great number of deep crevices. Usually, the smooth rock slopes down to the fissure on either side. Sometimes it is an interesting question to us whether the slope is not so steep that we cannot stand on it. Sometimes, starting down, we are compelled to go on, and we are not always sure that the crevice is not too wide for a jump, when we measure it with our eye from above. Probably the slopes would not be difficult if there was not a fissure at the lower end; nor would the fissures cause fear if they were but a few feet deep. It is curious how a little obstacle becomes a great obstruction, when a misstep would land a man in the bottom of a deep chasm. Climbing the face of a cliff, a man will walk along a step or shelf, but a few inches wide, without hesitancy, if the landing is but ten feet below, should he fall; but if the foot of the cliff is a thousand feet down, he will crawl. At last our way is cut off by a fissure so deep and wide that we cannot pass it. Then we turn and walk back into the country, over the smooth, naked sandstone, without vegetation, except that here and there dwarf cedars and piñon pines have found a footing in the huge cracks. . . .

Bradley, 21 July   Started this morning and by hard labor have made 8½ miles today. Rapids commenced about two miles from the junction and have now become continuous. We can't run them or rather we don't run many of them, on account of our rations. We are afraid they will spoil and if they do we are in a bad fix. Have let down with ropes much of the way. Made four portages and camp tonight in a place where we can only find sleeping ground by piling up rocks along the edge of the water and then collecting the scanty sand from between the huge bowlders. In that way, we have made comfortable beds. Have made two portages within 100 yds. above and there is another waiting not a hundred yds. below. So I conclude the Colorado is not a very easy stream to navigate.

The true portage, which involved unloading the boats and carrying the supplies over the talus, was backbreaking toil. Sometimes a trail had to be made over the rocks so that the men could gain footing.

Sumner, 21 July   Off again early and commenced the real work of exploration. Rowed through a very smooth channel for 5 miles when we came to a very bad rapid, but ran it all right. But we came to a worse one 200 yards below . . . for 200 yards and got into a . . . made 8½ miles, 4 portages and ran . . . rapids; swamped the small boat and lost . . . oars. Camped on the south side among the rocks.

Powell, 21 July   Came down river 8¼ miles. Bad rapids. 3 portages. Lost 3 oars from "Emma Dean." The flood plain is 18 to 20 ft. higher than river is now. Camped among rocks on the left bank. No. 11.

Powell Account of 21 July   We start this morning on the Colorado. The river is rough, and bad rapids, in close succession, are found. Two very hard portages are made during the forenoon. After dinner, in running a rapid, the "Emma Dean" is swamped, and we are thrown into the river; we cling to her, and in the first quiet water below she is righted and bailed out; but three oars are lost in this mishap. The larger boats land above the dangerous place, and we make a portage that occupies all the afternoon. We camp at night, on the rocks on the left bank, and can scarcely find room to lie down.

Bradley, 22 July   Made a short run today, only 1½ miles for Major wanted to determine what has so disarranged the strata here, and we have lost a pair of oars letting the little boat over a rapid he determined to lay by a day and make oars and climb the mountain. He with his brother climbed the nearest cliff which they found to be 1200 ft. high. The strata all along here dips both ways from the river which Major says is caused by sliding down of part of the mountain. Have looked below for two miles and we can run all the way for that distance though we can see rapids from there that think we can't run.

Sumner, 22 July   Made a portage and ran a mile and camped on the south side to make oars and repair boats. Professor and Walter climbed the south wall, height 1000 ft.; saw fresh moccasin tracks on the sand near camp.

Powell, 22 July   1¾ miles to confusion of rocks. Boys commenced to make oars. I examined the points of rock, before dinner. After dinner Walter and I climbed Mt. over camp. Easy found pitch. Unraveled the mystery of the rocks. Barometer obs. Camp scene. Supper, poor. Rhodes (Hawkins) takes instruments to determine the lat. and long. of the nearest pie.*

Powell Account of 22 July   This morning, we continue our journey, though short of oars. There is no timber growing on the walls within our reach, and no driftwood along the banks, so we are compelled to go on until something suitable can be found. A mile and three quarters below, we find a huge pile of driftwood, among which are some cottonwood logs. From these we select one which we think the best, and the men are set at work sawing oars. Our boats are leaking again, from the strains received in the bad rapids yesterday, so, after dinner, they are turned over, and some of the men are engaged in calking them.

Captain Powell and I go out to climb the wall to the east, for we can see dwarf pines above, and it is our purpose to collect the resin which oozes from them, to use in pitching our boats. We take a barometer with us, and find that the walls are becoming higher, for now they register an altitude, above the river, of nearly fifteen hundred feet.

Cataract Canyon

Bradley, 23 July   Another day of hard labor. Have made 5½ miles with three good long portages and all the way rapid. Much of the last three miles we

---

*This is the humorous incident that Major Powell also tells in his account of 19 July.

have let down with ropes. Rapids get worse as we advance and the walls get higher and nearly perpendicular. We camp tonight above a succession of furious cataracts. There are at least five in the next mile around which we shall have to make portages. Let it come. We know that we have got about 2500 ft. to fall yet before we reach Ft. Mohavie and if it comes all in the first hundred miles we shan't be dreading rapids afterwards for if it should continue at this rate much more than a hundred miles we should have to go the rest of the *way up hill* which is *not often the case with rivers.* Major estimates that we shall fall fifty feet on the next mile and he always underestimates. The heat is quite oppressive during the day. The thermometer indicates above 100 degrees most of the time and that heats the canon like an oven which lasts nearly all night, but usually gets quite cool by morning. The tide-mark* indicates that the water is sometimes 15 to 20 ft. higher than now and there must be fun here when it is at that height.

Powell, 23 July   Difficult rapids. 3 portages. Ran 5½ miles. West wall of canon vertical except ½ or ⅓ of height from base which has a steep talus. Camp on left bank. No. 13.

Sumner, 23 July   Ran 4 miles of good current, then rapids. Ran 5 bad ones and made 4 portages in ½ mile. Average width of river 80 yards; height of walls, 1800 ft.; north wall nearly all perpendicular. Camped on the south side on a sandbar.

Powell Account of 23 July   On starting, we come at once to difficult rapids and falls, that, in many places are more abrupt than in any of the canyons through which we have passed, and we decide to name this Cataract Canyon.

. . . From morning until noon, the course of the river is to the west; the scenery is grand, with rapids and falls below, and walls above, beset with crags and pinnacles. Just at noon we wheel again to the south, and go into camp for dinner.

While the cook is preparing it, Bradley, Captain Powell, and myself go up into a side canyon, that comes in at this point. We enter through a very narrow passage, having to wade along the course of a little stream until a cascade interrupts our progress. Then we climb to the right, for a hundred feet, until we reach a little shelf, along which we pass, walking with a great case, for it is narrow, until we pass around the fall. Here the gorge widens into a spacious,

---

*"Tide," or flood, marks as high as 35 to 40 feet above the river were observed elsewhere along the route. In 1872, the second party encountered water about 8 to 10 feet higher than the 1869 levels, and contended with much greater danger in the rapids.

sky-roofed chamber. In the farther end is a beautiful grove of cottonwoods, and between us and the cottonwoods the little stream widens out into three clear lakelets, with bottoms of smooth rock. Beyond the cottonwoods, the brook tumbles, in a series of white, shining cascades, from heights that seem immeasurable. Turning around, we can look through the cleft through which we came, and see the river, with towering walls beyond. What a chamber for a resting place is this! hewn from the solid rock; the heavens for a ceiling; cascade fountains within; a grove in the conservatory, clear lakelets for a refreshing bath, and an outlook through the doorway on a raging river, with cliffs and mountains beyond. . . .

We arrive, early in the afternoon, at the head of more rapids and falls, but, wearied with past work, we determine to rest, so go into camp, and the afternoon and evening are spent by the men in discussing the probabilities of successfully navigating the river below. The barometric records are examined, to see what descent we have made since we left the mouth of the Grand, and what descent since we left the Pacific Railroad, and what fall there yet must be to the river, ere we reach the end of the great canyons. The conclusion to which the men arrive seems to be about this: that there are great descents yet to be made, but, if they are distributed in rapids and short falls, as they have been heretofore, we will be able to overcome them. But, may be, we shall come to a fall in these canyons which we cannot pass, where the walls rise from the water's edge, so that we cannot land, and where the water is so swift that we cannot return. Such places have been found, except that the falls were not so great but that we could run them with safety. How will it be in the future! So they speculate over the serious probabilities in jesting mood, and I hear Sumner remark, "My idea is, we had better go slow, and learn to peddle."

Bradley, 24 July   Well, we got over or around three out of the five rapids. Had to take everything around by hand and around the second we had to carry our boats over the huge bowlders which is very hard work as two of them are very heavy, being made of oak. We had to slide them out on the rocks at the third rapid but not so far or so hard work as at the second. Have made only ¾ mile today and camp at another rapid which they tell me is not so bad as the others but I haven't been to look at it yet. They don't interest me much unless we can run them. That I like but portage don't agree with my constitution. We found part of the bones of what Major pronounces an alligator* tonight. He

---

*Despite Bradley's humor over the prospect of an alligator exploring the Colorado, we can assume Major Powell was referring to fossil remains.

must be on an independent exploring expedition, probably to discover the junction of Grand and Green and failed as many do for want of breath. All I have to say is he was sensible to die before he attempted to assend the next rapid for it has an almost direct fall of from 15 to 20 feet. We have met nothing to compare with it before. Weather is not quite so hot today. We are in good spirits. We are glad to get down our altitude before the canon gets narrower and higher as it will do when we come to hard rocks. In these rapid places the river narrows up unaccountably. Andy has been throwing stones across for amusement tonight.

Powell, 24 July   Only made ¾ mile today. 3 long portages where the river fell by estimate 42 ft. Huge rocks across the river. We camp among large rocks. I saw for an hour watching the waves—ridges at all angles to the direction of the river, mounds, and even cones with crests of foam that fall back. No. 14.

Sumner, 24 July   Hard at work early making a portage in the worst rapids we have seen so far. Made 4 portages in ¾ of a mile. "Kitty's Sister" had another narrow escape today. While crossing between rapids Howland broke an oar in a very bad place and came very near being drawn into a rapid that would smash any boat to pieces. Saw the tracks of an otter and mountain sheep on the sand. Walls. . . .? ft., ¾ blue marble, the remainder grey sandstone, lightly touched with red by a thin bed of red shale on the top, Driftwood 30 ft. high on the rocks. God help the poor wretch that is caught in the canon during high water. Camped on the south side among the rocks, 3 small hackberry bushes in sight of camp.

Powell Account of 24 July   We examine the rapids below. Large rocks have fallen from the walls—great, angular blocks, which have rolled down the talus, and are strewn along the channel. We are compelled to make three portages in succession, the distance being less than three-fourths of a mile, with a fall of seventy-five feet. Among these rocks, in chutes, whirlpools, and great waves, with rushing breakers and foam, the water finds it way, still tumbling down. We stop for the night, only three-fourths of a mile below the last camp. A very hard day's work has been done, and at evening I sit on a rock by the edge of the river, to look at the water, and listen to its roar. Hours ago, deep shadows had settled into the canyon as the sun passed behind the cliffs. Now, doubtless, the sun has gone down, for we can see no glint of light on the crags above. Darkness is coming on. The waves are rolling, with crests of foam so white they seem almost to give a light of their own. Nearby, a chute of water strikes the foot of a great block of limestone, fifty feet high, and the waters pile up against it, and roll back. Where there are sunken rocks, the water heaps up in mounds, or even in cones. At a point where rocks come very near the surface, the water forms a chute above, strikes, and is shot up ten or fifteen feet, and piles back in gentle curves, as in a fountain; and on the river tumbles and rolls.

Bradley, 25 July   Sunday brings no rest to us, no notice being taken of it. Have been working hard today to make 3½ miles. Two of the boats came in tonight leaking badly. Mine is now the only tight one we have left and fear she will not long remain so if we continue to meet such severe rapids. The river is still one foaming torrent, yet I believe there is a slight improvement today. We can see from the bluffs quite a long distance and it is all very rapid and covered with foam but we can't tell at this distance whether we can run it or not. We intended to remain here tomorrow and repair the boats but find we can't get out of the canon to get pitch so we shall move on in the morning. I hope for a longer run than we have had for the past few days.

Powell, 25 July   More rapids. Let down one long one. Ran one in which the "Emma Dean" was suddenly turned around, then ran 3 in a series before dinner. When Jack made a heavy oar—we ran down half a mile, let down past one rock, and run between 2 others.

Sumner, 25 July   Made a portage of 200 yards to begin with, then ran a bad rapid to get to another portage, made it and camped for the night at the head of another portage, north side. Made 3½ miles. Bad. run half a mile more, and let (down) a long rapid. Crossed over to right, for camp No. 15.

Powell Account of 25 July   Still more rapids and falls today. In one, the "Emma Dean" is caught in a whirlpool, and set spinning about; and it is with great difficulty we are able to get out of it, with the loss of an oar. At noon, another is made; and on we go, running some of the rapids, letting down with lines past others, and making two short portages. We camp on the right bank, hungry and tired.

Gypsum Canyon

Bradley, 26 July   Another day wasted foolishly. Run 1½ miles and finding a lateral canon Major wished to land and climb the mountains so five of us started on a wild-goose chase after pitch but it was so hot we all backed out except the Major who says he climbed the cliff, but I have my doubts. It is unaccountably hot in the mountains but being showery tonight the air feels a little cooler. Rapids continue. One below our present camp will give us another portage. Found the camp of an Indian today with meat bones that had been picked within two months.

Powell, 26 July   Ran a short distance after breakfast and then went into camp No. 16. Fix bars (barometers). Repairs boats. Made oar, lunch at 10:00 A.M. With Capt. P., Seneca, Bradley, and Andy* started up canon on left. Soon found pools of water, then brook, then amphitheater with deep pool clear and green. Climbed to left on shelf—to north first on a slide, large rocks, then up an irregular amphitheater on points that form steps and give hand hold, then up a cleft 25 to 30 ft., then up gorge along benches to left, away round point to left, still along benches up over grey sds.** to summit. Take obs. Collect pitch, use shirt sleeve for sack, hard rain—hail. Came down in mud, find Mt. Torrent rushing down over dry bed, water red and thick, reach camp about 10 minutes before creek. Little rain at camp. Camp 16.

Sumner, 26 July   Pulled out and ran a bad rapid in 1½ miles and camped on the south side to repair boats. 5 of the men tried to climb the cliff to get some rosin from the pine trees at the top but failed but the Professor, he being lucky enough to get about 2 lbs. Repaired our boats the best way we could and turned in. Rain this evening.

Powell Account of 26 July   ...About ten o'clock, Powell, Bradley, Howland, Hall, and myself start up a side canyon to the east. We soon come to pools of water; then to a brook, which is lost in the sands below; and, passing up the brook, we find the canyon narrows, the walls close in, are often overhanging, and at last we find ourselves in a vast amphitheater, with a pool of deep, clear, cold water on the bottom. At first, our way seems cut off; but we soon discover a little shelf, along which we climb, and, passing beyond the pool, walk a hundred yards or more, turn to the right, and find ourselves in another dome-shaped amphitheater. There is a winding cleft at the top, reaching out to the country above, nearly two thousand feet overhead. The rounded, basin-shaped bottom is filled with water to the foot of the walls. There is no shelf by which we can pass around the foot. If we swim across, we meet with a face of rock hundreds of feet high, over which a little roll glides, and it will be impossible to climb. So we can go no farther up this canyon. Then we turn back, and examine the walls on either side carefully, to discover, if possible,

---

*Walter Powell, Seneca Howland, George Bradley, Andrew Hall.

**Abbreviation for sandstone.

some way of climbing out. In this search, every man takes his own course, and we are scattered. I almost abandon the idea of getting out, and am engaged in searching for fossils, when I discover, on the north, a broken place, up which it may be possible for me to climb. The way, for a distance, is up a slide of rocks; then up an irregular amphitheater, on points that form steps and give hand-hold, and then I reach a little shelf, along which I walk, and discover a vertical fissure, parallel to the face of the wall, and reaching to a higher shelf. This fissure is narrow, and I try to climb up to the bench, which is about forty feet overhead. I have a barometer on my back, which rather impedes my climbing. The walls of the fissure are of smooth limestone, offering neither foot nor hand hold. So I support myself by pressing my back against one wall and my knees against the other, and, in this way, lift my body, in a shuffling manner, a few inches at a time, until I have, perhaps, made twenty-five feet of distance, when the crevice widens a little, I cannot press my knees against the rocks in front with sufficient power to give me support in lifting my body, and I try to go back. This I cannot do without falling. So I struggle along sidewise, farther into the crevice, where it narrows. But by this time my muscles are exhausted, and I cannot climb longer; so I move still a little farther into the crevice, where it is so narrow and wedging that I can lie in it, and there I rest. Five or ten minutes of this relief, and up once more I go, and reach the bench above. On this I can walk for a quarter of a mile, till I come to a place where the wall is again broken down, so that I can climb up still farther, and in an hour I reach the summit. I hang up my barometer, to give it a few minutes time to settle, and occupy myself in collecting resin from the piñon pines, which are found in great abundance. One of the principal objects in making this climb was to get this resin, for the purpose of smearing our boats; but I have with me no means of carrying it down. The day is very hot, and my coat was left in camp, so I have no linings to tear out. Then it occurs to me to cut off the sleeve of my shirt, tie it up at one end, and in this little sack I collect about a gallon of pitch. After taking observations for altitude, I wander back on the rock, for an hour or two, when suddenly I notice that a storm is coming from the south. I seek a shelter in the rocks; but when the storm bursts, it comes down as a flood from the heavens, not with gentle drops at first, slowly increasing in quantity, but as if suddenly poured out. I am thoroughly drenched, and almost washed away. It lasts not more than half an hour, when the clouds sweep by to the north, and I have sunshine again.

In the meantime, I have discovered a better way of getting down, and I start for camp, making the greatest haste possible. On reaching the bottom of the side canyon, I find a thousand streams rolling down the cliffs on every side, carrying with them red sand; and these all unite in the canyon below, in one great stream of red mud.

Traveling as fast as I can run, I soon reach the foot of the stream, for the rain did not reach the lower end of the canyon, and the water is running down a dry bed of sand; and, although it comes in waves, several feet high and fifteen or twenty feet in width, the sands soak it up, and it is lost. But wave follows wave, and rolls along, and is swallowed up; and still the floods come on from above. I find that I can travel faster than the stream; so I hasten to camp, and tell the men there is a river coming down the canyon. We carry our camp equipage hastily from the bank, to where we think it will be above the water. Then we stand by, and see the river roll on to join the Colorado. Great quantities of gypsum are found at the bottom of the gorge; so we name it Gypsum Canyon.

Bradley, 27 July ... We were so lucky as to get two sheep today which in the present reduced state of our ration is hailed as the greatest event of the trip. Weather showery but not much rain.

Powell, 27 July Let down boats over rapids, with portage. Another let down before dinner. One after dinner then through narrow cañon, with vertical walls for several hundred feet, above which the walls rise in steps. 10 or 12 ft. of the walls at the base was black with iron. Camp 17. At noon of 27th Capt. P. commenced with bar[ometer].

Sumner, 27 July Made a portage of 200 yds. and ran 11/12 mile passing 6 bad rapids. Killed 2 mountain sheep today—a Godsend to us, as sour bread and rotten bacon is poor diet for as hard work as we have to do. River today about 40 yards wide, walls 1000 ft. perpendicular except at side cañon. Camped on a sandbar.

Powell Account of 27 July ... Late in the afternoon, we pass to the left, around a sharp point, which is somewhat broken down near the foot, and discover a flock of mountain sheep on the rocks, more than a hundred feet above us. We quickly land in a cove, out of sight, and away go all the hunters with their guns, for the sheep have not discovered us. Soon, we hear firing, and those of us who have remained in the boats climb up to see what success the hunters have had. One sheep has been killed, and two of the men are still pursuing them. In a few minutes, we hear firing again, and the next moment down come the flock, clattering over the rocks, within twenty yards of us. One of the hunters seizes his gun, and brings a second sheep down, and the next minute the remainder of the flock is lost behind the rocks. We all give chase;

but it is impossible to follow there tracks over the naked rock, and we see them no more. Where they went out of this rock-walled canyon is a mystery, for we can see no way of escape. Doubtless, if we could spare the time for the search, we could find some gulch up which they ran.

We lash our prizes to the deck of one of the boats, and go on for a short distance; but fresh meat is too tempting for us, and we stop early to have a feast. And a feast it is! Two fine, young sheep. We care not for bread, or beans, or dried apples tonight; coffee and mutton is all we ask.

Narrow Canyon and the Mouth of the Dirty Devil

Bradley, 28 July   Had a very hard run this A.M. to make only two miles. Made two portages, the longest we have made on the Colorado, but since noon we have had an excellent run of 12½ miles. Most of the distance it was very rapid. The last few miles, however, it has been very still and we fear the rapids are going to quit us altogether for a while and then come on again as at this point the walls of the cañon are very low, not over 150 ft., and when they rise again we may have swifter water. We came tonight upon a stream that is not down upon any of our maps. It is larger than White River No. 2 and quite muddy, indicating recent rains in the mountains which we can see S.W. of us. The mountains are quite high. Think they are not snow-clad but it is so smoky we can't determine yet. We can tell in the morning. The creek comes in from the west and sweeps far out into the Colorado. It is not now much more than 30 to 50 yds. wide but has a channel much wider. Evidently at some seasons it is much larger and very noisy.

Powell, 28 July   Made 2 portages today, one very long at noon. After dinner ran a long chute, about half mile, very narrow, very rapid down the slope of the rocks. It had a marble floor. Then the cañon was rapid, narrow, straight, the walls rising from the water's edge, and running back with 2 grand steps that gradually come down to the water's edge. . . .

Sumner, 28 July   . . . Camped on the north side at the mouth of a stream 3 rods wide and 2 ft. deep. It is not laid down on any map. The water is about as filthy as the washing from the sewers of some large, dirty city, but stinks more than cologne ever did. It has been named "Dirty Creek." From the mouth of San Rafael River to 10 miles below the junction, the walls gradually increase in height and decrease from that point to the mouth of Dirty Creek [Dirty Devil]. At the mouth of dry gulch the limestone disappears, leaving the blue sandstone cut into every conceivable shape.

Powell Account of 28 July   We make two portages this morning, one of them very long. During the afternoon we run a chute, more than half a mile in length, narrow and rapid. This chute has a floor of marble; the rocks dip in the direction in which we are going, and the fall of the stream conforms to the inclination of the beds; so we float on water that is gliding down an inclined plane. At the foot of the chute, the river turns sharply to the right, and the water rolls up against a rock which, from above, seems to stand directly athwart its course. As we approach it, we pull with all our power to the right, but it seems impossible to avoid being carried headlong against the cliff, and we are carried up high on the waves—not against the rocks, for the rebounding water strikes us, and we are beaten back, and pass on with safety, except that we get a good drenching.

. . . At three o'clock we arrive at the foot of Cataract Canyon. Here a long canyon valley comes down from the east, and the river turns sharply to the west in a continuation of the line of the lateral valley. In the bend on the right, vast numbers of crags, and pinnacles, and tower-shaped rocks are seen. We call it Mille Crag Bend.

And now we wheel into another canyon, on swift water, unobstructed by rocks. This new canyon is very narrow and very straight, with walls vertical below and terraced above. The brink of the cliff is 1,300 feet above the water, where we enter it, but the rocks dip to the west, and, as the course of the canyon is in that direction, the walls are seen to slowly decrease in altitude. Floating down this narrow channel, and looking out through the canyon crevice away in the distance, the river is seen to turn again to the left, and beyond this point, away many miles, a great mountain is seen. Still floating down, we see other mountains, now to the right, now on the left, until a great mountain range is unfolded to view. We name this Narrow Canyon, and it terminates at the bend of the river below.

As we go down to this point, we discover the mouth of a stream, which enters from the right. Into this our little boat is turned. One of the men in the boat following, seeing what we have done, shouts to Dunn, asking if it is a trout stream. Dunn replies, much disgusted, that it is "a dirty devil" and by this name the river is to be known hereafter. The water is exceedingly muddy, and has an unpleasant odor.

Sumner Account of 28 July   As my journal has been lost for thirty years, I cannot give exact points, rapids, or incidents through Cataract Canyon.* At noon on the eighth day on the Colorado (July 28th) we rowed into camp just

---

*Sumner's diary covering 24 May through 28 June was sent by Powell to the *Missouri Democrat* and was therefore "lost" for many years. It was reprinted in the Spring 1969 issue of the *Utah Historical Quarterly*.

below a side stream coming in from the north which stinks bad enough to be the sewer from Sodom and Gomorrah, or even hell. I thought I had smelt some pretty bad odors on the battle field two days after action, but they were not up to the standard of that miserable little stream which I dubbed the "Dirty Devil" more than a generation ago. I am sure I beg the Devil's pardon, and I won't do it again if he will overlook it this time. And yet the source of that stream is in as pretty a mountain lake as ever the sun kissed, and swarming with trout.

While Major Powell and I were taking observations, some of the boys panned out a pan of gravel, and got a number of colors of gold, the first we had found. From the mouth of the North Wash just below the Dirty Devil all of the gravel bars contain placer gold, at least as far down as Paria Creek [Lee's Ferry]. It runs all the way from a few cents to as high as several dollars per yard in places. The gold is all of high grade, but very fine and therefore most difficult to save.

Hawkins Account of late July   Now our trouble begins, and plenty of bad rapids in the river. Dunn was the one who took the altitudes with the barometer, and it was here we had the first real trouble in the party, although Powell had named Dunn the "Dirty Devil." But the rest of the boys looked over that. At noon, while we were making a portage and letting the boats over a bad place, the ropes happened to catch Bill Dunn under the arms and came near drowning him, but he managed to catch the ropes and come out. While we were eating our dinner, Sumner said that Dunn came near being drowned and the Major's brother made the remark that it would have been but little loss. The Major spoke up and said that Dunn would have to pay thirty dollars for a watch belonging to him that had been soaked with water and ruined, and that if he did not he would have to leave the party.

Andy Hall and I were down at our boat, I having gone down after a cup and Andy had remained at the boat fitting one of his oars. When we returned to where they were eating, Sumner asked me what I thought of the Major's proposition, and I asked him what it was, and he then related what had been said. I asked the Major if that was his desire, and he said that it was. I made the remark that a part of his wishes could not be granted, as it was impossible to get out of the Canyon on account of the abrupt walls. He then said that it made no difference whether Dunn got out or not. I then said that I was sorry that Dunn had been jerked into the water and got the watch wet, and that I was sorry he felt that way with one of his party. The Major seemed to be offended at my remarks and said I had no right to pass on the matter, also that neither Hall nor myself, in the future of the party, would be expected to say anything, as we were too young. Hall made the remark that we had old heads on our shoulders anyway. Before this time everything seemed to be getting along fine, as each man had certain things to do, and I was doing the cooking, and I generally found plenty to do.

Our meal was ready and we all seated ourselves on the rocks to eat our dinner. Up to this time I had always helped the Major all I could and washed his hand (as he only had one) and generally found him a good place to sit at meals, sometimes a few feet from the rest. Before this it never made any difference to me, but now it did, for, as Andy Hall would say, he raised hell with himself in the break he had made with Dunn. I could see that there was a different feeling in the whole party at this time. The Major had sat down several feet from the rest of the party. I poured out each man a cup of coffee and one for him also and we all began to eat. He then asked me why I did not bring him his dinner as I had been doing before. I told him he had just said that he was going to make a change in the outfit, and I told him that I had made that change to start the ball rolling, and that he would have to come and get his grub like the rest of the boys.

His brother then handed his dinner to him. After dinner Sumner asked him if he had changed his mind in regard to Dunn and the watch and he said he had not, and that Dunn would either pay for the watch or leave the party. Dunn, Hall, Bradley, and myself were near the boat and about twenty feet from the Major and Sumner. We could not hear what they were talking about, but we had decided that if Dunn left the party we would go with him. Of course we expected opposition to what we intended to do, so after we had talked the matter over we wanted Bradley to go and tell the Major what we intended to do. But Bradley decided I had better go and tell him myself, as I had made the plan of going with Dunn. I went to where Sumner and the Major were talking with the two Howland boys.

I told the Major that Bradley, Hall, and I had decided to go with Dunn, and that we would take my boat (the cook boat) and some grub, and would pull out, and he could come when he got ready. He said he would not stand any such work, that it would be the ruin of his party. I told him that it was all his own fault, and that I had no more talk to make, and went back to the boat. I found Dunn, Bradley, and Hall waiting to see what had happened, but before I had time to tell them, Sumner came and began to talk to us, telling us to not feel put out, that the Major was hasty, and to give him another chance. Dunn remarked that the Major did not like him anyway. If he had, he would never have named the Escalante River the "Dirty Devil."

We camped at that place for the night and in the morning the Major said he would take thirty dollars for the watch and that he could pay for it when we got through. None of the party except the Major liked Capt. Powell. He had a bull-dozing way that was not then practiced in the West. He threatened to slap me several times for trying to sing as he did, but he never did slap anyone in the party. We all moved off down the river O.K., but our provisions began to run short, and rapids became more frequent, some of them very bad. But for a few days everything went all right. The boys would tell Indian adventures at night that someone had had. The remark was made that Dunn had nothing to say, and Captain Powell said he guessed Dunn did not know much about Indians. The Major chipped in and said, "Nor anything else." Sumner took it up for Dunn because he knew there would soon be trouble. He told Powell that Dunn had been wounded four times by the Comanches, so it all passed off.

The next day we had some very bad rapids, so bad that it was necessary to let the boats around some large rocks. In order to do this, and as Dunn was a fine swimmer, the Major asked him to swim out to a rock so the boat would swing in below. He made the rock all O. K. and was ready to catch the rope which was supposed to be thrown to him, so he could swing the boat in below, but the Major saw his chance to drown Dunn, as he thought, and he held the rope. That was the first time that he had interfered in the letting the boats around bad places, and the rope caught Dunn around the legs and pulled him into the current and came near losing the boat.

But Dunn held on to the rope and finally stopped in water up to his hips. We were all in the water but the Major and the Captain. Dunn told the Major that if he had not been a good swimmer he and the boat both would have been lost. The Major said as to Dunn that there would have been but little loss. One word brought on another, and the Major called Dunn a bad name and Dunn said that if the Major was not a cripple he would not be called such names.

Then Captain Powell said he was not crippled, and started for Dunn with an oath, and the remark he would finish Dunn. He had to pass right by me and I knew that he would soon drown Dunn, as he, so much larger could easily do. He was swearing and his eyes looked like fire. Just as he passed I caught him by the hair of his head and pulled him over back into the water. Howland saw us scuffling and he was afraid Cap would get hold of my legs. But Dunn got to me first and said, "For God's Sake, Bill, you will drown him!" By that time Howland was there and Cap had been in the water long enough and Dunn and Howland dragged him out on the sand bar in the rocks. After I got my hold in Cap's hair I was afraid to let go, for he was a very strong man. He was up in a short time, and mad! I guess he *was* mad! He cursed me to everything, even to being a "Missouri puke." I wasn't afraid of him when I got on dry ground. I could out-knock him after he was picked up twice.

He made for his gun and swore he would kill me and Dunn. But this talk did not excite me. As he was taking his gun from the deck of the boat, Andy Hall gave him a punch behind the ear and told him to put it back or off would go his head. Cap looked around and saw who had the gun, and he sure dropped his. This all happened before the Major got around to where we were. He soon took in the situation and came to me and made the remark that he would have never thought I would go back on him. I told him that he had gone back on himself, and that he had better help Cap get the sand out of his eyes, and that if he monkeyed with me any more I would keep him down next time.

Sumner and I had all we could do to keep down mutiny. There was bad feeling from that time on for a few days. We began not to recognize any authority from the Major. We began to run races with the boats, as the loads were almost all gone. It was fun for the first two days, but then the water began to get rough.

Mound Canyon

Bradley, 29 July   Run 20 miles with ease. Found small rapids or what we call *small* ones now but which would pass for full-grown *cataracts* in the States. We like them much for they send us along fast and easy and lower our altitude very much. Major named the new stream "Dirty Devil's Creek" and as we are the only white men who have seen it I for one feel quite highly complimented by the name, yet it is in keeping with his whole character which needs only a short study to be read like a book.* Those mountains we saw last night are not snow-clad. We passed them today leaving them on our right. They have considerable wood on them and are quite grand in appearance as they contain harder rocks than any we have before seen on the trip. Bazalt, granite, etc., which wears away slowly and gives them a very rough appearance. Hope we shan't meet any such right in our way but expect to do so before we get through, for all the explorers of the lower Colorado predict that there are Basaltic and Granite walls to the unknown cañon from 3000 to 5000 ft. high; if so we ought to meet them pretty soon for we are fast making distance into the unknown. We found an old ruin of a Moqui house today.** It was built in a desolate place where they could find a little grass and a little lowland on which to raise a few vegetables. It must be one or two hundred years since it was inhabited as every trace of paths or roof timbers are blotted out. It was built of

---

*Curiously enough, Bradley credits Powell with the name "Dirty Devil," Powell credits Dunn, and Sumner credits himself. To add to the confusion, Hawkins says Powell had referred to Dunn as a "dirty devil" before they came to the stinking river, which he then dubbed the "Dirty Devil," in reference to Dunn. This makes Bradley's reference to being complimented by the name and to reading "his whole character" somewhat ambiguous. On first reading one might assume this is a reference to Powell (if so, it is uncharacteristically critical for Bradley), but it could be a more subtle reference either to Dunn or to "The Devil."

**Pueblo (Moqui) remains. Moqui was the name applied by the Navajos to the Hopi Indians. The Major's diary gives fine sketch of the floor plan of this ruin.

stone with a thick strong wall some of which is still standing but most all has fallen down. It contained four rooms of the following dimensions 13 x 6, 13 x 18, 13 x 16, 13 x 28. There was also another not so well preserved, built under the bluff as if for a sort of kitchen or shelter for their cattle. We found many specimens of curiously marked fragments of crockery some of which I have saved, but may not be able to ever get them home. I would like very much to find one of their villages along the river for they are an hospitable people and retain more of the former customs of the old race than any other living tribe.

Powell, 29 July　Climbed rock on right. Going most of the day through Canon with low red walls. During the afternoon found ruins of house with fragments of pottery on rocky bluff to left at point of rock where it was overhanging. The remains of other walls were seen, perhaps 3 houses or compartments of one. Between the bluff and the river was a valley ⅓ mile long and 200-300 yards wide. Some mortar was yet left. Where the walls had not fallen, there was an opening in the wall at west near corner. Everything old looking; may be 2 or more centuries. After leaving ruins we ran down to camp 3 or 4 miles and I climbed the right wall and went back a mile or two. This monument formation is wonderfully rounded above into the mounds and cones. Deep holes are worn out. In one well I saw a true well 25 ft. deep. Mts. to N.W. Returned by dark and took obs. for lat. Camp No. 19.

Sumner, 29 July　Pulled out at 7 o'clock and ran down through a very crooked channel for 20¾ miles; passed 15 rapids, but none of them very bad. Passed an old Moqui ruin on a hill 30 ft. high, 200 yds. south of the river. One house or rather the remains of it, contained 4 rooms. Under the hill there are several more, but all have fallen to the ground leaving little but the foundation. How they contrived to live is a mystery to me, as the country around is as destitute of vegetation as a street. There is a small bench of a few acres between the hill and the river that might support half a dozen people if it was cleared of willows, cactus and horned toads. passed 2 small creeks coming in from the south side. Camped on the north side near a clump of oak trees.

Powell Account of 29 July　Two hours are given to the examination of these interesting ruins, then we run down fifteen miles farther, and discover another group. The principal building was situated on the summit of the hill. A part of the walls are standing, to the height of eight or ten feet, and the mortar yet remains in some places. The house was in the shape of an L with five rooms on the ground floor, one in the angle, and two in each entension. In the space in the angle, there is a deep excavation. From what we know of the people in the province of Tusayan, who are, doubtless, of the same race as the former inhabitants of these ruins, we conclude that this was a "kiva," or underground chamber, in which their religious ceremonies were performed.*

We leave these ruins, and run down two or three miles, to secure defensible positions. Just before sundown, I attempt to climb a rounded eminence, for which I hope to obtain a good outlook on the surrounding country. It is formed of smooth mounds, piled one above another. Up these I climb, winding here and there, to find a practicable way, until near the summit they become too steep for me to proceed. I search about, a few minutes, for a more easy way, when I am surprised at finding a stairway, evidently cut in the rock by hands. At one place, where there is a vertical wall of ten or twelve feet, I find an old, rickety ladder. It may be that this was a watchtower of that ancient people, whose homes we have found in ruins. On many of the tributaries of the Colorado I have heretofore examined their deserted dwellings. Those that show evidences of being built during the latter part of their occupation of the country are, usually, placed on the most inaccesible cliffs. Sometimes, the mouths of caves have been walled across, and there are many other evidences to show their anxiety to secure defensible positions. Probably the nomadic tribes were sweeping down upon them, and they resorted to these cliffs and canyons for safety. It is not unreasonable to suppose that this orange mound was used as a watchtower. Here I stand, where these now lost people stood centuries ago, and look over this strange country. I gaze off to great mountains, in the northwest, which are slowly covered by the night until they are lost, and then I return to camp. It is no easy task to find my way down the wall in the darkness, and I clamber about until it is nearly midnight, before I arrive.

Bradley, 30 July   Made another fine run of 21 miles though much of the way there was but little tide. The walls of the canon are yet quite low though somewhat higher than for the last few days. We are expecting to come up to the San Juan River, for by a Mormon map which we have it is only 50 miles from the junction and we have already come nearly twice that distance. By the official map from Washington it is put down as "probably" 100 miles, but as we have run farther west than they have marked the probable course of the Colorado, that will make the mouth of the San Juan further down though we shall

---

*These ruins were used by the Anasazi Indians in the last half of the twelfth century. No one knows for sure why they left, but authorities believe that a drought, combined with steady erosion of their small fields at the bottom of side canyons, was responsible. "Tusayan," Coronado's name for the Hopi villages, was apparently still in use in the 1860s.

probably strike it tomorrow. Begin to find occasional pieces of granite, which indicates that there are mountains of it near from which it has rolled down.

Powell, 30 July　Ran today through canon in monument form. Where the walls are broken down there are many gently rounded mounds and slopes towards the river. In the middle of the afternoon dip changed to a little N. or E. Canon walls gradually higher, and a terrace on the points. At noon I walked back some distance from river. The country runs back in broken ledges. At night I went up gulch and collected beautiful ferns found in dense masses. Camp on right. No. 20.

Sumner, 30 July　Off again at 7 o'clock and made a good day. Ran through a grayish sandstone canon, as destitute of vegetation (except where there is room on the river for walls) as the paper I write on. Passed 12 rapids, but none large enough to give us any trouble. Camp on the north side under a cliff 100 ft. high. Dunn killed a half-starved coyote near camp, the only sign of animal life we have seen for 3 days. Made 31 miles today.

Powell Account of 30 July　We make good progress today, as the water, though smooth, is swift. Sometimes, the canyon walls are vertical to the top; sometimes, they are vertical below, and have a mound-covered slope above; in other places, the slope, with its mounds, comes down to the water's edge. Still proceeding on our way, we find the orange sandstone is cut in two by a group of firm, calcareous strata, and the lower bed is underlaid by soft gypsiferous shales. Sometimes, the upper homogeneous bed is a smooth, vertical wall, but usually it is carved with mounds, with gently meandering valley lines. The lower bed, yielding to gravity, as the softer shales below work out into the river, breaks into angular surfaces, often having a columnar appearance. One could almost imagine that the walls had been carved with a purpose, to represent giant architectual forms.

In the deep recesses of the walls, we find springs, with mosses and ferns on the moistened sandstone.

Mouth of the San Juan and Monument Canyon

Bradley, 31 July　The last day of the month finds us at the mouth of the San Juan, and we find it about the size of White River No. 1, though not so deep as that was when we passed it. It has a very rapid tide and is quite muddy. It will add considerably to the amount of water and probably increase the speed for a little while. There is not a tree at its mouth and the place is most desolate and uninviting. Fear Major will conclude to remain here and observe the eclipse on the 7th but sincerely hope not for to find shelter we have to crawl into the rocks and let the evelike projection of the cliff shelter us, and the rocks are almost hissing hot. The thermometer seldom gets lower than 100 degrees except just before sunrise, when it falls a little. The air is so dry that there is generally over 40 degrees difference in the wet and dry thermometers. Have run 19½ miles today.

Powell, 31 July   Cool pleasant ride today through this part of Monument Canon. The large boats racing. Still more cones and rounded points. After dinner soon found the mouth of San Juan. Then I climbed Mt. Failed on obs. by reason of clouds, but obtained alt. of B. ceti [beta ceti, a star of 3.8 magnitude] in morning.* Camp No. 21.

Sumner, 31 July   Pulled out at 7 o'clock and rowed 18 miles against a strong head wind when we camped for dinner on the south side under an oak tree 15 inches in diameter and 15 ft. high. Found granite boulders at camp, the first on the trip. Pulled out at 1 o'clock and rowed 1½ miles—that brought us to the mouth of the San Juan River, a stream 30 yds. wide and 15 inches deep, dirty as can be, but not salty as most of the side streams are. Camped on the point between the 2 rivers and spent the whole of the afternoon in trying to find a place to get out, but failed to do so in any direction we wanted to. There is nothing growing at the junction but a few willows. One mile below on the south side of the Colorado River there is some scrubby oak. Canon walls from 300 to 800 ft. all sandstone, so steep and smooth that it is next to impossible to get out. Distance from Grand River, 116 miles. General course, due southwest. Country worthless to anybody or anything. Number of rapids run, 45. Portages 18.

Sumner Account of 31 July   Arriving at the mouth of the San Juan River we camped there a few days. Here I had another job of repairing instruments and cursing swarms of minute gnats, so small that they could hardly be seen but as full of venom as hell fire, or as a politician is full of tricks. Just above the San Juan we saw the first prominent "Moqui" houses, though we had seen some ruins farther up the river. These people were a strange folk. Remarkable that such frail things as corn shucks and leaves should last longer than the history of a nation!

From the San Juan we moved down a few miles and camped again to correct

---

*Powell is referring to obtaining his latitude from a reading of the angle of declination of the star beta ceti. He could then compute the longitude from consultation with a printed ephemeris, which gives dates and times for star positions.

the topographical work, as Howland had got things somewhat confused. Here occurred another spat between him and Major Powell. Will it never cease? Such silly business indulged in by educated men is liable to create a bad impression in the minds of frontier trappers. Military martinets and civilians very often disagree, however.

The Music Temple

Bradley, 1 August   Sunday finds us again on the move. Major tried in vain to climb the low cliffs on the south side of the San Juan. They are so very smooth that they defy his efforts and he becoming disgusted has moved down the river a mile or so to find a better camp. We are on the left side of the Colorado in a little bunch of oaks and willows which with a little fixing will afford a tolerable shelter. Just saw three sheep this A.M. but failed to get one of them. The rocks are so smooth it is impossible to follow them for they can run right up the side of a cliff where no man can get no foot-hold. Their feet are made cupping and the outer surface of the hoof is as sharp as a knife. They seem to have no fear of falling but will leap from rock to rock, never stumbling nor slipping though they will be a thousand ft. above us and a single miss-step would dash them to atoms. They are very good eating and we need meat very much, not having over 15 lbs. of bacon in the whole outfit. We are short of everything but flour, coffee and dried apples and in a few days our rations will be reduced to that.

Sumner, 1 August   Ran down 1¾ miles and found a good camp in some oak and willow bushes. Camped on the south side to repair boats and take obs. Thermometer, 104 degrees in the shade.

Powell Account of 1 August   We drop down two miles this morning, and go into camp again. There is a low, willow-covered strip of land along the walls on the east. Across this we walk, to explore an alcove which we see from the river. On entering, we find a little grove of box-elder and cottonwood trees; and, turning to the right, we find ourselves in a vast chamber, carved out of the rock. At the upper end there is a clear, deep pool of water, bordered with verdure. Standing by the side of this, we can see the grove at the entrance. The chamber is more than two hundred feet high, five hundred feet long, and two hundred feet wide. Through the ceiling, and on through the rocks for a thousand feet above, there is a narrow, winding skylight; and this is all carved out by a little stream, which only runs during the few showers that fall now and then in this arid country. The waters from the bare rocks back of the canyon, gathering rapidly into a small channel, have eroded a deep side canyon, through which they run, until they fall into the farther end of this camber. The rock at the ceiling is hard, the rock below, very soft and friable; and having cut through the upper harder portion down into the lower and softer, the stream has washed out these friable sandstones; and thus the chamber has been excavated.

Here we bring our camp. When "Old Shady" [Walter Powell] sings us a song at night, we are pleased to find that this hollow in the rock is filled with sweet sounds. It was doubtless made for an academy of music by its storm-born architect; so we name it Music Temple.

Bradley, 2 August In the same camp, doomed to be here another day, perhaps more than that for Major has been taking observations ever since we came here and seems no nearer done now than when he began. He ought to get the latitude and longitude of every mouth of a river not before known, and we are willing to face starvation if necessary to do it but further than that he should not ask us to wait and we must go on soon or the consequences will be different from what he anticipates. If we could get game or fish we should be all right but we have not caught a single mess of fish since we left the junction. Major has agreed to move on in the morning so we feel in good spirits tonight.

Sumner, 2 August In camp repairing and taking obs. Half a mile or less from camp there is a curious alcove worn in the sandstone by the rain water of a gulch. It is large enough to contain 200 people. Wall 200 ft. high and nearly closed in at the top. There are 3 cottonwood trees growing in the clear white sand floor and a little lake of pure water on one side. We christened it "Music Hall." Strong wind all day. Heavy shower at dark.

Powell Account of 2 August We still keep our camp in Music Temple today. I wish to obtain a view of the adjacent country, if possible; so, early in the morning, the men take me across the river, and I pass along by the foot of the cliff half a mile upstream, and then climb first up broken ledges, then two or three hundred yards up a smooth, sloping rock, and then pass out on a narrow ridge. Still, I find I have not attained an altitude from which I can overlook the region outside of the canyon; and so I descend into a little gulch, and climb again to a higher ridge, all the way along naked sandstone, and at last I reach a point of commanding view. I can look several miles up the San Juan, and a long distance up the Colorado; and away to the northwest I can see the Henry Mountains; to the northeast, the Sierra La Sal; to the southeast, unknown mountains; and to the southwest, the meandering of the canyon. Then I return to the bank of the river.

We sleep again in Music Temple.

Monument (or Glen) Canyon

Bradley, 3 August   Have made an easy run of 33 miles. Passed several rapids but none that we could not run easily. Have lowered our altitude finally. Over 750 ft. since we left the San Juan. This A.M. Jack was so fortunate as to kill a sheep which sets us up again and as the hills are a little more covered with grass we begin to hope that we may get an occasional sheep. If so we can live very well for they are very good eating and the one we got today is quite fat and will weigh about 80 lbs. dressed. There was another with it that we came near getting but it got away and perhaps it is well that it did for when we got two before part spoiled and we had to throw it away. We have taken the precaution to dry part of this so there is little danger of its spoiling. Fish were very plenty as we passed along today but they will not bite as they get plenty to eat all along; where the water is still we could see them catching small flies that the river seems covered with. The canon continues low and the sand-stone through which the river now runs has a strange tendency to form mounds and monuments from which Major has concluded to call it "Monument Canon" [later renamed Glen Canyon] from the mouth of the San Juan. Where we camp tonight there are pony tracks and evidences that the Indians can get in here. We think it must be through a little stream that comes in at this point but most such places become perpendicular if followed back a short distance. The weather continues very hot.

Sumner, 3 August   Pulled out early, made a good run. Saw 2 mountain sheep in a little valley on the south side. How they got there I will leave others to judge, as there is no outlet to the valley that a man can climb. Killed one and chased the other through the natural pasture for an hour and pulled out again. Made 33 miles and camped on the north side at the old Ute crossing between Utah and western Colorado and New Mexico. The trail on the north side comes down a side canon not more than 10 ft. wide with walls 200 ft. high, worn by a small, clear stream through sandstone. On the north side it is broken and easy to get out with ponies. The river is about 200 yards wide and when we were there, about 7 ft. deep.

Powell Account of 3 August   Start early this morning. The features of this canyon are greatly diversified. Still vertical walls at times. These are usually found to stand above great curves. The river, sweeping around these bends, undermines the cliffs in place. Sometimes, the rocks are overhanging; in other curves, curious, narrow glens are found. Through these we climb, by a rough stairway, perhaps several hundred feet, to where a spring bursts out from under an overhanging cliff, and where cottonwoods and willows stand, while, along the curves of the brooklet, oaks grow, and other rich vegetation is seen, in marked contrast to the general appearance of naked rock. We call these Oak Glens. . . .

On the walls, and back many miles into the country, numbers of monument-shaped buttes are observed. So we have a curious ensemble of wonderful features—carved walls, royal arches, glens, alcove gulches, mounds, and monuments. From which of these features shall we select a name? We decide to call it Glen Canyon.

Past these towering monuments, past these mounded billows of orange sandstone, past these oak-set glens, past these fern-decked alcoves, past these mural curves, we glide hour after hour, stopping now and then, as our attention is arrested by some new wonder, until we reach a point which is historic.

In the year 1776, Father Escalante, a Spanish priest, made an expedition from Santa Fe to the northwest, crossing the Grand and Green, and then passing down along the Wasatch Mountains and the southern plateaus, until he reached the Rio Virgen.* His intention was to cross to the Mission of Monterey; but, from information received from the Indians, he decided that the route was impracticable. Not wishing to return to Santa Fe over the circuitous route by which he had just traveled, he attempted to go by one more direct, and which led across the Colorado, at a point known as El vado de Los Padres. From the description which we have read, we are enabled to determine the place. A little stream comes down through a very narrow side canyon from the west. It was down this that he came, and our boats are lying at the point where the ford crosses. A well-beaten Indian trail is seen here yet. Between the cliff and the river there is a little meadow. The ashes of many campfires are seen, and bones of numbers of cattle are bleaching on the grass. For several years the Navajos have raided on the Mormons that dwell in the valleys to the west, and they doubtless cross frequently at this ford with their stolen cattle.

---

*The old Ute ford, El Vado de los Padres, and the Crossing of the Fathers are *all* names for the same ford, 39 miles above Lee's Ferry. Powell writes as if Father Escalante made the expedition by himself. Actually led by Fray Atanacio Dominguez, the expedition of approximately 10 men is now known as the Dominguez-Escalante Expedition, however, Fray Silvestre Valez de Escalante wrote the journal. They located the ford on the Colorado and crossed on 7 November 1776.

Mouth of the Paria River (Lee's Ferry) and Vermilion Cliffs

Bradley, 4 August   Another long run of 38¼ miles. Water very still all the way and a head wind which this P.M. has sometimes blown a perfect tornado with lightning and rain. The walls for the last 20 miles have been getting higher and the canon narrower. Tonight, however, we came suddenly to a point where the strata is very much broken and quite a basin is formed by the washing away of the upturned rocks, but just below a few miles the strata is again horizontal so that probably the break is only local. Jack and Bill D. have just come in from a short hunt and report that there seems to be quite an extensive plain off to the south of us. Where we are now encamped are signs of Indians such as brush cut for beds, and old bones—but quite old. We are at or very near the Ute trail where the Indians cross the river. Tomorrow or next day we ought to come to the Pah Rhear [Paria] River. A small trail where the Mormons have a ferry. Have made but little altitude today as the river has been too still, but just below our camp a fine rapid commences that is roaring pretty loud. . . .

Sumner, 4 August   Pulled out early and made a run of 38 miles, that brought us to the old Spanish Crossing between Salt Lake and New Mexico, called the Escalanta "El vade de los Padres." It is desolate enough to suit a lovesick poet. There is a small dirty stream coming in from the north called by the Mormons Pahria River. . . .*

Powell Account of 4 August   Today the walls grow higher, and the canyon much narrower. Monuments are still seen on either side; beautiful glens, and alcoves, and gorges and side canyons are yet found. After dinner, we find the river making a sudden turn to the northwest, and the whole character of the canyon changed. The walls are many hundreds of feet higher, and the rocks are chiefly variegated shades of beautiful colors—creamy orange above, then bright vermilion, and below, purple and chocolate beds, with green and yellow sands. We run four miles through this, in a direction a little to the west of north; wheel again to the west, and pass into a portion of the canyon where the characteristics are more like those above the bend. At night we stop at the mouth of a creek coming in from the right, and suppose it to be the Paria, which was described to me last year by a Mormon missionary.

Here the canyon terminates abruptly in a line of cliffs, which stretches from either side across the river.

---

*Paria River. Lee's Ferry was established here in 1872 by John D. Lee. Sumner is in error here; see note to 3 August.

Sumner Account of 4 August   Dropping down from Music Hall camp, we experienced nothing worthy of note excepting daily duckings and continuous fasting. We arrived at Paria Creek, a little stream coming in from the north. We camped there a day. Trails and ancient camps show that this point has been used for ages as a crossing place of the Colorado. There are great numbers of milling stones used by the Indians to grind, or rather pound, pinon nuts and grass seeds, mixed with dried grasshoppers and an occasional lizard, to make their daily—or rather weekly—bread. There is an ancient fort crowning a small butte near the crossing. Did the Moquis make a desperate stand here before they were wiped out by the northern hordes that swept everything before them from Puget Sound to the plains of Mexico? The invaders left barely enough of the Cliff Dwellers for seed. Their descendants, I believe, are the present Pueblo Indians, but I don't pretend to know, and I can't find any one to give me any better information.*

We saw fresh moccasin tracks at various places in a little valley, a fact which set me on the keenest watch to avoid a surprise. Indians rarely attack an unknown enemy unless they can surprise him. We were in no condition for a fight or a foot race. If the reds saw us, as they probably did, they could see plainly enough to satisfy them that to attempt to surprise us would be very hazardous. Accordingly, none showed up.

Marble Canyon

Bradley, 5 August   Well, I said yesterday that we had learned to like rapids, but we came to two of them today that *suit us too well.* They are furious cataracts. The first one we passed before we ate dinner and after dinner we run a few miles and came upon one that has lasted us all the P.M. But we are over it or rather around it for we had to take the boats out in one place. We have lowered our altitude today very much for this A.M. we had a series of rapids which we could run and which let us down very fast. Am very tired tonight. Hope a good sleep will do me good but this constant wetting in fresh water and exposure to a parching sun begins to tell on all of us. Run 12 miles today.

Powell, 5 August   A very long rapid to start with. Still more rapids. A portage, fall 14 ft. Dinner on right bank. Run of 2 or more miles, another long portage. Camp on right bank on sand.

---

*Although a small ring of rocks does exist on a low butte at Lee's Ferry, there is no evidence of battles between the northern Indians and the Moquis. He is right, however, about the Moqui descendents being the Pueblos (and of course, Hopis).

Sumner, 5 August　Pulled out early and ran a long rapid to begin with, then 12 more in 8 miles; made 2 portages over rapid of 15 ft. fall in 25 yds.; stove a hole in the *"Maid"* while lifting her over the rocks. Heavy wind and rain at night. Made 15 miles. Very hard work; camped on north side on a sandbar.

Powell Account of 5 August　With some feeling of anxiety, we enter a new cañon this morning. We have learned to closely observe the texture of the rock. In softer strata, we have a quiet river; in harder, we find rapids and falls. Below us are the limestones and hard sandstones which we found in Cataract Cañon. This bodes toil and danger. . . .

The cañon is narrow, with vertical walls, which gradually grow higher. More rapids and falls are found. We come to one with a drop of sixteen feet around which we make a portage, and then stop for dinner.

Then a run of two miles, and another portage, long and difficult then we camp for the night, on a bank of sand.

Bradley, 6 August　Another hard day for 10¾ miles. The cañon has lofty walls, much of the way perpendicular and wherever the rocks have fallen in or there is a side cañon we have a rapid. Where we can run the current is swift and we make a good speed. This forenoon we came upon a dangerous rapid where we had to cling to the smooth sides of the rocks until we could view the *situation* and having discovered a little foothold on the left at the top of the fall we succeeded in landing all our boats safely and climbing over the rocks that made the rapid. We carried our rations and then lowered our boats and were in and away again. Three times today we have had to carry everything around rapids, but the last few miles we came tonight we found the rapids less furious and I hope we are out of the worst of this series. Tomorrow is the eclipse so we have to stop and let Major climb the mountain to observe it. We have camped in a place where the rock is so much broken that possibly he may climb out but the chances are against him, for if he succeeds in reaching a point where he can see out, the probability is that it will be cloudy and rain about the hour for the eclipse as it has done for the past three or four days. The dip of the strata changes here to the west and the limestone is just in sight. It is fortunate that it changes for it always has given us trouble when that old hard marble comes up. It was that which gave us frightful cataracts when we first came into the Colorado and if we have escaped it we are lucky.

Powell, 6 August　Walls still get higher as down we go [in] to the lime-stone. Had a hard climb along benches and through cleft of rock to see rapids—made portage. Another after dinner—I went up lateral cañon found fossils, saw cascade of red mud. Camped at night on right bank.

Sumner, 6 August   Repaired the *"Maid"* and pulled out again into more rapids. Made 3 portages and ran 10 bad rapids in 10½ miles. Walls of cañon 2000 ft. and increasing as we go. River about 50 yds. wide, rapids and whirlpools all the way. Camped on the north side on a sandbar at dark.

Powell Account of 6 August   Cañon walls, still higher and higher, as we go down through strata. There is a steep talus at the foot of the cliff, and, in some places, the upper parts of the walls are terraced. . . .

Bradley, 7 August   Have been in camp all day repairing boats, for constant banging against rocks has begun to tell sadly on them and they are growing old faster if possible than we are. Have put four new ribs in mine today and calked her all around until she is as tight again as a cup. Hope it is the last time she will need repair on this trip. Major and brother have climbed the mountain to observe the eclipse but think it almost or quite a total failure for it has rained almost or quite all the P.M. We could see the sun from camp when it was about half covered but it clouded immediately and before the cloud passed it was behind the bluffs. Major has not yet come in. Cannot tell whether he saw it or not. If he did we shall have our longitude.* The river is very red and rising some. Hope it is caused only by these little showers for we now have all the water we want and any more would make it harder for us. Have pitched our tent for the first time since we left Uinta.

Powell, 7 August   Took obs. in morning. Climbed Mt. after dinner to observe eclipse. Failed, clouds. Slept on Mt. side, too dark to get all the way down.

Sumner, 7 August   In camp all day repairing boats and taking observations.

Powell Account of 7 August   The almanac tells us that we are to have an eclipse of the sun today, so Captain Powell and myself start early, taking our

---

*Longitude is obtained by observing the culmination of a star at the exact time predicted and listed in an ephemeris and by measuring the angle of declination. The difference in angle between what is predicted at Greenwich, England, and your location provides your longitude—as adjusted by latitude. Powell was anxious to obtain latitude and longitude so he could estimate how many miles of canyon lay ahead of him and his men.

instrument with us, for the purpose of making observations on the eclipse, to determine our longitude. Arriving at the summit, after four hours' hard climbing, to attain 2,300 feet in height, we hurriedly build a platform of rocks, on which to place our instruments, and quietly wait for the eclipse; but clouds come on, and rain falls, and sun and moon are obscured.

Much disappointed, we start on our return to camp, but it is late, and the clouds make the night very dark. Still we feel our way down among the rocks with great care, for two or three hours, though making slow progress indeed. At last we lose our way, and dare proceed no further. The rain comes down in torrents, and we can find no shelter. We can neither climb up nor go down, and in the darkness dare not move about, but sit and "weather out" the night.

Redwall Cavern

Bradley, 8 August   Major and brother were in the bluffs all last night. They looked at the eclipse and at the river and mountains until they could not get to camp before it got too dark, for one cannot come down perpendicular walls unless he has daylight for it. The sun clouded at the moment the eclipse passed off so we know no more about our longitude now than when we came here. Though it is Sunday it brings no rest for us. We have found five rapids today around which we have had to make portages. Have run only 3½ miles today. Never made so many portages in one day for we have never had so little to carry around them as now. The weather is more pleasant tonight and the river is clearer but it is very muddy yet. . . . We begin to be a ragged looking set for our clothing is wearing out with much rough labor and we wear scarce enough to cover our nakedness for it is very warm with a sun pouring down between sand-stone walls 2000 ft. high. They are that height now and gradually rising though Major says that 12 or 15 miles ahead seems to be a slight valley or break, probably where the Pah Rhear comes in, and just beyond that are very high snow-clad mountains. . . . The limestone is coming up again and there are some of the most beautiful marbles I ever saw, not excepting those in the Cap. [Capitol] at Washington. They are polished by the waves, many of them, and look very fine. Should like specimens of them but the uncertainty of adequate transportation makes it vain to collect even a foccil, not to speak of plain rocks. We are interested now only in how we shall get through the canon and once more to civilization through we are more than ever sanguine of success. Still our slow progress and wasting rations admonish us that we have something to do. Fortunately we are a happy-go-lucky set of fellows and look more to our present comfort than our future danger and as the cook has a fine lot of beans cookings with every prospect that his sweating and swearing will issue in an ample breakfast in the morning, we shall make our beds tonight and no doubt sleep as soundly as if surrounded with all the comforts of "happy home" instead of in a cave of the earth.

Powell, 8 August   Five portages today. Beautiful marble, cream and pink and grey, purple with light red tints, etc. Curious effect of the water's dashing against foot of pile of rocks. Alcoves and arches of water. . . . Camp in Cave. Camp 27. [Redwall Cavern]

Sumner, 8 August   Pulled out early and did a terrible hard work. Made 5 portages in 3¼ miles. Camped on the south side under a marble cliff; walls increasing in height. Gathered little twigs of driftwood to cook our bread and make coffee.

Powell Account of 8 August   Daylight comes, after a long, oh! how long a night, and we soon reach camp.

After breakfast we start again, and make two portages during the forenoon.

The limestone of this canon is often polished, and makes a beautiful marble. Sometimes the rocks are of many colors—white, gray, pink, and purple, with saffron tints. It is with very great labor that we make progress, meeting with many obstructions, running rapids, letting down our boats with lines, from rock to rock, and sometimes carrying boats and cargo around bad places. We camp at night, just after a hard portage, under an overhanging wall, glad to find shelter from the rain. We have to search for some time to find a few sticks of driftwood, just sufficient to boil a cup of coffee.

The water sweeps rapidly in this elbow of river, and has cut its way under the rock, excavating a vast half circular chamber, which, if utilized for a theater, would give sitting to fifty thousand people.* Objections might be raised against it, from the fact that, at high water, the floor is covered with a raging flood.

Vasey's Paradise

Bradley, August 9   We made but little distance on Sunday but today we have run 16 miles, made three portages and passed 31 rapids, some of them very bad ones. Have had a little better running this P.M. Am in hopes that this series of heavy rapids is about ended. We have now run down our altitude until we are no longer apprehensive on that score. The limestone continues to rise

---

*He is referring to Redwall Cavern. This entry is out of order since he comes to Vasey's Paradise on the following day, 9 Aug. Redwall Cavern is a mile below Vasey's.

fast. Think there is about one thousand ft. up now but as the bottom part is softer than that which came up first it wears faster and makes a better bed for the river. We passed a beautiful cascade today but the rapids were so furious and the walls so nearly vertical we could not stop to examine it. To me it was the prettiest sight of the whole trip—The green ferns around it formed a pleasing contrast with the unending barrenness of the cañon.

Powell, August 9   Scenery on grand scale. Marble walls polished by the waves. Walls 2000-2200 ft. high. 3 portages before dinner. This afternoon I had a walk of a mile on a marble pavement, polished smooth in many places, in others embossed in a thousand fantastic patterns. Highly colored marble. Sun shining through cleft in the wall and the marble sending back the light in iridescence. At noon a cleft or canon on left, quite narrow with a succession of pools one above another, going back and connected by a little stream of clear water. The pavement a little too wide for a Boston street. Pot holes filled with clear water. Banded marble at noon, 20 ft. out of the water. After dinner we found a spring gushing from an orifice in the marble, as silvery foam glad to see the light released from prison. A bank of brilliant verdure (ferns chiefly) on the talus below.

Many little springs this afteroon with patches of verdure below. A huge canon ½ mile below spring. Vast number of caves and domed alcoves in this region. Walls about 2500 ft. high. At 3 p.m. just below spring the high water mark comes down to 10 to 12 ft., and the first mesquite seen. Camp in Mesquite Grove.

Sumner, 9 August   Hard at work early. Made 4 portages and ran 27 bad rapids in 13 miles. Passed a beautiful spring pouring out of the cliff 100 ft. above the river. The white water over the blue marble made a pretty show. I would not advise anybody to go there to see it. The walls of the canons are about 3000 ft. nearly perpendicular and it can not be climbed from the river. Made 16 miles and camped on the south side on a sandbar.

Powell Account of 9 August   And now, the scenery is on a grand scale. The walls of the cañon, 2,500 feet high, are of marble, of many beautiful colors, and often polished below by the waves, or far up the sides, where showers have washed the sands over the cliffs.

At one place I have a walk, for more than a mile, on a marble pavement, all polished and fretted with strange devices, and embossed in a thousand fantastic patterns. Through a cleft in the wall the sun shines on this pavement, which gleams in iridescent beauty.

I pass up into the cleft. It is very narrow, with a succession of pools standing at higher levels as I go back. The water in these pools is clear and cool, coming down from springs. Then I return to the pavement, which is but a terrace or bench, over which the river runs at its flood, but left bare at present. Along the pavement, in many places, are basins of clear water, in strange contrast to the red mud of the river. At length I come to the end of this marble terrace, and take again to the boat.

Riding down a short distance, a beautiful view is presented. The river turns sharply to the east, and seems inclosed by a wall, set with a million brilliant gems. What can it mean? Every eye is engaged, everyone wonders. On coming nearer, we find fountains bursting from the rock, high overhead, and the spray in the sunshine forms the gems which bedeck the wall. The rocks below the fountain are covered with mosses, and ferns, and many beautiful flowering plants. We name it Vasey's Paradise, in honor of the botanist who traveled with us last year.*

We pass many side cañons today, that are dark, gloomy passages, back into the heart of the rocks that form the plateau through which this cañon is cut.

It rains again this afternoon. Scarcely do the first drops fall, when little rills run down the walls. As the storm comes on, the little rills increase in size, until great streams are formed. Although the walls of the cañon are chiefly limestone, the adjacent country is of red sandstone; and now the waters, loaded with these sands, come down in rivers of bright red mud, leaping over the walls in innumerable cascades. It is plain now how these walls are polished in many places.

At last, the storm ceases, and we go on. We have cut through the sandstones and limestones met in the upper part of the canon, and through one great bed of marble a thousand feet in thickness. In this, great numbers of caves are hollowed out, and carvings are seen, which suggest architectural forms, though on a scale so grand that architectural terms belittle them. As this great bed forms a distinctive feature of the cañon, we call it Marble Cañon.

It is a peculiar feature of these walls, that many projections are set out into the river, as if the wall was buttressed for support. The walls themselves are half a mile high, and these buttresses are on a corresponding scale, jutting into the river scores of feet. In the recesses between these projections there are dancing eddies or whirlpools. Sometimes these alcoves have caves at the back, giving them the appearance of great depth. Then other caves are seen above, forming vast, dome-shaped chambers. The walls, and buttresses, and chambers are all of marble.

The river is now quiet; the cañon wider. Above, when the river is at its flood,

*Naturalist George Vasey accompanied Powell on his "Rocky Mountain Scientific Exploring Expedition" during the summer of 1868.

the waters gorge up, so that the difference between high and low water mark is often fifty or even seventy feet; but here, high water mark is not more than twenty feet above the present stage of the river. Sometimes there is a narrow floodplain between the water and the wall.

Here we first discover *mesquite* shrubs, or small trees, with finely divided leaves and pods, somewhat like the locust.

Sumner Account of 9 August   Below Paria Creek we soon encounter some pretty bad rapids. The rapids themselves were not so bad, but there was a vicious undertow and backwater at the tail of all of them that was a holy terror. If a boat kept the dividing line between the main current and the back current it went through all right. If the bow caught in the back current the least bit, the boat was whirled around quick enough to take the kinks out of a ram's horn. The boat was sure to fill with water and was usually capsized. . . .

Near the center of Marble Caynon is the prettiest spring I ever saw. [Vasey's Paradise] It comes out of a straight marble wall, four or five hundred feet high, through a round hole probably six or eight feet in diameter and pitches into the river in a magnificently graceful curve of white foam. . . .

From Paria Creek [or Lee's Ferry] to the Rio De Lino, Flax River or Little Colorado, there is marble enough of all kinds to build forty Babylons, walls and all, with enough to spare to build forty other cities before it would be missed. If geology is true—and it certainly is, if anything is—what vast ages the little insects must have worked to furnish the material for two thousand feet of marble! And what a length of time it took to form the miles of lime and sandstone that overlie the marble! . . . And then, how long did it require the Colorado River to cut its channel through all the sedimentary rocks and twelve hundred feet and more into the Archean formation? Who knows? The testimony of the rocks cannot be impeached. I think Moses must be mistaken in his chronology as recorded in Biblical history. From Green River, Wyoming, to the Virginia River is one continuous geological book. You can turn leaf after leaf from the Quatenary to the Archean. Whoever can read it is a master for sure.

Mouth of the Flax River or Little Colorado

Bradley, 10 August   About noon today Major concluded that our course south, our extreme southern latitude and our continuous falling of altitude all indicate that we had passed the Pah Rhear River and were fast approaching some other, probably the Chiquito, or Little Colorado. He told us so at noon and at 2 P.M. we came upon it. It is a loathesome little stream, so filthy and muddy that it fairly stinks. It is only 30 to 50 yds. wide now and in many places a man can cross it on the rocks without going in to his knees. There are signs of Indians here but quite old. Cannot tell whether they are Moquis or Apaches.* I think more likely the latter for the Moquis keep close to their villages. We now conclude that we passed the Ute trail Aug. 3 where we saw the pony tracks, and that the loathsome little stream that came in where we found the strata so broken Aug. 4 is no other than the Pah Rhear [Paria] River. The Colorado continues very rapid, indeed it seems more like an overgrown brook than it does like a large river. We have run 13¾ miles today in which we passed 35 rapids. We run them all though some of them were bad ones. One was the largest we have run in the Colorado for we have gone more cautiously in it than we did in the Green. I think we have had too much caution and made portages where to run would be quite as safe and much less injurious to the boats. We shall have to stop here two or three days to get latitude and longitude as this point has not been determined though it is said a man went through from here on a raft to Callville in eleven days. If so we have little to fear from waterfalls below. But I place but little reliance on such reports though his story has been published with much show of reason and Major has seen the man.** We are sorry to be delayed as we have had no meat for several days and not one sixth of a ration for more than a month, yet we are willing to do all that we can to make the trip a success. Weather showery.

Powell, 10 August Walls still higher. Water very swift. Falling rapidly [altitude]. Timber-clad ridges run to right. Reach Flax River at 2 P.M. Camp No. 29.

Sumner, 10 August Pulled out at 7 o'clock and ran 14 miles, passing 20 rapids many of them bad. Came to mouth of Flax or Little Colorado River, as disgusting a stream as there is on the continent; 3 rods wide and 3 ft. deep, half of its volume and ⅔ of its weight is mud and silt. There are a few mesquite bushes growing on the south side of Flax River, nothing on the Colorado. Walls about 4000 ft. high, inaccessible except on a very few points. Camped under a ledge of rocks, 100 yards below Flax River, and ¼ of a mile from the Colorado.

---

*Anasazi—referred to as "Moquis"—ruins were evident at the mouth of the Little Colorado in 1869. These ruins were rebuilt in 1890 to serve as a cabin for a prospector named Ben Beamer. (No Apaches ever lived in the canyon).

**Bradley is referring to the claim by James White that in 1867 he rafted from the junction of the Grand and Green to Callville, Nevada. See note page 2.

Powell Account of 10 August   Walls still higher; water, swift again. We pass several broad, ragged canons on our right, and up through these we catch glimpses of a forest-clad plateau, miles away to the west.

At two o'clock, we reach the mouth of the Colorado Chiquito. This stream enters through a cañon, on a scale quite as grand as that of the Colorado itself. It is a very small river, and exceedingly muddy and salty. I walk up the stream three or four miles, this afternoon, crossing and recrossing where I can easily wade it. Then I climb several hundred feet at one place, and can see up the chasm, through which the river runs, for several miles. On my way back, I kill two rattlesnakes, and find, on my arrival, that another has been killed just at camp.

Bradley, 11 August   Have been in camp all day for I have nothing to wear on my feet but an old pair of boots in which I cannot climb the mountains and which are my only reliance for making portages. In the boat and much of the time in camp I go bare-foot, but I have a pair of camp moccasins to slip on when the rocks are bad or the sand is too hot. I have given away my clothing until I am reduced to the same condition of those who lost by the shipwreck of our boats. I cannot see a man of the party more destitute than I am. Thank God the trip is nearly ended for it is no place for a man in my circumstances but it will let me out of the Army, and for that I would almost agree to explore the river Styx. I have rigged a stone table and chair and have commenced again to copy my notes. Have copied some from time to time and find it much easier than to do it all at once. Shall get them copied to date if we stay here tomorrow and I fear we shall have to stay several days. . . . Our camp is under the shelving edge of a cliff on the south side of the Chiquito and is protected from both sun and rain by overhanging rocks though it is filthy with dust and alive with insects. If this is a specimen of Arrazona a very little of it will do for me. The men are uneasy and discontented and anxious to move on. If Major does not do something soon I fear the consequences, but he is contented and seems to think that biscuit made of sour and musty flour and a few dried apples is ample to sustain a laboring man. If he can only study geology he will be happy without food or shelter but the rest of us are not afflicted with it to an alarming extent.

Powell, 11 August   Capt. and Sumner take obs. I walk up Flax 5 miles. Old Indian camp seen, trails footpaths. Flax tumbling down over many falls. Water very muddy, salty. P.M. Walter and I walk down river. Old path well worn. No lunar on account of clouds. Same camp under rocks.

Sumner, 11 and 12 August   In camp taking observations and measuring walls. . . .

Powell Account of 11 August   We remain at this point today for the purpose of determining the latitude and longitude, measuring the height of the walls, drying our rations, and repairing our boats.

Captain Powell, early in the morning, takes a barometer, and goes out to climb a point between the two rivers.

I walk down the gorge to the left at the foot of the cliff, climb to a bench, and discover a trail, deeply worn in the rock. . . .

I return to camp about three o'clock, and find that some of the men have discovered ruins, and many fragments of pottery; also, etchings and hieroglyphics on the rocks.

We find, tonight, on comparing the readings of the barometers, that the walls are about three thousand feet high—more than half a mile—an altitude difficult to appreciate from a mere statement of feet. The ascent is made, not by a slope such as is usually found in climbing a mountain, but is much more abrupt—often vertical for many hundreds of feet—so that the impression is that we are at great depth; and we look up to see but a little patch of sky. . . .

Sumner Account of 11 August   After about a week of daily duckings and some dangers we passed Marble Canyon and arrived at the mouth of the Little Colorado, a miserably lonely place indeed, with no signs of life but lizards, bats, and scorpions. It seemed like the first gates of hell. One almost expected to see Cerberus poke his ugly head out of some dismal hole and growl his disapproval of all who had not Charon's pass.*

We camped near the mouth of the Little Colorado one and a half days—made repairs, took observations, and checked up our records. Walter Powell took a barometer and climbed the cliff between the two rivers. We could see him as he reached the top. He looked like a mote in a sunbeam. Major Powell climbed the cliff below the Little Colorado and was gone so long I was afraid he was lost, as he went up an old Indian trail, and would never carry any arms. As we were on the edge of the Apache and Havasupai Indian country, his act was foolish, to say the least. However, he returned about dark and reported seeing nothing worse than two large rattlesnakes.

---

*Charon is the boatman of the River Styx, the entrance to the Afterworld in Greek mythology, and Cerberus is his dog.

Bradley, August 12   Have copied my notes to date and now am anxious to be on the move. Major got latitude last night by which we find ourselves as far south as Callville so that what we run now must be west from this point. Major's brother is out on the mountains with the barometer so we shall know their height when he comes in. There remains nothing more to be done that is absolutely necessary for lat. and long. are sufficient and we ought to be away in the morning. Don't know whether we shall or not. It is looking like a shower tonight. I am surprised to find it raining nearly every night in a country where they say rain seldom falls.

Powell, 12 August   Take obs. Capt. climbed Mt.

Powell Account of 12 August   . . . This morning, I spend two or three hours in climbing among these shelves, and then I pass above them, and go up a long slope, to the foot of the cliff, and try to discover some way by which I can reach the top of the wall; but I find my progress cut off by an amphitheater. Then, I wander away around to the left, up a little gulch, and along benches, and climb, from time to time, until I reach an altitude of nearly two thousand feet, and can get no higher. From this point, I can look off to the west, up side cañons of the Colorado, and see the edge of a great plateau, from which streams run down into the Colorado, and deep gulches, in the escarpment which faces us, continued by cañons, ragged and flaring, and set with cliffs and towering crags, down to the river. I can see far up Marble Canon, to long lines of chocolate-colored cliffs, and above these, the Vermilion Cliffs. I can see, also, up the Colorado Chiquito, through a very ragged and broken cañon, with sharp salients set out from the walls on either side, their points overlapping, so that a huge tooth of marble, on one side, seems to be set between two teeth on the opposite; and I can also get glimpses of walls, standing away back from the river, while over my head are mural escarpments, not possible to be scaled. . . .

Marble Cañon is 65½ miles long. And its head, it is 200 feet deep, and steadily increases in depth to its foot, where its walls are 3,500 feet high.

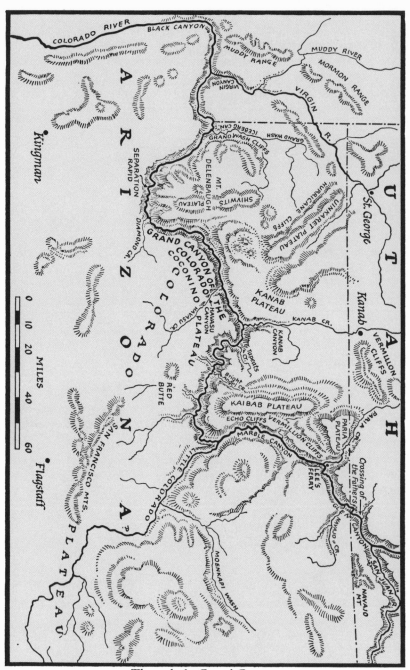

Through the Grand Canyon.

VII. The Little Colorado to the Foot of the Grand Canyon

I t was clear to Powell, as they left the junction with the Little Colorado behind, they were entering the most grandiose canyon of all. As he wrote in his account of 13 August, "we are ready to start on our way down the Great Unknown." So high were the canyon walls and so complex the gothiclike formations, that to Powell "the great river shrinks into insignificance . . . and we are but pigmies. . . . We have an unknown distance yet to run; an unknown river yet to explore."

Although they were only 217 miles and 18 days from the end of their pilgrimage, this final act of their drama was the most difficult to play out; it demanded all the strength and courage and resolve they had left. It battered their boats and depleted their food and equipment until they were forced, in their final ordeal, to act out of utter and perhaps foolhardy helplessness. What had started as an amateurish scientific expedition ended in a struggle for no more than survival. The fact that three of the crew did not survive the final act to take their curtain calls, gives testimony to the severity of their final challenge.

Even Major Powell, the happy geologist and cartographer, began to look like he had seen a ghost and wrote in his account that occasional jests of his men sounded "ghastly" to him. The others spoke of the Grand Canyon as if they were in prison; its sublime desert splendor was to their weary and frightened eyes, ". . . the worst hole in America." Sumner looked at his companions and saw in their eyes "the stern look" of troops "forming for a charge in battle."

Since most of the crew members were in uniform during the war, remind-
ers of the battle zone may have been common among them. Not only was their
food supply nearly exhausted, their boats needed repairs and recaulking nearly
every day. They began to have dreams of gargantuan meals that awaited their
release from prison. In addition to scalding temperatures of 115 degrees, they
were hampered by hard rains and a swollen river. The techniques they had
developed upriver of scouting rapids from shore and lining or portaging where
needed, were nullified by the steep granitic walls and the vastly increased
volume and speed of the river. At times they were forced to run the rapids
headlong, with seemingly reckless abandon.

Even if Major Powell or one of the others had written a novel of their
adventure, it could hardly be more dramatic than the story told by Bradley,
Powell, Sumner, and Hawkins of their final days in the great unknown. What
unfolds is a story of stories, as each narrator interprets the final days as a
culmination of all that had gone before. Perhaps Hawkins and Sumner were
right in reading the departure of Dunn and the Howlands as a response to their
conflict with the Major. Or perhaps, as Powell told it, the three were terrified
of the river and felt they had a better chance of survival by abandoning the
Colorado for the desert lands above. In his typically noncommital way, Bradley
merely reported that "there is discontent in camp tonight. . . ." What was
thought and spoken that fateful night of 27 August at Separation Rapids will
never be known, but for those who stayed with Powell on the river, Bradley
predicted accurately when he wrote that night, "'tis darkest just before the day'·
and I trust our day is about to dawn."

Bradley, 13 August   Started about 9 A.M. and have made 15 miles. The
rapids are almost innumerable, some of them very heavy ones full of treacherous rocks. Three times today we have let down with ropes but without making a
portage. Our rations are so much reduced now that they make but little
difference to the boats. We camp tonight at the head of the worst rapid we have
found today and the longest we have seen on the Colorado. The rocks are seen
nearly all over it for half a mile or more—indeed the river runs through a vast
pile of rocks. I am convinced that no man has ever run such rapids on a raft,
though it is possible he might pass along the shore and build another raft
below and so work his way out. . . . Major has just come in and says the granite
is coming up less than a mile down the river. . . . One thing is pretty certain—
no rocks ever made can make much worse rapids than we now have.

Powell, 13 August   15 miles of very rapid river. Walls much broken. Come
to granite at night. Ind. camp nearby. I climb wall, still more rapids before us.

Sumner, 13 August   Pulled out at 8 o'clock and enter into another nest of rapids. Ran 30 and let down with ropes; passed 3 more in 15 miles travel. Ran out of the old red sandstone about 4 miles below the mouth of Flax River; 6 miles below there are the remains of an old volcano. Camped on the north side at the head of a rapid about 1 mile long with a fall of 50 or 60 ft. that has about 100 rocks in the upper half of it. How anyone can ride that on a raft is more than I can see.* Mr. White may have done so but I can't believe it. At the lower end of the rapid the granite rises for the first time. There is no granite whatever (except boulders) from Green River City to the head of this rapid.

Powell Account of 13 August   We are now ready to start on our way down the Great Unknown. Our boats tied to a common stake, are chafing each other, as they are tossed by the fretful river. They ride high and buoyant, for their loads are lighter than we could desire. We have but a month's rations remaining. The flour has been resifted through the mosquito net sieve; the spoiled bacon has been dried, and the worst of it boiled; the few pounds of dried apples have been spread in the sun, and reshrunken to their normal bulk; the sugar has all melted, and gone on its way down the river; but we have a large sack of coffee. The lighting of the boats has this advantage: they will ride the waves better, and we shall have but little to carry when we make a portage.

We are three-quarters of a mile in the depths of the earth, and the great river shrinks into insignificance, as it dashes its angry waves against the walls and cliffs, that rise to the world above; they are but puny ripples, and we but pigmies, running up and down the sands, or lost among the boulders.

We have an unknown distance yet to run; an unknown river yet to explore. What falls there are, we know not; what rocks beset the channel, we know not; what walls rise over the river, we know not. Ah, well! we may conjecture many things. The men talk as cheerfully as ever; jests are bandied about freely this morning; but to me the cheer is somber and the jests are ghastly. . . . With great care, and constant watchfulness, we proceed, making about four miles this afternoon, and camp in a cave.**

Sumner Account of 13 August   It was not long before we could plainly foresee trouble, as the formation was rising and we knew that the next leaf or

---

*The rapid Sumner refers to is probably Unkar, located 11 miles below the mouth of the Little Colorado River. In his longer account, also dated 13 August, Sumner probably refers to Hance Rapid, located just over 15 miles below the Little Colorado.

**The cave Powell refers to is uncertain. His location would place it very near the Hopi Salt Mines, which are actually caves, about 2½ miles below the Little Colorado.

chapter would be granite or gneiss. We were not long held in suspense. Sure enough, as we rounded a curve—biff! up came the old Archean granite with its usual trimmings, a very bad rapid. And if any men ever did penance for their sins, we did a-plenty for the next two hundred miles. To add to our troubles, there was a nearly continuous rain and a great rise in the river that created such a current and turmoil that it tried our strength to the limit. We were weakened by hardships and ceaseless toil for twenty out of twenty-four hours of the day. Starvation stared us in the face. I felt like Job: it would be a good scheme to curse God and die, but, like him, I did not do it. Frequently something laughable would turn up to drive away the blue devils. . . .

About fifteen miles below the Little Colorado the first bad rapid occurs, in what I wanted to name Coronado Canyon. Major Powell told me it should bear my name if he got through and ever had the opportunity to place it on the Government map. Well, he got through all right, but he forgot his vows and named it Grand Canyon. The name is appropriate enough, but as there are a dozen "Grand Canyons" in the southwestern part of the United States, the name is liable to mislead the stranger.*

Landing at the head of the first great rapid in the granite, we soon saw that it would not do to try to run it. So we let down with lines. The work was very hard and trying, as the water was icy cold and full of rocks. Seeing there was no help for it, all hands worked manfully and we got through it a little before night. Then we proceeded a short distance and ran into another bird of the same foul blood. We camped at the head of it and made the best of it for the night.

Major Powell spent the following day geologizing, as he was a nuisance in the work of portaging. His imperious orders were not appreciated. We had troubles enough with him. There was another spat between the Major and Howland at this point. Tackling the next rapid as soon as Hawkins, the cook, had called coffee and sour dough and we disposed of it, into the rapid we went, and ran it all right. Two oars were broken, and the side of the "Emma Dean" was cracked. We repaired this damage, and hunted another rapid. That did not take us long, for they are plentiful and easily found in the Grand Canyon. . . .

Inner Gorge of the Grand Canyon

Bradley, 14 August   Well, this is emphatically the wildest day of the trip so far. We let down the first rapid this morning, run the one at its foot—a very

---

*If Sumner is accurate, Powell later decided against naming the canyon after Sumner. Known earlier as Big Canyon, the name "Grand Canyon" first appeared on a railroad map in 1868. Powell's reports, however, gave final permanence to the name Grand Canyon.

heavy one—and then a succession of very rough ones until near noon when we came to the worst one we had seen on the river and the walls being vertical or rather coming to the water on both sides we had to run it and all being ready, away we went each boat following close to the one next before. The little boat being too small for such a frightful sea, filled soon after starting and swung around head up river almost unmanageable but on she went and by the good cool sense of those on board she was kept right side up through the whole of it (more than half a mile). My boat came next and the first wave dashed partly over us with fearful force striking one oar from the hand of Major's brother but did not fill the boat. She rose to battle with the next one and by good luck we kept her head to the waves and rode them all taking less water than we sometimes do on much smaller rapids. Bill R. [Hawkins] came next and quite as lucky as we were he escaped with a good shaking up and slight ducking. The waves were frightful beyond anything we have yet met and it seemed for a time that our chance to save the boats was very slim but we are a lusty set and our good luck did not go back on us then. This P.M. we have kept up the game, until tonight we find ourselves six miles from where we started and in about the middle of a tremendous rapid fully half a mile long.* We have lowered the boats to this point by clinging to the side of the granite cliff and working them along as best we could. It injures them very much and if I could have my say we should run it for the risk is no greater and we can run it in a few moments while this will take us nearly another half day. We have but poor accommodations for sleeping tonight. No two except Major and Jack can find space wide enough to make a double bed and if they don't lie still we shall "hear something drop" and find one of them in the river before morning. I sleep in a wide seam of the rocks where I can't roll out. Andy has his bed just above the water on a fragment at the water's edge scarce wide enough to hold him. The rest are tucked around like eve-swallows wherever the cliff offers sufficient space to stretch themselves with any degree of comfort or safety.

Powell, 14 August   Made no portage from camp then run 2 miles to bad falls in narrow chute, no talus, no foothold of any kind, must run it or abandon the enterprise! Good luck! Little boat fills with water twice. Chute ½ mile long. Fall 30 ft. probably, huge waves. Then run of 2 or 3 rapids, then a long portage. Dinner in a cave. Camp at night on rocks in middle of long portage on right bank.

---

*On this day the expedition ran Sockdolager Rapid, Mile 78.5, a very difficult rapid. They spent the night huddled on the right bank of Grapevine Rapid, trying to sleep in a tiny boulder field almost in the river.

Sumner, 14 August   Made a portage of half the rapid and ran the rest to get into a half dozen more bad ones in . . . when we came to a fearful looking . . . a long rapid with a fall of 30 ft. and no foothold to make a portage. Climbed up the side of the canon wall as far as we could to get a partial view of the thing. Returned to the boat. Fastened down the hatches of the cabins and pulled out into the waves. The two large boats went through without getting more than half full of water. But the small boat filled in the first waves and drifted ¾ of a mile through a perfect hell of waves, but came out all right. Bailed out our boats, laughed over the scrape and pulled out again in some more, one of which filled *"Kitty's Sister."* At 2 o'clock came to a rapid that cannot be run by any boat, half a mile long, 75 yds. wide, fall of 50 ft. and full of rocks. Landed on the north side and worked hard till sunset to get half way down. Ate our supper of some bread and coffee and went to sleep on the bare, rough granite rock. Made 7 miles; 12 rapids, all bad. River very narrow. Granite 1000 ft. high.

Powell Account of 14 August   At daybreak we walk down the bank of the river, on a little sandy beach, to take a view of a new feature in the cañon. Heretofore, hard rocks have given us bad river; soft rocks, smooth water; and a series of rocks harder than any we have experienced sets in. The river enters the granite. . . .

Sumner Account of 14 August   We finally encountered a stretch of water and canyon that made my hair curl. I don't know how it affected the other boys. The walls were close on both sides, with a fall of probably thirty feet in six hundred yards, a white foam as far down as we could see, with a line of waves in the middle, fifteen feet high. And as the canyon curved to the left and shut out the view below, we were puzzled for awhile. I had charge of the leading boat, the "Emma Dean," from the start at Green River. Owing to the petty quarrels between Major Powell and the Howland brothers and Dunn, I had undertaken much of the running part of the expedition. I decided to run it, though there was a queer feeling in my craw, as I could see plainly enough a certain swamping for all the boats. But what was around the curve below out of our sight?

A fall below meant certain destruction to all. I stated the case and asked, "Who follows?" I can still hear the ringing voices of Hawkins and Hall: "Pull out! We'll follow you to tidewater or hell!" Carefully fastening the hatches and directing the other boats to keep a hundred yards apart, I started out. The "Emma Dean" had not made a hundred yards before an especially heavy wave struck her and drove her completely under water. Though it did not capsize her or knock any one out, the wave rendered her completely unmanageable. Dunn and I laid out all our surplus strength to keep her off the rocks, while Major Powell worked like a Trojan to bail her out a little. . . .

The other boats had disappeared around a curve, and had encountered we knew not what. Giving the "Emma Dean" all the speed we possibly could, we passed through the rapid, ducked at every wave, but as we struck them just right we did not fill. After half a mile of such work we caught up with the other boats, landed in a quiet cove. They greeted us with a ringing cheer as we rounded in. We compared notes, Hall in a rollicking way saying he felt sorry for us as they passed by, and regretted that he hadn't a picture of us.

Howland was very grave and silent. I have often asked myself this question: did he have a premonition of his death soon to come? I have been in a cavalry charge, charged the batteries, and stood by the guns to repel a charge. But never before did my sand run so low. In fact, it all ran out, but as I had to have some more grit, I borrowed it from the other boys and got along all right after that.

After running probably another mile we encountered another rapid, or rather a fall—the only direct fall we had encountered on the river. It was a direct straight fall, reaching entirely across the river, with a drop of about eight feet. As we could see there was no great danger below, I determined to run it, a decision that all agreed to. So out we pulled and made for it full speed, and jumped it like jumping a hurdle with a bucking horse—and didn't ship enough water to moisten a postage stamp. The fall gave off a peculiar sound at intervals of about ten seconds that sounded precisely like a minute gun at sea. Hence it was called Minute Gun Falls.* And so it went—rapids, daily duckings, and "heap hungry" all the time. Through hard usage all the boats were getting short on oars. We therefore looked anxiously for a drift log to make them from. The river is so terrific it seems to smash everything into pieces, leaving nothing large enough to make an oar.

Bright Angel Creek

Bradley, 15 August   This morning (Sunday) we lowered the little boat with great labor and it nearly stove her so we volunteered to run my boat through and putting in the rations away we went. . . . We went like the wind and as luck would have it took in but little water, only one sea which was not quite thick enough to get on board but swept our stern with terrible force. Caught by the whirlpools below we whirled round and round until out of them and then rowed into the eddy and laid on our oars to have the fun of seeing Bill R. run it which he did after a while, but not getting out quite far enough from shore his boat nearly filled and he broke one oar. We have already (12 M.) made 4 miles and after we let down past the rapid at which we now lie we may made a good

---

*Probably Hance Rapids.

run yet. We don't expect it, however, for the granite raises Cain with the river. Have run only 3¼ miles this P.M. for Howland had the misfortune to lose his notes and map of the river from Little Colorado down to this point so we have camped at the first landing, which happens to be an excellent camping ground shaded by a fine weeping-willow which throws a greatful shadow over a wide circle. There is also a fine creek or river as they would call it in this country coming in from the north, clear as crystal and quite swift and wide. Bright Angel Creek. There are fish in it but Howland has tried in vain to catch them so they can't be trout. Think they are only whitefish. The boys have just come in from a walk up the creek and report good oar-timber a few miles up the creek which has drifted down so we shall probably stay a day or two and make oars....

Powell, 15 August   Finish portage, and make a short one where Billy runs his boat to opposite shore failing to reach us. After dinner short run and portage and camp early, at mouth of Silver Creek. [later named Bright Angel Creek] I have a long walk up creek; find oar timber. Camp No. 32.

Sumner, 15 August   Finished the portage and ran 12 more bad rapids and made 2 portages in 8 miles travel. Camped about 4 miles at the mouth of a clear trout stream coming in from the north. There is a large willow growing on a sand bar a few rods above the creek that affords a splendid camp. Stretched our weary bodies on the sand under the willow and rested the remainder of the day.

Powell Account of 15 August   This morning we find we can let down for three or four hundred yards, and it is managed in this way: We pass along the wall, by climbing from projecting point to point, sometimes near the water's edge, at other places fifty or sixty feet above, and hold the boat with a line, while two men remain aboard, and prevent her from being dashed against the rocks, and keep the line from getting caught on the wall. In two hours we have brought them all down, as far as it is possible, in this way. A few yards below, the river strikes with great violence against a projecting rock, and our boats are pulled up in a little bay above. We must now manage to pull out of this, and clear the point below. The little boat is held by the bow obliquely up the stream. We jump in, and pull out only a few strokes, and sweep clear of the dangerous rock. The other boats follow in the same manner, and the rapid is passed.

It is not easy to describe the labor of such navigation. We must prevent the waves from dashing the boats against the cliffs. Sometimes, where the river is swift, we must put a bight of rope about a rock, to prevent her being snatched from us by a wave; but where the plunge is too great, or the chute too swift, we must let her leap, and catch her below, or the undertow will drag her under the falling water, and she sinks. Where we wish to run her out a little way from shore, through a channel between rocks, we first throw in little sticks of driftwood, and watch their course, to see where we must steer, so that she will pass the channel in safety. And so we hold, and let go, and pull, and lift, and ward, among rocks, around rocks, and over rocks.

And now we go on through this solemn, mysterious way. The river is very deep, the cañon very narrow, and still obstructed, so that there is no steady flow of the stream; but the waters wheel, and roll, and boil, and we are scarcely able to determine where we can go. Now, the boat is carried to the right, perhaps close to the wall; again, she is shot into the stream, and perhaps is dragged over to the other side, where, caught in a whirlpool, she spins about. We can neither land nor run as we please. The boats are entirely unmanageable; no order in their running can be preserved; now one, now another, is ahead, each crew laboring for its own preservation. In such a place we come to another rapid. Two of the boats run it perforce. One succeeds in landing, but there is no foothold by which to make a portage, and she is pushed out again into the stream. The next minute a great reflex wave fills the open compartment; she is water-logged, and drifts unmanageable. Breaker after breaker rolls over her, and one capsizes her. The men are thrown out; but they cling to the boat, and she drifts down some distance, alongside of us, and we are able to catch her. She is soon bailed out, and the men are aboard once more; but the oars are lost, so a pair from the "Emma Dean" is spared. Then for two miles we find smooth water. . . .

Early in the afternoon, we discover a stream, entering from the north, a clear, beautiful creek, coming down through a gorgeous red cañon. We land, and camp on a sand beach, above its mouth, under a great, overspreading tree, with willow-shaped leaves.

Bradley, 16 August Have been at work hard getting out oars for the stick we found was large and we had but poor tools to work with. Have got out three but mine is left until last and is not finished. They have come to think that my boat should carry all the rations, go into all dangerous places first and get along with least. So be it. The trip is nearly ended and when it is up perhaps I shall be just as well off but one can't help minding an imposition even in a wilderness so far from civilization. There is another old Moqui ruin where we are camped tonight. Have found the same little fragments of broken crockery as we did before. Have saved a few little specimens. An unpleasant little accident occurred today which we shall feel keenly all the rest of the trip. The cook, having spread all the rations to dry, was engaged making oars when the boat swung around by the eddy tide; the rope caught the box of soda and drew it all into the river so we must eat "un-leavened bread" all the rest of the trip. Major has called the stream coming in at this point "Silver Creek." [Bright Angel Creek]

Powell, 16 August   Make oars and take obs. Same camp.

Sumner, 16 August   In camp today and repair and rest. Made some oars from a pine log we found half mile up the creek. The Professor named the stream "Silver Creek." Very hot all day.

Powell Account of 16 August   We must dry out rations again today, and make oars.

The Colorado is never a clear stream, but for the past three or four days it has been raining much of the time, and the floods, which are poured over the walls, have brought down great quantities of mud, making it exceedingly turbid now. The little affluent, which we have discovered here, is a clear, beautiful creek, or river, as it would be termed in this western country, where streams are not abundant. We have named one stream, away above, in honor of the great chief of the "Bad Angels," and, as this is in beautiful contrast to that, we conclude to name it "Bright Angel."*

Early in the morning, the whole party starts up to explore the Bright Angel River, with the special purpose of seeking timber, from which to make oars. A couple of miles above, we find a large pine log, which has been floated down from the plateau, probably from an altitude of more than six thousand feet, but not many-miles back. On its way, it must have passed over many cataracts and falls, for it bears scars in evidence of the rough usage which it has received. The men roll it on skids, and the work of sawing oars is commenced. . . .

Late in the afternoon I return, and go up a little gulch, just above this creek, about two hundred yards from camp, and discover the ruins of two or three old houses, which are originally of stone, laid in mortar. Only the foundations are left, but irregular blocks, of which the houses were constructed, lie scattered about. In one room I find an old mealing stone, deeply worn, as if it had been much used. A great deal of pottery is strewn around, and old trails, which in some places are deeply worn into the rocks, are seen.

It is ever a source of wonder to us why these ancient people sought such inaccessible places for their homes. . . .

----

*Powell first named it "Silver Creek," as indicated in the Bradley and Sumner entries. After the expedition, in December 1869, Powell renamed it "Bright Angel Creek," probably to stand in dramatic contrast to the muddy tributary they named "Dirty Devil."

Sumner Account of 16 August   By great caution and good luck we reached Bright Angel Creek, a small clear stream coming out of the Kanab Plateau region, where we turned in and camped one and a half days. We found here some red spruce logs out of which oars were made by ripping them out with a common hand saw, considerable of a task. The creek is about ten feet wide in low water and a foot deep, clear enough but in August warm as dishwater. We saw no indication that white men had ever visited the valley of the Bright Angel before. There were plenty of old Indian camps, milling stones, and wikiups. Here was lost the last remnant of our soda. Hawkins put it on the bank in a gold pan. The bank caved in and away it went, pan and all. After that we had rotten flour mixed with Colorado River water, not a very palatable mixture. But after eating the "sinkers" we knew we had dined!

After making oars and inspecting everything, we pulled out again for more of the Great Unknown. There was not much talk indulged in by the grim squad of half-starved men with faces wearing that peculiar stern look always noticed on the faces of men forming for a charge in battle. It is not handsome by any means, but all the same it has a fascination about it that always attracts attention.

This part of the canyon is probably the worst hole in America, if not in the world. The gloomy black rocks of the Archean formation drive all the spirit out of a man. And the excessive drenching and hard work drive all the strength out of him and leave him in a bad fix indeed. We had to move on or starve. As starving was not on the program, we took our medicine—but I am afraid we did not look pleasant.

Bradley, 17 August   We have run a succession of rapids and made three portages today. One portage lasted us nearly all the P.M., and as soon as we had finished it we came upon another very bad one and knowing we could not pass it tonight we have not tackled it at all but some of the boys have gone out hunting as we began to see signs of sheep again. The granite peaks begin to get gradually lower but they are very irregular for we sometimes see them only about 300 ft. and immediately come to another almost or quite 1000 ft. The old red sand-stone rests on the granite and then the marble above so that a little way back from the river the hills rise to from 4000 to 5000 feet and are covered with pines. . . .

Powell, 17 August   Make run of 10¼ miles today, with 2 bad portages. Camp at night just above one. Walk up creek 3 miles. Grand scenery. Old Indian camps. Through this Cañon the limestone overlies the granite and runs down near the river in sharp wall-like points. To the summit of this the highest rocks that can be seen at any point. I estimate the height at 4000 ft. may be only 3500. Camp No. 33.

Sumner, 17 August   Pulled out at 8 o'clock and ran a continuous rapid for 3 miles; then came to a portage; while letting the *"Maid"* down with a line she struck a rock and loosened her head block badly. Repaired damages and pulled out again into more rapids. Made 2 heavy portages and ran 12 bad rapids in traveling 9¾ miles. Camped on south side at the head of another portage. Supper of unleavened bread.

Powell Account of 17 August   Our rations are still spoiling; the bacon is so badly injured that we are compelled to throw it away. By an accident, this morning, the saleratus is lost overboard. We have now only musty flour sufficient for ten days, a few dried apples, but plenty of coffee. We must make all haste possible. If we meet with difficulties, as we have done in the cañon above, we may be compelled to give up the expedition, and try to reach the Mormon settlements to the north. Our hopes are that the worst places are passed, but our barometers are all so much injured as to be useless, so we have lost our reckoning in altitude, and know not how much descent the river has yet to make.

The stream is still wild and rapid, and rolls through a narrow channel. We make but slow progress, often landing against a wall, and climbing around some point, where we can see the river below. Although very anxious to advance, we are determined to run with great caution, lest, by another accident, we lose all our supplies. How precious that little flour has become! We divide it among the boats, and carefully store it away so that it can be lost only by the loss of the boat itself.

. . . We make ten miles and a half, and camp among the rocks, on the right. We have had rain, from time to time, all day, and have been thoroughly drenched and chilled; but between showers the sun shines with great power, and the mercury in our thermometers stands at 115°, so that we have rapid changes from great extremes, which are very disagreeable. It is especially cold in the rain tonight. The little canvas we have is rotten and useless; the rubber ponchos, with which we started from Green River City, have all been lost; more than half the party is without hats, and not one of us has an entire suit of clothes, and we have not a blanket apiece. So we gather driftwood, and build a fire; but after supper the rain, coming down in torrents, extinguishes it, and we sit up all night, on the rocks, shivering, and are more exhausted by the night's discomfort than by the day's toil.

Bradley, 18 August   Hard work and little distance seems to be the characteristic of this cañon. Have worked very hard today and have advanced but four miles. Rapids very numerous and very large. A great many lateral cañons come in almost as large as the one in which the river runs and they sweep down immense quantities of huge rocks which at places literally dam up the river, making the worst kind of a rapid because you can see rocks rising all over them with no channel in which to run them. If we could we would run more of them because our rations are not sufficient to anything more than just to sustain life. Coffee and *heavy* bread cannot be called *light rations* but one feels quite light about the stomache after living on it a while. We have just lowered our boats over a very treacherous rapid and camped at its foot, for just below us is another all ready to start on in the morning with a fine chance for a man to see what strength he has gained by a night's rest. This P.M. we have had a terrible thunder-shower. We had to fasten our boats to the rocks and seek shelter from the wind behind bowlders. The rain poared down in torrents and the thunder-peals echoed through the cañon from crag to crag making wild music for the lightning to dance to. After a shower it is grand to see the cascades leap from the cliffs and turn to vapor before they reach the rocks below. There are thousands of them of all sizes, pure and white as molten silver. The water of the river is now very muddy from the continual showers which we have. It is not fit to drink but fortunately we find better among the rocks most of the time. The river at this point runs 25° North of West.

Powell, 18 August   Bad rapids, portages and rain. Camped on right bank among the rocks. Wagon sheet makes but poor cover.

Sumner, 18 August   Made 3 portages in 4 miles; camped on the north side on account of a terrible storm. Rained all night.

Powell Account of 18 August   The day is employed in making portages, and we advance but two miles on our journey. Still it rains.

While the men are at work making portages, I climb up the granite to its summit, and go away back over the rust-colored sandstones and greenish-yellow shales, to the foot of the marble wall. I climb so high that the men and boats are lost in the black depths below, and the dashing river is a rippling brook; and still there is more canon above than below. All about me are interesting geological records. The book is open, and I can read as I run. All about me are grand views, for the clouds are playing again in the gorges. But somehow I think of the nine day's rations, and the bad river, and the lesson of the rocks, and the glory of the scene is but half seen.

I push on to an angle, where I hope to get a view of the country beyond, to see, if possible, what the prospect may be of our soon running through this plateau, or, at least, of meeting with some geological change that will let us out of the granite; but, arriving at the point, I can see below only a labyrinth of deep gorges.

Inner Gorge of the Grand Canyon

Bradley, 19 August   The rapid we started with this morning gave us to understand the character of the day's run. It was a wild one. The boats labored hard but came out all right. The waves were frightful and had any of the boats shipped a sea it would have been her last for there was no still water below. We ran a wild race for about two miles, first pulling right—then left, now to avoid the waves and now to escape the bowlders, sometimes half full of water and as soon as a little could be thrown out it was replaced by double the quantity. Our heavy boat run past the lead boat and we dashed on alone, whirling and rushing like the wind—looking for a place to land. At length we succeeded in checking her and landed in an eddy where we bailed the boat and waited for the others to come up. Coming to one we could not run we were forced to make a short portage and lower with ropes for ¼ of a mile which took us until after 12 o'clock. We took dinner on the side of a cliff where the cook could scarcely find a place large enough to hold his fire, for if there happens to be sufficient wood to cook with we don't dare look further for we should be quite likely to come to another rapid where we should not be able to find wood. It commenced raining last night and has hardly abated until 4 o'clock this P.M. Doubt if we don't have more before morning. All our clothing and bedding is wet and I expect a miserable night of it. Hardly had we started after dinner before we came to a furious rapid which seemed to have but few rocks and we resolve to run it. The little boat took the lead but was not equal to the task for she swamped at once and we rushed on to her assistance hardly heeding the danger we ourselves were in. The whirlpools below caught us and our furious speed threw us against the rocks with terrible force. Fortunately we struck with the cut-water which is the strongest part of our boat. We cleared the shore and reached the little boat which by this time was nearly sunk and the crew were all in the water holding her up. We took them in and towed them into an eddy below where we built a fire and have been lying ever since drying the instruments, etc. Fortunately nothing was lost but a pair of oars. Have run only 5¾ miles.

Powell, 19 August   Run bad rapid, and two more below. Make portage. Dinner in rain among the rocks. After dinner little boat swamps. Bradley comes up with boat in good time. Camp on left bank, dig out a sleeping place, dry out by fire.

Sumner, 19 August   Made 3 heavy portages and ran 3 very dangerous rapids; in one the small boat was swamped again. Made 5¾ miles. Camped on the south side. Rain all day and most of the night.

Powell Account of 19 August   Rain again this morning. Still we are in our granite prison, and the time is occupied until noon in making a long, bad portage....

Bradley, 20 August   We did not have rain last night nor have we had any today though last night our bedding was so wet that before morning we got very cold and uncomfortable. The sun came up clear this A.M., reached us about 8½ o'clock and as all was wet we concluded it was best to stay where we were and dry out. So we stayed until noon, had dinner, and the loaded up our boats having dried everything nicely. We have had a good little run this P.M. of 8¼ miles. Made one portage and lowered the boats with ropes twice. Rapids continue heavy but this P.M. seem a little farther apart. We must be getting near to where the Mormons run the river for they have run it 65 miles above Callville and one would think we had run rapids enough already to be allowed a respite soon.*

Powell, 20 August   Remained in camp until noon. Made 2 portages in afternoon. Came at night to the "old red." Found remains of old Moquis village on bank, stone houses and pottery....

Sumner, 20 August   Laid over till noon to dry out what little we had left. Pulled out at noon and ran one dangerous rapid to begin with, then 3 portages in 8¼ miles. Camped on the north side near a lot of Moqui ruins. Course of river 15 miles 25° north of west.

Powell Account of 20 August   The characteristics of the cañon change this morning. The river is broader, the walls more sloping, and composed of black slates, that stand on edge. These nearly vertical slates are washed out in places—that is, the softer beds are washed out between the harder, which are left standing. In this way, curious little alcoves are formed, in which are quiet bays of water, but on a much smaller scale than the great bays and buttresses of Marble Cañon.

---

*Bradley's guess as to the distance to Callville was very inaccurate. Actually, he and the Powell party were probably 200 miles upstream from Callville when this was written. In 1867, a small Mormon party led by Jacob Hamblin boated from Pearce's Ferry to Callville, a distance of about 65 miles, all of which is now covered by Lake Mead.

The river is still rapid, and we stop to let down with lines several times, but make greater progress as we run ten miles. We camp on the right bank. Here, on a terrace of trap, we discover another group of ruins. There was evidently quite a village on this rock. Again we find mealing stones, and much broken pottery, and up in a little natural shelf in the rock, back of the ruins, we find a globular basket, that would hold perhaps a third of a bushel. It is badly broken, and, as I attempt to take it up, it falls to pieces. There are many beautiful flint chips, as if this had been the home of an old arrow maker.

Bradley, 21 August   Have run 21 miles today and it stands first for dashing wildness of any day we have seen or *will see* if I guess rightly, for we have been all day among the rapids furious and long but we have managed to run all but one of them which was I think the roughest-looking one we have met. The granite rose up in huge slabs running far out into the river and the fall was furious. The granite disappeared this P.M. but to my surprise we had no fall or even bad rapid where the sand-stone commenced. I thought that running out of hard rock into sandstone would make a fall where the two met but it made nothing of the sort. I feel more unwell tonight than I have felt on the trip. I have been wet so much lately that I am ripe for any disease and our scanty food has reduced me to poor condition but I am still in good spirits and am threatening all sorts of revenge when I get to decent food once more.

Powell, 21 August   Good run today. Many bad rapids, let down one near camp in morning. Made about 20 miles. The rocks near the river after leaving the granite were shelving and vertical then a sloping terrace. Then marble walls with terraces. Camp on left bank.

Sumner, 21 August   Made a portage within half a mile of camp, then ran 6 bad rapids in 7 miles when we came to a perfect hell—a rapid with a fall of 30 ft in 300 yds.* Made a portage on the south side, then pulled out again and ran 14 miles, passing 20 rapids, but ran them all without trouble. Ran the granite up and down again. Made 22 miles. Camped on the south side of a sand bar; a few willows the first since leaving Silver Creek and second since Flax River. Near camp average width of river 60 yds.; height of walls 4000 ft. but getting less. Course of river northwest.

---

*This could possibly be Deubendorff Rapid, which at low water is very difficult.

Powell Account of 21 August   We start early this morning, cheered by the prospect of a fine day, and encouraged, also, by the good run made yesterday. A quarter of a mile below camp the river turns abruptly to the left, and between camp and that point is very swift, running down in a long, broken chute, and piling up against the foot of the cliff, where it turns to the left. We try to pull across, so as to go down on the other side, but the waters are swift, and it seems impossible for us to escape the rock below; but, in pulling across, the bow of the boat is turned to the farther shore, so that we are swept broadside down, and are prevented, by the rebounding waters, from striking against the wall. There we toss about for a few seconds in these billows, and are carried past the danger. Below, the river turns again to the right, the canon is very narrow, and we see in advance but a short distance. The water, too, is very swift, and there is no landing place. From around this curve there comes a mad roar, and down we are carried, with a dizzying velocity, to the head of another rapid. On either side, high over our heads, there are overhanging granite walls, and the sharp bends cut off our view, so that a few minutes will carry us into unknown waters. Away we go, on one long, winding chute. I stand on deck, supporting myself with a strap, fastened on either side to the gunwale, and the boat glides rapidly, where the water is smooth, or striking a wave, she leaps and bounds like a thing of life, and we have a wild, exhilarating ride for ten miles, which we make in less than an hour. The excitement is so great that we forget the danger, until we hear the roar of a great fall below; then we back on our oars, and are carried slowly toward its head, and succeed in landing just above, and find that we have to make another portage. At this we are engaged until some time after dinner.

Just here we run out of the granite!

Ten miles in less than half a day, and limestone walls below. Good cheer returns; we forget the storms, and the gloom, and cloud-covered cañons, and the black granite, and the raging river, and push our boats from the shore in great glee. . . .

Bradley, 22 August   It rained some last night and as we had no tent up I took my overcoat and went into the cliff where I found good quarters for the rest of the night. Has been raining considerably today and we have pitched the tent which may perhaps *prevent rain tonight*. We have found about five miles of granite today for the river has been running within five degrees of east much of the time. What it means I don't know, but if it keeps on in this way we shall be back where we started from, which would make us feel very much as I imagine the old hog felt when he moved the hollow log so that both ends came on the outside of the fence. Fortunately we can see below our present camp where it turns again to the west and south. We have made 11¼ miles today. . . .

Powell, 22 August   Today made a long detour to N.E. Ran back again into the granite. Camp on right bank early, on account of rain, at the head of long portage.

Sumner, 22 August   Made 11¼ miles—nearly all rapids, one heavy portage. Course of river northeast. Camped on north side on some lava. Ran the granite up and down again today. Rain all day.

Powell Account of 22 August   We come to rapids again, this morning, and are occupied several hours in passing them, letting the boats down, from rock to rock, with lines, for nearly half a mile, and then have to make a long portage. While the men are engaged in this, I climb the wall on the northeast, to a height of about two thousand five hundred feet, where I can obtain a good view of a long stretch of cañon below. . . .

After my return to the boats we run another mile, and camp for the night.

We have made but little over seven miles today, and a part of our flour has been soaked in the river again.

Deer Creek Falls

Bradley, 23 August   Have had another hard day of it. Made only two miles this A.M., but this P.M. we got out of the granite rock and have made 10¼ miles making 12¼ miles for the day, which is somewhat encouraging seeing that the river has now got back to its proper direction again. Just below our camp tonight is another rapid around which they talk of making another portage. Hope they will feel better about it in the morning and run it for it is an easy and safe one.

Powell, 23 August   After portage run short distance to dinner camp. In afternoon found beautiful fall from a curiously worn hole in lateral canon 100 ft. high, when we ran into the marble. Wall almost vertical. Canon still grand. Very bad portage on right bank this afternoon. Camp on left.

Sumner, 23 August   Made 3 portages and run 20 bad rapids in 12¼ miles. Passed 2 cold streams coming in from the north, one of them pouring off a cliff 200 ft. high. Camped on the south side between perpendicular walls 2000 ft. high, all marble.

Powell Account of 23 August   Our way today is again through marble walls. Now and then we pass, for a short distance, through patches of granite, like hills thrust up into the limestone. At one of these places we have to make another portage, and taking advantage of the delay, I go up a little stream, to the north, wading it all the way, sometimes having to plunge into my neck; in other places being compelled to swim across little basins that have been excavated at the foot of the falls. Along its course are many cascades and springs gushing out from the rocks on either side. Sometimes a cottonwood tree grows over the water. I come to one beautiful fall, of more than a hundred and fifty feet, and climb around it on the right, on the broken rocks. Still going up, I find the canon narrowing very much, being but fifteen or twenty feet wide; yet the walls rise on either side many hundreds of feet, perhaps thousands; I can hardly tell.

In some places the stream has not excavated its channel down vertically through the rocks, but has cut obliquely, so that one wall overhangs the other. In other places it is cut vertically above and obliquely below, or obliquely above and vertically below, so that it is impossible to see out overhead. But I can go no farther. The time which I estimated it would take to make the portage has almost expired, and I start back on a round trot, wading in the creek where I must, and plunging through basins, and find the men waiting for me, and away we go on the river.

Just after dinner we pass a stream on the right, which leaps into the Colorado by a direct fall of more than a hundred feet, forming a beautiful cascade. There is a bed of very hard rock above, thirty or forty feet in thickness, and much softer beds below. The hard beds above project many yards beyond the softer, which are washed out, forming a deep cave behind the fall, and the stream pours through a narrow crevice above into a deep pool below.* Around on the rocks, in the cave-like chamber, are set beautiful ferns, with delicate fronds and enameled stalks. The little frondlets have their points turned down, to form spore cases. It has very much the appearance of the Maiden's Hair fern, but is much larger. This delicate foliage covers the rocks all about the fountain, and gives the chamber great beauty. But we have little time to spend in admiration, so on we go. . . .

We camp tonight in a marble cave, and find, on looking at our reckoning, we have run twenty-two miles.

---

*The waterfall he describes is almost certainly the spectacular Deer Creek Falls, which is quite visible from the river.

Bradley, 24 August   Have run 22¾ miles today after making a bad portage this morning and letting down with ropes this noon. This A.M. we run only one hour and made over seven miles. Our boats are getting so very leaky that we have to calk them very often. We are still running a succession of rapids but this P.M. have run all we came to expect the one at our present camp, which we shall run in the morning. Did not run it tonight for just above it is a singular recess or alcove in the rock about 100 ft. long and 50 ft. wide forming a fine shelter and was fast commencing to rain when we arrived so Major camped here where all can find shelter without pitching tents. We are now in the marble rock again so tonight it will not be strange if we "dream we dwelt in marble halls." We are much surprised to find the distance to Grand Wash lengthened out so much beyond the Mormon estimate for we have now run over 120 miles and they estimate it at from 70 to 80 miles. The reason probably is that ours is distance by river while theirs is the actual distance by land for the river has run very crooked since we passed the Little Colorado. We cannot now be very far from it unless the river turns back again which it shows no sign of doing. As we advance the river widens and the tide slackens.

Powell, 24 August   Good run today of 22 miles. Many rapids. High water mark coming down. River widening. Camp under rock.

Sumner, 24 August   Made a portage on the start. Ran a few miles to get another—made it. Ate dinner of unleavened bread and pulled out again and ran 15 miles through a narrow gorge, between walls 1500 ft. high—all marble. Passed 12 rapids, 4 bad ones, but ran them all, as they were clear of rocks. Made 22¼ miles and camped on the south side under a ledge of rocks on a bed of lime and magnesia.

Powell Account of 24 August   The cañon is wider today. The walls rise to vertical height of nearly three thousand feet. In many places the river runs under a cliff, in great curves, forming amphitheaters, half-dome shaped.

Though the river is rapid, we meet with no serious obstructions, and run twenty miles. It is curious how anxious we are to make up our reckoning every time we stop, now that our diet is confined to plenty of coffee, very little spoiled flour, and very few dried apples. It has come to be a race for a dinner. Still, we make such fine progress, all hands are in good cheer, but not a moment of daylight is lost.

Vulcan's Anvil and Lava Falls

Bradley, 25 August   Have run 35 miles today all the way rapid. About 10 o'clock A.M. came to volcanic lava which had been poared out since the river had reached its present bed. It had at some time filled up the channel as high as 1500 ft., but was worn down so as only to leave a cataract, yet it was a bad one and we had to slide our boats out around it. The country begins to look a little more open and the river still improves. Came very near having an unpleasant accident today for as we were letting one of the heavy boats down the iron strap on the bow that holds the rope gave way. Fortunately there were four of us in the water holding and guiding the boat and we succeeded in getting a line to the ringbolt in the stern and turning her without accident. We commenced our last sack of flour tonight.

Powell, 25 August   Good run in forenoon, 14 miles. Canon still with marble walls. Sds. [sandstone] in distance now and then. Come to lava monument in middle of river [Vulcan's Anvil], then to lava falls. These falls must have been very great at one time. Lava comes down to high water mark—may be lower—and 1500 ft. high on either side. The canon was filled. Vast piles of gravel below point where lava crossed 100 ft. high. Limestone and sds. in lava. The falls now are among boulders some distance below the ancient fall. . . . 35 miles today. Camp 41.

Sumner, 25 August   Ran a bad rapid to begin our day's work, then a dozen more in 14½ miles, when we came to a fall, or the nearest approach to it of any on the river; about 5 miles above the falls the canon has been completely filled up with lava when it was as deep as it is now, and has all been cut out the second time except at the falls, where there is a large lot of basalt still in the river, making a fall of about 15 ft. in 40 yds. On the south side of the river, ¼ mile below the falls, there are a number of springs that flow more water combined than Flax River does, but they are so strongly impregnated with lime as to scald the mouth when drank. Made a portage on the south side, had dinner and pulled out again and ran a dozen more rapids, some bad ones. . . .

Powell Account of 25 August   We make twelve miles this morning, when we come to monuments of lava, standing in the river; low rocks, mostly, but some of them shafts more than a hundred feet high. Going on down, three or four miles, we find them increasing in number. Great quantities of cooler lava and many cinder-cones are seen on either side; and then we come to an abrupt cataract. Just over the fall, on the right wall, a cinder-cone, or extinct volcano, with a well-defined crater, stands on the very brink of the cañon. This, doubtless, is the one we saw two or three days ago. From this volcano vast floods of lava have been poured down into the river, and a stream of the molten rock has run up the cañon, three or four miles, and down, we know not how far. Just where it poured over the cañon wall is the fall. The whole north side, as far as we can see, is lined with the black basalt, and high up on the opposite wall are patches of the same material, resting on the benches, and filling old alcoves and caves, giving to the wall a spotted appearance.*

The rocks are broken in two, along a line which here crosses the river, and the beds, which we have seen coming down the cañon for the last thirty miles, have dropped 800 feet, on the lower side of the line, forming what geologists call a fault. The volcanic cone stands directly over the fissure thus formed. On the side of the river opposite, mammoth springs burst out of this crevice, one or two hundred feet above the river, pouring in a stream quite equal in volume to the Colorado Chiquito.

This stream seems to be loaded with carbonate of lime, and the water, evaporating, leaves an incrustation on the rocks; and this process has been continued for a long time, for extensive deposits are noticed, in which are basins, with bubbling springs. The water is salty.

We have to make a portage here, which is completed in about three hours, and on we go.

We have no difficulty as we float along, and I am able to observe the wonderful phenomena connected with this flood of lava. The cañon was doubtless filled to a height of twelve or fifteen hundred feet, perhaps by more than one flood. This would dam the water back; and in cutting through this great lava bed, a new channel has been formed, sometimes on one side, sometimes on the other. The cooled lava, being of firmer texture than the rocks of which the walls are composed, remains in some places; in others a narrow channel has been cut, leaving a line of basalt on either side. It is possible that the lava cooled faster on the sides against the walls, and that the center ran out; but of this we can only conjecture. . . .

What a conflict of water and fire there must have been here! Just imagine a river of molten rock, running down into a river of melted snow. What a seething and boiling of the waters; what clouds of steam rolled into the heavens!

Thirty-five miles today. Hurray!

Indian Camp

Bradley, 26 August   Another 35 mile run with but one let down, which was more choice than necessity. We happened to land on the wrong side to run it so we let the boats over it. This A.M. we run out of the lava which flowed down the river for many miles and which made or helped to make many rapids. We are now in the granite again and I anticipate trouble if it continues for we never

---

*Vulcan's Anvil, Mile 178, or about 1½ miles above Lava Falls. Powell's description of the lava flows is still fairly accurate.

strike it without trouble. The country which has been very broken for some miles begins to close in upon us and the river narrows and shoots through the granite like a brook in some places. We found an Indian camp today with gardens made with considerable care. The Indians are probably out in the mountains hunting and have left the gardens to take care of themselves until they return. They had corn, mellons, and squashes growing. We took several squashes, some of them very large, and tonight have cooked one and find it very nice. Wish we had taken more of them. The corn and mellons were not up enough to be eatable. There were two curious *rugs* hung up under the cliff made of wildcat skins and sewed like a mat. They were quite neat looking and very soft, probably used for beds. They had no regular lodges but seemed to live in booths covered with brush and corn-stalks. From signs and scraps of baskets we judge they are Utes, probably Pah-Utes [Paiutes].*

Powell, 26 August   Found Indian camp today—gardens. Good run of 35 miles. Camp 42.

Sumner, 26 August   Made 35 miles. Ran 31 rapids and made one portage. Passed melon garden. Camped on north side.

Powell Account of 26 August   ... Since we left the Colorado Chiquito, we have seen no evidences that the tribe of Indians inhabiting the plateaus on either side ever come down to the river; but about eleven o'clock today we discover an Indian garden, at the foot of the wall on the right, just where a little stream, with a narrow flood-plain, comes down through a side canon. Along the valley, the Indians have planted corn, using the water which burst out in springs at the foot of the cliff, for irrigation. The corn is looking quite well, but is not sufficiently advanced to give us roasting ears; but there are some nice, green squashes. We carry ten or a dozen of these on board our boats, and hurriedly leave, not willing to be caught in the robbery, yet excusing ourselves by pleading our great want. We run down a short distance, to where we feel certain no Indians can follow; and what a kettle of squash sauce we make! True, we have no salt with which to season it, but it makes a fine addition to our unleavened bread and coffee. Never was fruit so sweet as these stolen squashes.

After dinner we push on again, making fine time, finding many rapids, but

---

*This Indian garden could possibly have been at the mouth of Whitmore Wash, Mile 188, where pictographs have been found. Whitmore Wash is a broad valley that provided seasonal homes to wandering Southern Paiute Indians. These primitive Indians practiced agriculture where possible, while hunting occasionally for rabbits and other small animals. One of their chief food plants was *mescal,* or Agave. Shelters were of brush. They have lived in the area since about A.D. 1300.

none so bad that we cannot run them with safety, and when we stop, just at dusk, and foot up our reckoning, we find we have run thirty-five miles again.

What a supper we make; unleavened bread, green squash sauce, and strong coffee. We have been for a few days on half rations, but we have no stint of roast squash.

A few days like this, and we are out of prison.

Separation Rapids

Bradley, 27 August Run 12 miles today but at noon we came to the worst rapid yet seen. The water dashes against the left bank and then is thrown furiously back against the right. The billows are huge and I fear our boats could not ride them if we could keep them off the rocks. The spectacle is appalling to us. We have only subsistence for about five days and have been trying half a day to get around this one rapid while there are three others in sight below. What they are we cannot tell only that they are huge ones. If we could get on the cliff about a hundred yards below the head of this one we could let our boats down to that point and then have foot-hold all the rest of the way, but we have tried all the P.M. without success. Shall keep trying tomorrow and I hope by going farther back in the mountains and then coming down opposite we may succeed. Think Major has now gone to try it. There is discontent in camp tonight and I fear some of the party will take to the mountains but hope not. This is decidedly the darkest day of the trip but I don't despair yet. I shall be one to try to run it rather than take to the mountains. "'Tis darkest just before the day" and I trust our day is about to dawn.

Powell, 27 August Run 12 miles. At noon came to bad rapid. Spent afternoon in exploration. Camp on left bank in gulch 43.

Sumner, 27 August Made 12 miles. Ran dozen bad rapids then came to cross gulches were Howland senior and Dunn left 169¾ miles.

Powell Account of 27 August This morning the river takes a more southerly direction. The dip of the rocks is to the north, and we are rapidly running into lower formations. Unless our course changes, we shall very soon run again into the granite. This gives us some anxiety. Now and then the river turns to the west, and excites hopes that are soon destroyed by another turn to the south. About nine o'clock we come to the dreaded rock. It is with no little misgiving that we see the river enter these black, hard walls. At its very entrance we have to make a portage; then we have to let down with lines past some ugly rocks. Then we run a mile or two farther, and then the rapids below can be seen.

About eleven o'clock we come to a place in the river where it seems much worse than any we have yet met in all its course. A little creek comes down from the left. We land first on the right, and clamber up over the granite pinnacles for a mile or two, but can see no way by which we can let down, and to run it would be sure destruction. After dinner we cross to examine it on the left. High above the river we can walk along on the top of the granite, which is broken off at the edge, and set with crags and pinnacles, so that it is very difficult to get a view of the river at all. In my eagerness to reach a point where I can see the roaring fall below, I go too far on the wall, and can neither advance nor retreat. I stand with one foot on a little projecting rock, and cling with my hand fixed in a little crevice. Finding I am caught here, suspended 400 feet above the river, into which I should fall if my footing fails, I call for help. The men come, and pass me a line, but I cannot let go of the rock long enough to take hold of it. Then they bring two or three of the largest oars. All this takes time which seems very precious to me; but at last they arrive. The blade of one of the oars is pushed into a little crevice in the rock beyond me, in such a manner that they can hold me pressed against the wall. Then another is fixed in such a way that I can step on it, and thus I am extricated.

Still another hour is spent in examining the river from this side, but no good view of it is obtained, so now we return to the side that was first examined, and the afternoon is spent in clambering among the crags and pinnacles, and carefully scanning the river again. We find that the lateral streams have washed boulders into the river, so as to form a dam, over which the water makes a broken fall of eighteen or twenty feet; then there is a rapid, beset with rocks, for two or three hundred yards, while, on the other side, points of the wall project into the river. Then there is a second fall below; how great, we cannot tell. Then there is a rapid, filled with huge rocks, for one or two hundred yards. At the bottom of it, from the right wall, a great rock projects quite half-way across the river. It has a sloping surface extending up stream, and the water, coming down with all the momentum gained in the falls and rapids above, rolls up this inclined plane many feet, and tumbles over to the left. I decide that it is possible to let down over the first fall, then run near the right cliff to a point just above the second, where we can pull out into a little chute, and having run over that in safety, we must pull with all our power across the stream, to avoid the great rock below. On my return to the boat, I announce to the men that we are to run it in the morning. Then we cross the river, and go into camp for the night on some rocks, in the mouth of the little side cañon.

After supper Captain Howland asks to have a talk with me. We walk up the little creek a short distance, and I soon find that his object is to remonstrate against my determination to proceed. He thinks that we had better abandon the river here. Talking with him, I learn that his brother, William Dunn, and himself have determined to go no farther in the boats. So we return to camp. Nothing is said to the other men.

For the last two days, our course has not been plotted. I sit down and do this now, for the purpose of finding where we are by dead reckoning. It is a clear night, and I take out the sextant to make observations for latitude, and find that the astromonic determination agrees very nearly with that of the plot—quite as closely as might be expected, from a meridian observation on a planet. In a direct line, we must be about forty-five miles from the mouth of the Rio Virgen. If we can reach that point, we know that there are settlements up that river about twenty miles. This forty-five miles, in a direct line, will probably be eighty or ninety in the meandering line of the river. But then we know that there is comparatively open country for many miles above the mouth of the Virgen, which is our point of destination.

As soon as I determine all this, I spread my plot on the sand, and wake Howland, who is sleeping down by the river, and show him where I suppose we are, and where several Mormon settlements are situated.

We have another short talk about the morrow, and he lies down again; but for me there is no sleep. All night long, I pace up and down a little path, on a few yards of sand beach, along by the river. Is it wise to go on? I go to the boats again, to look at our rations. I feel satisfied that we can get over the danger immediately before us; what there may be below I know not. From our outlook yesterday, on the cliffs, the cañon seemed to make another great bend to the south, and this, from our experience heretofore, means more and higher granite walls. I am not sure that we can climb out of the cañon here, and, when at the top of the wall, I know enough of the country to be certain that it is a desert of rock and sand, between this and the nearest Mormon town, which, on the most direct line, must be seventy-five miles away. True, the late rains have been favorable to us, should we go out, for the probabilities are that we shall find water still standing in holes, and, at one time, I almost conclude to leave the river. But for years I have been contemplating this trip. To leave the exploration unfinished, to say that there is a part of the cañon which I cannot explore, having already almost accomplished it, is more than I am willing to acknowledge, and I determine to go on.

I wake my brother, and tell him of Howland's determination, and he promises to stay with me; then I call up Hawkins, the cook, and he makes a like promise; then Sumner, and Bradley, and Hall, and they all agree to go on.

Hawkins Account of late August   The trouble with the Howland boys began away back at Disaster Falls, where their boat was lost, but with Dunn it began only a few weeks before he left the party. At noon one day when the boats were being let over a bad place, Dunn was down by the water's edge with a barometer, taking the altitude. He was also assigned the post to look after the rope fastened to the boat and held by Sumner and others. By some means Dunn was thrown into the river, but he caught the rope and finally got out. In this he got wet a watch that belonged to the Major. At dinner the same day Major Powell told Dunn that he would have to pay for the watch or leave the party, which was impossible at that point. Dunn told him a bird could not get out of that place, thinking the Major was joking, but all of us were quickly convinced that every word the Major said was meant. Dunn siad he could not leave then, but that he would go as soon as he could get out. The Major then said he would have to pay one dollar a day for his board until such time as he could get out of the canyon. The rest of us sat listening as we ate our dinner. As Sumner was the oldest of our crowd, that is, the two Howlands, Dunn, Hall, and myself, we naturally looked at him as our spokesman.

Sumner told the Major he was surprised at what he had said to Dunn, and the Major said he was running the expedition. But Sumner said that was one thing he could not do—compel Dunn to leave the party or make him pay for his board. Walter Powell, better known as Captain Powell, took up the quarrel and thereby came near getting shot. We all considered the Captain demented because of his imprisonment in Andersonville prison. Had it not been for this, I doubt very much if the Captain would have made the entire trip.

The Separation

Bradley, 28 August　Tried in vain to get around or down the cliff and came to the determination to run the rapid or perish in the attempt. Three men refused to go farther (two Howlands and Wm. Dunn) and we had to let them take to the mountains. They left us with good feelings though we deeply regret their loss for they are as fine fellows as I ever had the good fortune to meet.

We crossed the river and carried our boats around one bad point with great labor and leaving the *"Emma Dean"* tied to the shore, all the remainder of the party (six all told) got into the two large boats and dashed out into the boiling tide with all the courage we could muster. We rowed with all our might until the billows became too large to do anything but hold on to the boats and by good fortune both boats came out at the bottom of the rapid, well soaked with water of course but right side up and not even an oar was lost. The three boys stood on the cliff looking at us and having waved them adieu we dashed through the next rapid and then into an eddy where we stopped to *catch our breath* and bail out the water from our now nearly sunken boats. We had never such a rapid before but we have run a worse one since that this P.M. We got a good little run over an almost continuous rapid until about the middle of the P.M. we came to some more of the lava and a tremendous rapid. Thinking it possible to let our boats around by the cliff I got into mine to keep her off the rocks and the men took the rope (130 ft. long) and went up on the cliff to let her down, not dreaming but what it was a comparatively easy task. For a time it worked finely but the cliff rising higher as they advanced and the tide getting stronger as we neared the rapid the task became more difficult until the rope was no longer long enough and they were obliged to hold it just where it was and go back to the other boat for more rope. The water roared so furiously that I could not make them hear and they could not see me, I was so far under the cliff, but where they held me was just on a point of the crag where the tide was strongest. With four feet more of rope I could have got in below the point and kept the boat steady but where I was she would sheer out into the tide and then come in with terrible force against the rocks. I got out my knife to cut the rope but hoped relief would come soon, and one look at the foaming cataract below kept me from cutting it and then I was suffering all the tortures of the rack, but having sufficient sense left to look out the best channel through if anything should give-way, and it was lucky I did so, for after what seemed quite half an hour and just as they were uniting the two ropes, the boat gave a furious shoot out into the stream. The cut water rope and all flew full thirty ft. in air and the loosened boat dashed out like a war-horse eager for the fray. On I went and sooner than I can write it was in the breakers but just as I always am, afraid while danger is approaching but cool in the midst of it, I could steer the boat as well as if the water was smooth. By putting an oar first on one side then on the other I could swing her around and guide her very well, and having passed the worst part of it and finding that the boat was eaquel to the task I swung my hat to the boys on the cliff in token of "All's Well." Major says nothing ever gave him more joy than to see me swing my hat, for they all thought that the boat and I too were gone to the "Happy hunting grounds" until them. The Major's Bro. and Jack climbed along the cliff with rope to come to my assistance but Major not thinking I should be able to land the boat or hold her if I did, got into the other boat with Bill and Andy and came through after me. Their boat got turned around and they came very near going against the rocks. They found me safely stowed around in an eddy bailing out the boat when they came. It stands A No. 1 of the trip. Run 14 miles.

Powell, 28 August   Boys left us. Ran rapid. Bradley boat. Make camp on left bank.

Sumner, 28 August   O. G. Howland and W. H. Dunn decided to abandon the outfit and try to reach the settlements on the head of Virgin River. Each took a gun and all the ammunition he wanted and some provisions and left us to go it or swamp. The remaining 6 men lifted the 2 large boats over the rock past some of the rapids, abandoned the small boat as useless property, and pulled out and ran the rest of the damned rapid with a ringing cheer, though at great risk, as the boats shipped nearly half full in a perfect hell of foam. Bailed out and pulled out again and ran 10 more rapids in 6 miles, when we came to another hell. There is a . . . pouring in from the south . . . of large rocks that . . . to make a very bad . . .

Powell Account of 28 August   At last daylight comes, and we have breakfast, without a word being said about the future. The meal is as solemn as a funeral. After breakfast, I ask the three men if they still think it best to leave us. The elder Howland thinks it is, and Dunn agrees with him. The younger Howland tries to persuade them to go with the party, failing in which, he decides to go with his brother.

Then we cross the river. The small boat is very much disabled, and unsea-worthy. With the loss of hands, consequent on the departure of the three men, we shall not be able to run all of the boats, so I decided to leave my "Emma Dean."

Two rifles and a shot gun are given to the men who are going out. I ask them to help themselves to the rations, and take what they think to be a fair share. This they refuse to do, saying they have no fear but that they can get something to eat; but Billy, the cook, has a pan of biscuits prepared for dinner, and these he leaves on a rock.

Before starting, we take our barometers, fossils, the minerals, and some ammunition from the boat, and leave them on the rocks. We are going over this place as light as possible. The three men help us lift our boats over a rock twenty-five or thirty feet high, and let them down again over the first fall, and now we are all ready to start. The last thing before leaving, I write a letter to my wife, and give it to Howland. Sumner gives him his watch, directing that it be sent to his sister, should he not be heard from again. The records of the expedition have been kept in duplicate. One set of these is given to Howland, and now we are ready. For the last time, they entreat us not to go on, and tell us that it is madness to set out in this place; that we can never get safely through it; and, further, that the river turns again to the south into the granite, and a few miles of such rapids and falls will exhaust our entire stock of rations, and then it will be too late to climb out. Some tears are shed; it is rather a solemn parting; each party thinks the other is taking the dangerous course.

My old boat left, I go on board of the "Maid of the Cañon." The three men climb a crag, that overhangs the river, to watch us off. The "Maid of the Cañon" pushes out. We glide rapidly along the foot of the wall, just grazing one great rock, then pull out a little into the chute of the second fall, and plunge over it. The open compartment is filled when we strike the first wave below, but we cut through it, and then the men pull with all their power toward the left wall, and swing clear of the dangerous rock below all right. We are scarcely a minute in running it, and find that, although it looked bad from above, we have passed many places that were worse. . . . Just after dinner we come to another bad place. A little stream comes in from the left, and below there is a fall, and still below another fall. Above, the river tumbles down, over and among the rocks, in whirlpools and great waves, and the waters are lashed into mad, white foam. . . . When I arrive I find the men have let one of [the boats] down to the head of the fall. She is in swift water, and they are not able to pull her back; nor are they able to go on with the line, as it is not long enough to reach the higher part of the cliff, which is just before them; so they take a bight around a crag. I send two men back for the other line. The boat is in very swift water, and Bradley is standing in the open compartment, holding out his oar to prevent her from striking against the foot of the cliff. Now she shoots out into the stream, and up as far as the line will permit, and then, wheeling, drives headlong against the rock, then out and back again, now straining on the line, now striking against the rock. As soon as the second line is brought, we pass it down to him; but his attention is all taken up with his own situation, and he does not see that we are passing the line to him. I stand on a projecting rock, waving my hat to gain his attention, for my voice is drowned by the roaring of the falls. Just at this moment, I see him take his knife from its sheath, and step forward to cut the line. He has evidently decided that it is better to go over with the boat as it is, then to wait for her to be broken to pieces. As he leans over, the boat sheers again into the stream, the stem post breaks away, and she is loose. With perfect composure Bradley seizes the great scull oar, places it in the stern rowlock, and pulls with all his power (and he is an athlete) to turn the bow of the boat down stream, for he wishes to go bow down, rather than to drift broadside on. One, two strokes he makes, and a third just as she goes over, and boat is fairly turned, and she goes down almost beyond our sight, though we are more than a hundred feet above the river. Then she comes up again, on a great wave, and down and up, then around behind some great rocks, and is lost in the mad, white foam below. We stand frozen with fear, for we see no boat. Bradley is gone, so it seems. But now, away below, we see something coming out of the waves. It is evidently a boat. A moment more, and we see Bradley standing on deck, swinging his hat to show that he is all right. But he is in a whirlpool. We have the stem post of his boat attached to the line. How badly she may be disabled we know not. I direct Sumner and Powell to pass along the cliff and see if they can reach him from below. Rhodes, Hall, and myself run to the other boat, jump aboard, push out, and away we go over the falls. A wave rolls over us, and our boat is unmanageable. Another great wave strikes us, the boat rolls over, and tumbles and tosses, I know not how. All I know is that

Bradley is picking us up. We soon have all right again, and row to the cliff, and wait until Sumner and Powell can come. After a difficult climb they reach us. We run two or three miles farther, and turn again to the northwest, continuing until night, when we have run out of the granite once more.

Hawkins Account of 28 August   When we came to the rapid where the Howland boys and Dunn decided to leave the party, we all looked at it and Hall and I had our course picked out on that rapid for the morning. The Major and some of the other boys went across the river to look to see if there was any chance to let the boats over it by ropes. On the following morning when I raised up from my bed about daybreak, I saw the Major walking up and down on a patch of sand and I called to Andy Hall, who shared the bed with me, and asked what the Major meant. He said he saw some of the boys and the Major in council the evening before, but could not find out what was the matter.

By the time the Major walked up to where I was making a fire and said, "Billy, how much flour have you now?" I said, "Very little," and showed it to him, and he told me to make it all into biscuits as near one size as possible. I asked no questions, excepting if we wanted any dried apples cooked, as we had about 100 pounds of them, and about 75 pounds of coffee. That was our entire stock of provisions. The Major said I need not cook any apples.

Andy Hall drew my attention to a group of the boys that were off to one side counciling among themselves. Bradley came up to the fire and I asked him if it was not coming to a show-down. He said he could not understand the Major, but there was something going to happen. I did not know or care what happened, as I was sure Andy and Bradley would stand by me in anything that was reasonable.

I called out to come to coffee. All came and drank the coffee and ate the bread, and there was not one word said, one to another. When we got through the Major said, "Billy, you take this bread and divide it just as equally as you can." I made nine piles and put one biscuit in each pile till my supply was gone. I don't remember how many there were to the man, but there were three or four left over and I said we would give these to the Major, but he said his share would have to do him.

The Major, the Howland brothers, Dunn, and Sumner went off to one side to hold another council. Bradley came over to where Andy Hall and I were standing and completely broke down and shed tears, and said such actions made him feel like a child again. By that time the Major came up to where we were standing and said, "Well, Billy, we have concluded to abandon the river for the present," stating that on account of the scarcity of provisions and because the rapids were getting more severe, he thought the better thing to do was to leave the river, as it could not be more than one hundred miles to some settlement in Utah, and that we would get a new supply of grub and return and complete our journey. By that time all the boys were standing and listening to him. When he finished his say, I asked him if he would sell the boat to Andy and me. He said if we would come back and finish the trip he would give us the boat. I told him I proposed to finish my part of it then.

I said, "Major, you have always looked to Hall and me as being too young to have anything to say in your council, but Hall and I are going to go down this river whether you or any of the rest go or not." And I told him that if he left the river I would not think of following him one foot on land, that my mind was set. Then the Major said, "Well, Billy, if I have one man that will stay with me I will continue my journey or be drowned in the attempt." I told him that Bradley, Hall, and I had made up our minds to continue and that I thought the worst of the rapids were passed, and that if he had taken me into his council he would have soon found out my attitude on that point.

Sumner spoke up and said, "Stay with it, Billy, and I will be with you." It did not take long to settle the rest of it. The Howland brothers and Dunn had made up their minds and would not change them. Of course, we knew what was the reason Dunn left. As for any fear, he did not possess it. And as for the other boys, they never showed any signs of fear. The elder of the Howlands had been in the boat with me since his own boat was wrecked.

We all crossed over to the north side, hid our supplies and instruments, and left one boat for the boys. It is my opinion that if the Howland boys had not agreed to leave the river in the council I referred to, they would have come with us. But they were sore about the way Dunn had been treated. I will admit that at that time they had more than an even chance to get out by land. We lifted our boats up about thirty feet over a ledge or rock and put them in a little bay in a crevice or crack between the rocks which was some twenty feet in width and thirty-five or forty feet in length. Here the water was still, but it ran like lightning in front of the crevice.

We had the two boats. The other one we left with the Howland brothers and Dunn. We again asked them to come with us. Dunn held me by the hand and tears came into his eyes as he said he hated to leave Sumner and me, that we had had many a hard and daring time together before we ever saw the Colorado River. "But," he said, "Billy, you cannot blame me." I could not answer. For once in my life I was hurt to the very heart, and in silence I shook his hand for the last time in this world. All this time Sumner and Hall were talking with the Howland boys.

The Major came into my boat, and we started first, but when we struck the main current it was so swift that it sent us back in the eddy in the little cove. By this time things were getting interesting, and again Dunn and the Howland brothers said we would never make it. I said, "Watch my smoke this time!" I told Hall to put all his strength in the oars, and I would do the rest. The Major got a firm hold with his left hand and sat down in the bottom of the boat. I headed for the lower side of the cove so as to strike the main current more on a down stream course than before. It was perhaps thirty feet from the mouth of the cove to the middle of the high waves which were over fifteen feet in height, but Hall had the boat under such headway that I could manage it with my steering oar, so I caught the side of the main waves, then cut them for the other side, which we made all right and landed below. Then came Bradley, and Sumner and Captain Powell in the other boat.

We took in perhaps only thirty gallons of water in my boat. The other boat did not fare so well, as it struck the rapid too high up, but it got through all right. We all landed and hallooed to the other boys that we left on the rock to come, but they would not.

It was here Major Powell took off his life preserver and handed it to me, saying he would have no more use for it and would make me a present of it. I told him he had better keep it on, but he said that he felt safe with any man who could come through the way I did between the rocks, and that he would make me a present of it. I thanked him, and said I would keep it to remember the Major and the daring trip and hardships down through the entire length of the Colorado River Canyons. I have the life preserver now in my possession, although it is unfit for use by reason of old age.*

Sumner Account of 28 August   Finally we arrived at a peculiarly bad rapid, or rather three rapids, that did not look a bit good. I call them Separation Rapids as here was where the Howland brothers and Dunn left the party and met their deaths at the hands of treacherous villains destitute of all traces of courage or humanity. . . .

Arriving at Separation, or Desertion, Rapid, just as you have a mind to call it, about ten o'clock in the morning, we appeared to be up against it sure. There were two side canyons coming into the Colorado nearly opposite each other, the river not being over fifty yards wide and running like a race horse. The first part of the rapid is caused by the big rocks carried out of the side canyon coming in from the south. The second part of the rapid is formed by rocks from the north side canyon and granite reef that reaches one-third of the way across the river, making a Z-shaped rapid. We spent the day trying to solve the problem.

Howland and Dunn told me at noon that they did not care about taking any more chances on the river, and proposed to leave and try to make the Mormon settlements north of the river. I did what I could to knock such notions out of

---

*Major Powell's life preserver is on display in the Smithsonian.

their heads, but as I was not sure of my own side of the argument, I fear I did not make the case very strong, certainly not strong enough to dissuade them from their plans. I talked with Major Powell quietly on the subject. He seemed dazed by the proposition confronting us. I then declared that I was going on the river route, and explained my plans to him how to surmount the difficulty, plans which were carried out next morning. I explained to the boys, the Howlands and Dunn, how we could pass the rapid. In this they agreed with me. But what was below? We knew that we were less than seventy miles from the mouth of the canyon, but had no idea what kind of river we had to encounter below where we were.

As O. G. Howland, who appeared to be the leader of the three, had fully made up his mind to quit, since the rapids had become a holy terror to him, I saw that further talk was useless, and so informed Major Powell. I suggested that we make duplicate copies of our field notes, and give the men the latitude and longitude and a draft of the location of the Mormon settlements as far as we knew. Major Powell and I were up most of the night to get an observation, and he worked out the calculations while I kept a light burning for him with mesquite brush. At daylight we crossed back to the north side of the river and commenced to make the portage, which was accomplished in this way:

All hands took hold and we lifted the boats over the granite reef, about twenty-five feet high. By then taking a bight with the rope around the channels worn in the granite, we managed to let the boats down into a little cove formed below the reef. There was hardly room for two boats to lie, but after getting them there we saw that by striking the main current bows up stream we could make it. If we struck it that way it was my opinion that the current would have a tendency to throw the boats to the opposite side of the river, and thus enable us to avoid the dangerous rock some fifty yards below.

After getting all ready we had a short talk with the boys (the Howlands and Dunn) and urged them to join us. It proved a failure, so we gave them duplicate notes, two watches, and some money. Then Major Powell took his seat in the first or outside boat, while I held it to the bank till all was ready. When the word was given I shoved the boat out as far as I could. The first start was not successful, but the second time away they went. The current took hold of the bow and whirled the boat round in a flash, but shot her nearly across the river, and cleared the dangerous rock and fountain waves below. We watched them till they passed the two falls farther down and saw them turn in and land on a sandy beach a half-mile beyond.

We repeated the same tactics with the other boat and I rounded in beside them. We waited about two hours, fired guns, and motioned for the men (the Howlands and Dunn) to come on, as they could have done by climbing along the cliffs. The last thing we saw of them they were standing on the reef, motioning us to go on, which we finally did. If I remember rightly, Major

Powell states it was not as bad as it looked, and that we had run worse. I flatly dispute that statement. At the stage of water we struck, I don't think there would be one chance in a thousand to make it by running the whole rapid.

Before starting I tied the little "Emma Dean" at the head of the rapid. Here we cached two barometers and a bunch of beaver traps. Everything was probably washed into the river at the next flood, as the rise in the river at that point is very great. . . . While we repaired the boats the boys discussed the conduct and the fate of the three men left above. They all seemed to think the red bellies would surely get them. But I could not believe that the reds would get them, as I had trained Dunn for two years in how to avoid a surprise, and I did not think the red devils would make open attack on three armed men. But I did have some misgiving that they would not escape the double-dyed white devils that infested that part of the country. Grapevine reports convinced me later that that was their fate.*

Grand Wash

Bradley, 29 August   This is the first Sunday that I have felt justified in running but it has now become a race for life. We have only enough flour to last us five days and we do not know how long we may be winding around among these hills but we are much encouraged by the constant improvement in the looks of the country. We run down the granite about 10 A.M. and then the country began to open and we expect that we are now in the vicinity of Grand Wash though we may pass it without knowing it. Indeed we may have passed it before this for we have worked hard today and have run 42½ miles. We are quite worn out tonight but with a good night's rest we shall, I trust, be able to renew the race in the morning. We have run all the rapids we found today without stopping to look at them for we have no time to waste in looking. The rapids grow less as we advance and we hope and expect that the worst of the trip is over. All we regret now is that the three boys who took to the mountains are not here to share our joy and triumph. We have run some distance north today which will drive them far out of their course for if the river runs north the cañons running into it must run east and their proper course from where they left us is about N.W.

Sumner, 29 August   We came out to a low rolling desert, and saw plainly that our work of danger was done—gave 3 cheers and pulled away steady strokes till 5 o'clock when we camped on the south side and summed up the log and found we had run 42½ miles.

---

*See the Afterword for Powell's definitive report on the fate of the Howlands and Dunn.

Powell Account of 29 August   We start very early this morning. The river still continues swift, but we have no serious difficulty, and at twelve o'clock emerge from the Grand Cañon of the Colorado.

We are in a valley now, and low mountains are seen in the distance, coming to the river below. We recognize this as the Grand Wash. . . .

Tonight we camp on the left bank, in a *mesquite* thicket.

The relief from danger, and the joy of success, are great. When he who has been chained by wounds to a hospital cot, until his canvas tent seems like a dungeon cell, until the groans of those who lie about, tortured with probe and knife, are piled up, a weight of horror on his ears that he cannot throw off, cannot forget, and until the stench of festering wounds and anaesthetic drugs has filled the air with its loathsome burthen, at last goes out into the open field, what a world he sees! How beautiful the sky; how bright the sunshine; what "floods of delirious music" pour from the throats of birds; how sweet the fragrance of earth, and tree, and blossom! The first hour of convalescent freedom seems rich recompense for all—pain, gloom, terror.

Something like this are the feelings we experience tonight. Ever before us has been an unknown danger, heavier than immediate peril. Every waking hour passed in the Grand Cañon has been one of toil. We have watched with deep solicitude the steady disappearance of our scant supply of rations, and from time to time have seen the river snatch a portion of the little left, while we were ahungered. And danger and toil were endured in those gloomy depths, where ofttimes the clouds hid the sky by day, and but a narrow zone of stars could be seen at night. Only during the few hours of deep sleep, consequent on hard labor, has the roar of the waters been hushed. Now the danger is over; now the toil has ceased; now the gloom has disappeared; now the firmament is bounded only by the horizon; and what a vast expanse of constellations can be seen!

The river rolls by us in silent majesty; the quiet of the camp is sweet; our joy is almost ecstasy. We sit still long after midnight, talking of the Grand Cañon, talking of home, but chiefly talking of the three men who left us. Are they wandering in those depths, unable to find a way out? are they searching over the desert lands above for water? or are they nearing the settlements?

The Virgin River

Bradley, 30 August   We got started at sunrise this morning expecting a long hard pull of it and worked hard until a little past noon, making 26 miles, the country all the while improving and opening, when we came somewhat unexpectedly to the mouth of the Virgin River, a quite large but muddy stream coming in from Utah, along which the Mormons have many settlements. We found three men and a boy (Mormons) fishing just below and immediately landed to learn where we were for we could hardly credit that all our trials were over until they assured us that we were within 20 miles of Callville and all right. They immediately took us to their cabin (they are fishermen) and cooked all they could for us of fish, squashes, etc., and we ate until I am very much like the darkey preacher, too full for utterance. As soon as we got here we sent an Indian up to St. Thomas (about 25 miles) where we are assured Col. Head has sent our mail to, for none of us have had a letter since leaving Greenriver City, almost 3½ months. I wrote a line and sent it to Lucy to assure Mother I was all right, but I was so intoxicated with joy at getting through so soon and so well that I don't know what I wrote to her.

Sumner, 30 August Pulled out at sunrise, and made 24 miles by noon, seeing nothing but smooth water and rolling desert till 10 o'clock when we came to the palatial residence of a Piute Indian; found the paternal head of a large family without even the fig leaf wallowing in the hot sand and ashes under some weeds thrown over 2 poles. Her ladyship's costume was nice and light and cool. It consisted of half a yard of dirty buckskin and a brass ring. She was as disgusting a hag as ever rode a broomstick. Camped for dinner on the north side. Pulled out at 1 o'clock and rowed about 7 miles, when we came to the mouth of Virgin River, where we found 3 white men and a boy fishing with a net. Stopped, and dispatched a Piute Indian after the mail at St. Thomas, 25 miles up the Virgin; set the men cooking fish, settled back on our dignity till the fish were cooked, when we laid our dignified manners aside and assumed the manner of so many hogs. Ate as long as we could and went to sleep to wake hungry.

Powell Account of 30 August We run through two or three short, low cañons today, and on emerging from one, we discover a band of Indians in the valley below. They see us, and scamper away in most eager haste, to hide among the rocks. Although we land, and call for them to return, not an Indian can be seen.

Two or three miles farther down, in turning a short bend in the river, we come upon another camp. So near are we before they can see us that I can shout to them, and, being able to speak a little of their language, I tell them we are friends; but they all flee to the rocks, except a man, a woman, and two children. We land, and talk with them. They are without lodges, but have built little shelters of boughs, under which they wallow in the sand. The man is dressed in a hat; the woman in a string of beads only. At first they are evidently much terrified; but when I talk to them in their own language and tell them we are friends, and inquire after people in the Mormon towns, they are soon reassured, and beg for tobacco. Of this precious article we have none to spare. Sumner looks around in the boat for something to give them, and finds a little piece of colored soap, which they receive as a valuable present, rather as a thing of beauty than as a useful commodity, however. They are either unwilling or unable to tell us anything about the Indians or white people, and so we push off, for we must lose no time.

We camp at noon under the right bank. And now, as we push out, we are in great expectancy, for we hope every minute to discover the mouth of the Rio Virgen.

Soon one of the men exclaims: "Yonder's an Indian in the river." Looking for a few minutes, we certainly do see two or three persons. The men bend to their oars, and pull towards them. Approaching, we see that there are three white men and an Indian hauling a seine, and then we discover that it is just at the mouth of the long sought river.

As we come near, the men seem far less surprised to see us than we do to see them. They evidently know who we are, and, on talking with them, they tell us that we have been reported lost long ago, and that some weeks before, a messenger had been sent from Salt Lake City, with instructions for them to watch for any fragments or relics of our party that might drift down the stream.

Our new-found friends, Mr. Asa and his two sons, tell us that they are pioneers of a town that is to be built on the bank.

Eighteen or twenty miles up the valley of the Rio Virgen there are two Mormon towns, St. Joseph and St. Thomas. Tonight we dispatch an Indian to the last mentioned place, to bring any letters that may be there for us.

Our arrival here is very opportune. When we look over our store of supplies, we find about ten pounds of flour, fifteen pounds of dried apples, but seventy or eighty pounds of coffee.

Hawkins Account of 30 August   The Major said to me "Now, as to the money you are to receive for your goods and horses, I expect to get it from the Government and also to pay your transportation back," explaining that he had money with him, and that he would let me have what I needed during the trip, and that he would be responsible to me for the remainder. He gave me a receipt for the amount due me at that time. Sumner told me that he was to receive good prices for his supplies and stores and good pay for his work, and that he would have several thousand dollars coming to him when he got through, and that he was to receive it all when we got to the end of the river journey. Later in the fall, Major Powell told me that if he could get the Government to appropriate $12,000 there would be $1,000 for each of us and $2,000 for himself for the trip.

When we finally got to the mouth of the Virgin River, the Major and his brother left us. I cannot tell how much money he paid to each one, but he gave each man some. He gave me $60 and Hall $60, and said that he would send us a government voucher for the rest, also for what he was to pay me for the provisions and animals I sold him. As we had not come to Cottonwood Island, I asked him how about my traps that he was to make good. There was thirty-six of them, and I had paid $3.00 a piece for them.

"Well," the Major said, "they got lost in Green River."

"Yes," I replied, "but you agreed to make them good when we got to Cottonwood Island."

Then he said he would allow me $2.50 for each trap and would find out what the transportation was, and send me a voucher for the whole amount. The voucher is still coming. All I ever received was $60, at the mouth of the Virgin River. Sumner is out a good deal more than I am. I saw the Major after that and asked him about it, and he told me he was still expecting an appropriation from the government. Then he would pay me.*

Sumner Account of 30 August   About noon the doors of the Grand Canyon were opened, and we could see all around us, a thing we had not been able to do for many a day unless we climbed the cliff. It was a strange and delightful sensation. For my part, I felt as Dante probably felt as he crowded up from Hades. Paddling along slowly, we acted like schoolboys let out for recess, and "Old Shady" [Walter Powell] made the valley ring with songs. Hall, trying to follow suit, made a failure, and Hawkins told him to shut up or he would drown him. We went into noon camp on the left bank of the river and had a dinner of "sinkers," pure and simple.** We saw here the first California quail we had ever seen. There were moccasin and barefoot tracks at our camp, and I thought it a good scheme to get out some reserve cartridges that I had previously stored away in a rubber boot leg, and sealed with pinon pitch. As it happened, we did not need them.

After dinner we ran perhaps three miles. A squaw suddenly bounced out of some mesquite bushes and cut out down the sand at a gait that would have thrown dust in the eyes of Maud S. As she was clothed only in chastity and appeared to have some business down farther, we did not interview her ladyship. A half-mile farther we turned a bend in the river and came to a wikiup with one of Nature's noblemen squatting in front. As we approached the mansion, our Lady Godiva (this one, however, traveled on foot) put in an

---

*Sumner and Hawkins apparently never received any additional pay from Powell.

**Sinkers are the heavy, unleavened wheatcakes that Hawkins had fried, using the remaining flour, and divided among the two parties at Separation Rapids.

appearance, evidently to protect her lord. As her first salutation was, "Heap hungry! Towae (tobacco)!" we knew there must be white men in the neighborhood. We tossed the Indians some tobacco and Hawkins threw a cake of fancy-colored soap to one of the papooses. He caught it with the dexterity of a monkey and proceeded to devour it without further ceremony. Running about three miles farther, we came in sight of three men seining a mile below us. With the telescope I saw at once that they were white men. I yanked the colors out of the locker and hoisted them at the bow. We had played our hand out and won against desperate odds! Whether the game was worth the powder or not, I leave to the judgment of others.

Rounding in at the camp of the whites, we found we were at the mouth of the Virgin River, and that the men were some Saints starting a new settlement. They had no horses, so we hired a buck Indian to go up to the Mormon town of St. Thomas after mail. We proceeded to take a rest after catching a lot of fish, which Hawkins baked at once in an outdoor oven. Here comes in a strange case of superstition or some other nonsense. When the fish were gone, we offered a good portion to the Indians who stood around us. They would not touch them, but at once rounded up and caught a score of lizards about a foot long. These they ate, not going to the trouble of killing and dressing them. They took them raw as a white man does his oysters. I presume it is a matter of education. The Navajos claim they drove the ancient cliff dwellers in the Colorado River and they turned to fish. Therefore, these Indians will not eat fish of any kind.

Sumner, 31 August   Laid over to fill up and rest all. Our mail carrier came in at noon with word that the Mormon bishop was on his way down with mail, flour and melons for us. He did not make his appearance till dark when we talked and ate melons till the morning star could be seen. The Prof. and Walter concluded to leave and go to Salt Lake City rather than to go to Yuma and take the stage to San Franzisco. Distance from mouth of Uintah River to junction of Green and Grand rivers 248 miles. General course 10° west of south. Rapids run 61—Portages—4—⁹⁄₁₀ of the distance. Cañon and all worthless.

Powell Account of 31 August   This afternoon the Indian returns with a letter, informing us that Bishop Leithhead, of St. Thomas, and two or three other Mormons are coming down with a wagon, bringing us supplies. They arrive about sundown. Mr. Asa treats us with great kindness, to the extent of his ability; but Bishop Leithhead brings in his wagon two or three dozen melons, and many other little luxuries, and we are comfortable once more.

Sumner Account of 31 August   Toward evening of the second day the Indian we had sent for mail returned, and with him came Bishop Leithhead of the Mormon Church and Andy Gibbons, a noted scout and guide. They brought a load of melons and other garden truck and two sacks of flour with them. After reading our letters and eating a square meal of "biscuit bread," we commenced formulating some plans for the rescue of the Howland brothers and Dunn. As we described the men and the locality in which they left us, we were listened to in respectful silence. But when Major Powell made the foolish break of telling them the amount of valuables the boys had, I noticed a complete change in the actions of a certain one of the men present. From one with a listless demeanor he instantly changed to a wide-awake, intensely interested listener, and his eyes snapped and burned like a rattlesnake's, particularly when Major Powell told him of an especially valuable chronometer for which he had paid six hundred and fifty dollars.

I believe when Major Powell got up into the Mormon settlements he sent out a party to look for our lost men. I heard about two months afterwards, while in Fort Yuma, California, that they brought in the report that the Howland brothers and Dunn came to an Indian camp, shot an Indian, and ravished and shot three squaws, and that the Indians then collected a force and killed all three of the men. But I am positive I saw some years afterwards the silver watch that I had given Howland. I was with some men in a carousal. One of them had a watch and boasted how he came by it. I tried to get hold of it so as to identify it by a certain screw that I had made and put in myself, but it was spirited away, and I was never afterwards able to get sight of it. Such evidence is not conclusive, but all of it was enough to convince me that the Indians were not at the head of the murder, if they had anything to do with it.

Powell, 1 September, Last Account   This morning Sumner, Bradley, Hawkins, and Hall, taking on a small supply of rations, start down the Colorado with the boats. It is their intention to go to Fort Mojave, and perhaps from there overland to Los Angeles.

Captain Powell and myself return with Bishop Leithhead to St. Thomas. From St. Thomas we go to Salt Lake City.

Sumner, Last Account   The Powells left us next morning, going with the Bishop Leithhead to Salt Lake City, leaving the necessary instruments with me to finish up the work to connect onto Lieutenant Ives's work, made from the gulf up the river in 1857–58.* I collected the stuff and we leisurely pulled out and down the river. Our party was reduced to four, Hawkins, Bradley, Hall, and myself. We drifted down to the old town of Callville, then entirely deserted. We went on and camped that night at the head of Black Canyon. We stopped over at Camp Eldorado, a mining camp where there were about fifty men, and had, of course, to listen to that silly story of James White's navigating the Colorado River on a raft. He was probably some renegade horse thief that had to leave between two days, and very likely struck the Colorado River at the mouth of the Grand Wash.

After taking on some snake medicine, we pulled down to Fort Mojave, Arizona, a two-company post in command of Colonel Stacy, who treated us very kindly. Here we drew four months' supplies and stopped several days. After writing up my journal and getting wind, chart, and weather notes, and other data of interest, we pulled on down to Camp Colorado, where a company of infantry was stationed. Bradley and Hawkins went on down the river while Hall and I were stopping at Mojave. The party was then mighty small, just Hall and myself. We soon passed the other men at Ehrenburg, a small shipping station for Prescott and the adjacent mining country, and then on to Fort Yuma, California, opposite the mouth of the Gila River. After camping there several days to get weather records from the post and take in the sights, we dropped down the river and camped at Bowman Ferry. From there we rowed down through the dismal mud flats of the lower Colorado and camped on an island.

Pulling out from our island camp, we dropped past the squaws and wikiups of the Cocopas, and about noon came to tidewater at the head of the Gulf of California. Not wishing to locate a ranch there, we stayed only two hours. Starting back up the river, we made good progress by using a wagon sheet for a sail. I believe Hall and I are the only men that ever navigated the Green and Colorado rivers for so long a distance—from Green River Station, Wyoming, to tidewater at the head of the Gulf of California.

As I shared the blankets with Major J.W. Powell for two years, I believe I knew him—perhaps not. He gave very scant credit to any of his men. It was all "Captain Powell and I," when as a matter of fact Captain Walter Powell was about as worthless as a piece of furniture as could be found in a day's journey. O.G. Howland was far his superior physically and morally and, God knows, away above him mentally. I have seen it in print that Captain Powell suffered so

---

*Lt. Joseph C. Ives attempted to travel upstream from the mouth of the Colorado with his steamer *Explorer* in 1857–58. The *Explorer* crashed in Black Canyon, confirming suspicion that the river was not navigable by steamboat. Ives later continued his exploration on horseback to as far as Cataract Canyon.

much in Confederate prisons that it unbalanced his mind. He is still living in Los Angeles, California. [He died 10 March 1915].

Major Powell paid me but $75.00 for my two years' work. I paid out of my own pocket more than a thousand dollars to make the trip a success. I have seen it in print, too, that the Major spent great sums of his own money to help the expedition along. May I kindly ask when and to whom he paid it? But he has passed over the range, and the Bookkeeper is there. He was a man of many traits, good, bad, and indifferent. He was vastly over-estimated *as a man,* as so many others have been. As a scholar and scientist he was worthy of all praise. His body has gone to the dust and his soul back to the God who gave it. Let us cast a mantle of charity over his faults.

I know it is decidedly bad form for me to write as I have done. My only defense is that in the Report the Major tries to make a bad impression against the Howland brothers and Bill Dunn. Bill Dunn was no saint, but he was, or rather would have been, another Jim Bludsoe, had the opportunity presented itself.* Hall is also dead—fell in defense of the United States mail which he was carrying at the time, fighting one against four, and held it to the last. Two of his assailants were hanged and two were serving life sentences in the Arizona penitentiary. Bradley died some years ago at San Diego, California, from injuries received in an accident. Hawkins is still living at Eden, Graham County, Arizona. I saw him in 1900. [Hawkins died 21 June 1919]. As for myself, it is not for me to speak. I have heard it said, "Success is a virtue and failure is a crime." Nearly all of my companions have passed over the range, and I am still left behind.

"Ho! Stand to your glasses steady!
'Tis all we have left to prize.
A cup for the dead already—
Hurrah for the next that dies!"* *

---

*The reference is to "Jim Bludse of the Prairie Belle," a poem by John Hay.

* *Sumner's toast comes from "The Revel," a poem by Bartholomew Dowling. Sumner died on 5 July 1907.

Climbing the Grand Canyon.

Afterword

T hus ends what historian William Culp Darrah has called, "the last great exploration into unknown and unmapped country in the United States." The drama over, the curtain descends and the actors soon scatter to their various destinations. As with any complex text expressing multiple points of view and conflicting opinions, this narrative leaves the reader with many loose ends and jagged edges. Each narrator experienced his own Great Unknown in the canyons of the Colorado; each journal projects its own palpable presence and personality.

As Powell and his five fellow survivors arrived at Grand Wash, they met a small community of Mormons at the mouth of the Virgin River and soon received food sufficient to drive away their monumental hunger. Although the Major and Captain Powell were bone weary of the river and anxious for news of the Howlands and Dunn, the other four (Sumner, Hawkins, Hall, and Bradley), soon decided to continue on downriver. Bradley and Sumner voyaged as far as Yuma, while Hawkins and Hall continued on, running the entire river to tidewater at the Gulf of California.

The two Powells sent out an inquiry by Mormon scouts about their missing crew, and before long received reply from the community of St. George that the three had been slain by Shivwit Indians. With this unhappy news, the two Powells headed east by train, reading the papers that were by then full of stories of their exploits and losses. Since there had been several "authoritative" newspaper reports that Powell's entire party had perished on the river, the Major soon discovered that the story of their survival had caught the public's fancy, and he was a national hero. Powell began to capitalize on this fame with a lecture tour and various publications, for he had already realized how much work lay ahead of him in mapping and describing this complex, still-unknown territory and its equally complex matrix of Indian societies.

But what accomplishments can actually be attributed to the first exploration of the Colorado, other than notoriety and personal fame for Powell? It had been no more than a quasiscientific exploration, for not even the Major had received thorough scientific training. Further, toward the end of the voyage the crew was forced to give up any efforts at measurement, observation, and sample collecting to focus all their skill and energy on survival.

At the very least, Powell's first exploration provided this rich narrative of America's last great exploration of unknown and unmapped lands. Ironically, although Powell wished to establish his scientific credibility for further surveying of the West, his voyage provided far more valuable cultural than scientific information. Powell also placed his indellible mark upon this landscape not only by describing it, but also by naming its principal features. To travel by boat or overland through this region, even today, is to encounter dozens and dozens of names given to the features of the Colorado Plateau by Powell and his men. Beyond these, as Wallace Stegner has pointed out, Powell discovered here the great challenge and work of his career: the exploring, mapping and describing of this vast arid region, and the planning of public policy for its wise settlement and use.

A man of great energy and resolve to achieve his goals, Powell continued his studies of the Colorado Plateau country. Before long he had received a congressional appropriation of $25,000 for the continuation of his "Survey of the Colorado River and the West," which was placed under the jurisdiction of the Department of the Interior. Powell's Colorado River Survey continued to receive support until 1877 and included many field workers and a number of exploring and surveying trips. Notable among these was his second Colorado River expedition of 1871–72, an enterprise far better financed and equipped and with a better quotient of scientific expertise than the first. During this period, Powell devoted much of his effort to learning Indian languages and cultures. With the help of Mormon scout and frontiersman Jacob Hamblin, Powell visited many of the Indian villages of the Colorado Plateau. He learned the languages, cultural patterns, and rituals of the Utes, Paiutes, and Hopi (or Moqui); he was also on friendly terms with the Shivwits. He became known to many of them as *Ka-Pur-Ats* (One-Arm-Off), as he visited their villages and learned their languages and cultures. In fact, one night, while visiting a Shivwits village, he heard the tale of how their braves killed the Howland brothers and Dunn in their sleep, mistaking them for a group of prospectors who had attacked and then killed a squaw. As difficult as his restraint must have been, Powell felt the greater good lay in understanding and trust, rather than in seeking revenge.

In the midst of this activity, which was making him an authority on western Indians, Powell published his report of the 1869 exploration, serially, in *Scribners Magazine.* With a few changes and additions, this became his *Report on the Exploration of the Colorado River,* published by the Smithsonian in 1875. Powell wanted a single book that would bring the work of his surveys and Indian studies to the public. Even though he had lead two river expeditions, he chose to tell the story of the more dramatic first voyage. Since his account was based on his sketchy river journal plus his memory and the more recent second voyage, it is no wonder there are numerous inaccuracies. Powell's long, embellished, and rather dramatic descriptions indicate his eye was on an audience thirsting for news and literature of the unknown West. Following the elaborate style of nineteenth-century travel literature, he wrote for educated easterners and perhaps their elected representatives, rather than for the scientific community.

Although his report was well received, his next and more serious publication, *Report on the Arid Lands of the United States* (1877) was generally ignored and its initial influence was slight. In it he proposed a system for classification of western lands according to their resource capability and especially their access to water and suitability for irrigation. He stipulated that all homesteads must include water rights, and that grazing farms should include not less than 2,560 acres. If Powell's plan had become law it might have averted great human hardship, especially during the drought of 1890, and might have greatly increased the success ratio of homesteading in the arid West.

In 1879, Major Powell was appointed first director of the Bureau of Ethnology within the Smithsonian Institution. This was entirely appropriate since Powell had been contributing field notes, orthographies, cultural artifacts, and thousands of Indian photographs to the Smithsonian over the previous decade. In fact, the materials contributed by the Powell Survey became the basic collection of the new bureau that was dedicated to the study and preservation of the languages, artifacts, and cultures of American Indians.

Not long afterward, Powell was appointed to succeed Clarence King as director of the U.S. Geological Survey. During the 1880s, the activities of the survey expanded rapidly under his guidance to include all aspects of geological work from basic to applied research, from paleontology to water resources and irrigation. The survey is generally acknowledged to have set a world standard in geological research. Toward the end of Powell's years with the organization, it received funding for an irrigation survey and certified locations for reservoir sites and dam construction. Powell resigned in 1894, but continued his career-long work with the Bureau of Ethnology. He died in 1902.

Readers wishing more information about John Wesley Powell, his explorations and achievements, should first consult Wallace Stegner's comprehensive study, *Beyond the Hundredth Meridian: The Exploration of the Grand Canyon and the Second Opening of the West*. Notable among a sizeable list of books about Powell and the Colorado, is William Culp Darrah's *Powell of the Colorado*. The complaints lodged against Powell by Sumner and Hawkins in their later accounts have been extensively examined by R. B. Stanton and J. M. Chalfant in *Colorado River Controversies*, and by W. W. Bass in *Adventures in the Canyons of the Colorado*. Their arguments have also been rebutted by Wallace Stegner.

Because the positions are well argued in earlier studies, it has not been the intention of this edition to dwell on the Colorado controversies or to favor one position or another regarding Powell's treatment of his crew either during or after the expedition. The effect, however, of honoring only Powell and of keeping only his account of the experience in print, has been to deny all but historians access to the full ensemble of voices that constitute the story of *The Great Unknown*. Any argument that the Hawkins and Sumner accounts should be ignored is as faulty as an argument that Powell's account be disqualified because it collapses his two expeditions (1869 and 1871–72) into one narrative, makes numerous errors in fact and date, and fails to mention the second expedition and its crew. Despite their idiosyncrasies and limitations, each narrative voice plays its distinctive part in this drama of adventure and discovery.

The current tendency in historical and literary study is to recognize that language and literature by nature struggle against unitary readings and resist closure. This trend, plus a growing interest in fragments, unfinished texts, multiple voices, and readings, encourages the publication of editions of this sort. The voices and narratives that are woven into the story of this book have jogged and clashed indirectly with each other ever since they were written. Now that they are forced to coexist within the same book, it is even less likely they will tolerate isolated readings. Fortunately, most enduring texts contain such internal diversity and complex ambivalence that they continue to attract and perplex readers across the years. Let us hope *The Great Unknown* will become just this kind of book, and find its place among the enduring literature of the American West.

Marble Canyon.

Selected Bibliography

Baker, Pearl. *Trail on the Water.* Boulder: Pruett Publishing Co., 1969.

Bartlett, Richard A. *Great Surveys of the American West.* Norman: University of Oklahoma Press, 1962.

Corle, Edwin. *Listen, Bright Angel.* New York: Duell, Sloan and Pearce, 1946.

Darrah, William Culp. *Powell of Colorado.* Princeton: Princeton University Press, 1951.

Dellenbaugh, Frederick S. *A Canyon Voyage.* New Haven: Yale University Press, 1972.

Derby, George Horatio. *Derby's Report on Opening the Colorado, 1850-1851.* Albuquerque: University of New Mexico Press, 1969.

Gilbert, Grove Carl. *John Wesley Powell.* Chicago, 1903.

Goetzman, William H. *Exploration and Empire.* New York: Alfred A. Knopf, 1966.

Goldwater, Barry M. *Delightful Journey Down the Green and Colorado Rivers.* Tempe, Arizona: Arizona Historical Foundation, 1970.

Hillers, John. *Photographed All the Best Scenery.* Salt Lake City: University of Utah Press, 1972.

Kolb, Ellsworth L. *Through the Canyon from Wyoming to Mexico.* New York: The Macmillan Company, 1914.

McKee, Edwin D. *Evolution of the Colorado River in Arizona.* Flagstaff: Museum of Northern Arizona, 1967.

Nims, Franklin A. *Photographer and the River.* Sante Fe, New Mexico: Stagecoach Press, 1967.

Powell, John Wesley. *Canyons of the Colorado.* New York: Argosy, 1964. (Originally published in 1895).

—— *The Exploration of the Colorado River.* Introduction by Wallace Stegner. Chicago: University of Chicago Press, 1957.

—— *The Exploration of the Colorado River.* New York: Anchor Books, 1961 (Originally published in 1875).

Stanton, Robert B. *Down the Colorado.* Norman: University of Oklahoma Press, 1965.

Stegner, Wallace. *Beyond The Hundredth Meridian.* New York: Houghton Mifflin, 1954.

Utah Historical Quarterly, vols. 15, 37. (Journals of Bradley, Sumner and Hawkins).

Watkins, Tom H. *The Grand Colorado; the story of the river and its canyons.* Palo Alto, California: American West Publishing Co., 1969.

Index

(Does not include references to Powell and his crew or to the Colorado, Green and Grand rivers)